EXILE ENDS IN GLORY

EXILE ENDS IN GLORY

The Life of a Trappistine
MOTHER M. BERCHMANS, O.C.S.O.

Thomas Merton

Paulist Press
New York / Mahwah, NJ

Cover image courtesy of the Merton Legacy Trust
Cover design by Trace Murphy
Book design by Lynn Else

Ex parte Ordinis
Nihil obstat: Fr. M. Gabriel O'Connell, O.C.S.O.
Fr. M. Anthony Chassagne, O.C.S.O.
Imprimi potest: Fr. M. Dominique Nogues, O.C.S.O., Abbot General

Nihil obstat: John A. Schulien, S.T.D., Censor librorum
Imprimatur: Moyses E. Kiley, Archiepiscopus Milwaukiensis
Die 4 Novembris, 1947

Originally published in 1948 by The Bruce Publishing Company, Milwaukee

Paulist Press edition published in 2015

Library of Congress Control Number: 2015930563

ISBN 978-0-8091-4909-4 (paper)
ISBN 978-1-58768-453-1 (e-book)

Published by Paulist Press
997 Macarthur Boulevard
Mahwah, New Jersey 07430

www.paulistpress.com

Printed and bound in the
United States of America

In The Charity of Christ
These Pages are Dedicated by the
Author to His Brethren,
The American Cistercian Pioneers,
Founders of Our Lady of the Holy Ghost,
In Georgia, 1944,
And Our Lady of the Most Blessed Trinity,
Utah, 1947, as well as to the Cistercian Nuns
Destined by God
to Found The First Convent of Trappistines
In Our Land

CONTENTS

CONTENTS

PREFACE

It has fallen to our lot, in the Providence of God, to put the finishing touches to this biography of a Trappistine foundress on the very day when the founders of a new American monastery of Strict Cistercians, or Trappists, are about to leave their mother house and enter into regions of labor, hardship, and uncertainty as Mother Berchmans did before them. Thirty-two Cistercians are ready for the three-day train journey that will take them to the little improvised monastery of army huts that awaits them in the Rocky Mountains of Utah. And probably there is not one of them who does not feel, in his heart, something of the strange indefinable mixture of anguish and of peace that filled the heart of this heroic little nun as she embarked for Japan some forty-five years ago.

What lends even more significance to this book is the other circumstance that it was begun just at the time when the founders of the first filiation of Gethsemani were leaving for Georgia, in 1944. And finally, during the last year, with marvelous rapidity, plans have been shaping for the first convent of Trappistines in the United States, in the archdiocese of Boston.

Clearly the story of Mother Berchmans has been given to us at this precise time in order that these pioneers and all their countrymen, Catholic and non-Catholic alike, may acquire a deeper appreciation of the sanctity God has destined for those whom He calls to follow Him by this particular path of obscurity, poverty, labor, and exile.

But first of all, lest we seem to exaggerate the interior sacrifice that is required in these religious souls, it is necessary to explain that exile is something that must necessarily be endowed with a very special poignancy for Cistercians who all make vows of *stability*, at their profession. With us, it is a virtue to get attached to a single monastery, to sink our roots deep in the soil with the intention of never going away. Indeed, one of the marks of a good Trappist is a single-minded love for the community of his profession. We monks are supposed to cling to the walls of our monastery like ivy. And, as a matter of fact, the whole tenor of our life of labor, silence, prayer in community, binds us so strongly together into a single organism that separation is, for us, almost like the amputation of a limb.

God has His own way of sanctifying His elect. And those who are called to a more intimate union with Him soon discover that His most terrible purifications are those in which He seems even to be contradicting Himself. He makes us love our monastery under pain of displeasing Him; and then suddenly He turns around and tears us away from our monastery under circumstances that would make it an infidelity to grace to look back at one's old home. What is even more terrible, He teaches us to love prayer and to prize the intimate knowledge of Him that is given us in the silence of contemplation above all other gifts and activities; and then suddenly he makes prayer impossible, and throws us headlong into lives of active responsibility in which He hides Himself behind a smoke screen of distractions and leaves us to struggle with the danger of losing the fine edge of the interior spirit with which He had endowed us in the time of recollection.

But the answer to these problems is that every soul called by God to the religious life has his own special place, his own all-important function to perform in building up the kingdom of God, the Mystical Body of Christ. Our sanctity must inevitably be determined by our readiness to fit in with God's plans for us and for His Church, especially when it demands the sacrifice of our own most cherished desires and ideals.

We are called to sacrifice everything, our very selves; and that means, above all, our judgment, our own will. And therefore the trials that are calculated to purify us the most are precisely the ones which escape the capacity of our own understanding and which flatly contradict the most fundamental tendencies of our own will. But the sacrifices that are thus required of us do not necessarily have to be, in themselves, the most spectacular. What God wants is to liberate us from the things that keep us back from Him. These things may be very trifling—indeed, they may be perfectly legitimate and praiseworthy in themselves. All that matters is the fact that we are attached to them. God, being (for our own sakes) a jealous God, intends to pursue with His implacable vengeance the slightest obstacle to His own immense love, no matter what that obstacle may be.

Mother Mary Berchmans was one of those people who never knew what it was to commit a serious sin. Indeed, in the opinion of those who knew her, she was already a saint before she entered the convent of Trappistines. But God knew how much work there yet remained to be done in her soul, and the chief means He chose for doing it was: exile.

Mother Berchmans had a gentle, tender, and affectionate heart, one that readily attached itself to persons and to places. It was a heart that loved all the most beautiful things in life, and which delighted above all in solitude and prayer. It was a heart that God had made for love; but He had made it for Himself. He wanted her to love creatures, but to love them in Him and for Him, for only thus could she be delivered from bondage to their attraction.

It is not surprising that God took Mother Berchmans away from the big, fervent community of Laval where she was happy and secure, loved and admired, and sent her to that poor little cottage in Japan. It is not even surprising that He made her work so hard that she had little time for contemplation before the tabernacle. But how could He mean to detach her even from the love of such holy things as her virtues? Yet He allowed her to undergo trials that revealed her to herself in all her weakness and poverty, her nothingness, her helplessness to accomplish anything without Him, in order that she might live, not merely to "acquire virtues," not to "weave herself a crown," but to love Him, to seek Him, to live in and for and by Him alone. For thus she would be living by love alone; and love transcends and includes all the other virtues. For "many waters cannot quench charity, nor can the floods drown it: if a man should give all the substance of his house for love he shall despise it (that is, the sacrifice) as nothing" (Cant. 8:7).

The story of this sacrifice was first written down by the man who was her spiritual director in Japan, himself a Cistercian, Father Robert Lepasquier, sent to the Orient from the monastery of Bricquebec in Normandy. It is from that manuscript that most of the material of the present work was drawn. Thanks to the generosity of the present Rev. Abbess of Our Lady of the Angels, Rev. Mother Cecilia Hirato, O.C.S.O., and the cooperation of Mother Léonie, of the same monastery, we have been able to obtain some other documents from the archives of that house together with the photographs which illustrate the present volume. Rev. Mother Cecilia was one of Mother Berchmans' novices, and Mother Leonie was her contemporary and co-pioneer in Japan.

Our thanks are also due to the generous assistance of the American army chaplains, stationed in Japan, who transmitted our mail to the Sisters there although the ways were not yet open for normal postal communication.

Monastery of Our Lady of Gethsemani
July 7, 1947

CHAPTER I

THE CONVENT OF THE REDEMPTION

It is March twenty-fourth, 1880. Tomorrow will be the feast of the Annunciation. Indeed, this book begins and ends with a feast of the Virgin Mother of God. It is the story of someone who was led and guided and taught and formed by the Mother of God, secretly, through the grace of Christ her Son, to a life of prayer, sacrifice, penance, and reparation.

It is a story that begins with sacrifice and ends with the consummation of a holocaust. It is the life of a Cistercian nun, a Trappistine.

On March twenty-fourth, 1880, we are standing in a street of the great, dark, French industrial city of Lyons. Over the roofs of the buildings, huddled together at the confluence of two rivers, we see the towers of the shrine of Our Lady of Fourvières, that dominates the city. But we are standing in front of a convent. It is the Convent of the Redemption, an orphanage and foundling home.

As we stand and look, we see a young woman approach, holding by the hand a little child, a girl, some four years old. She rings the doorbell, and presently the door is opened and admits them both. After some time it opens again, and the woman comes out alone. She hurries up the street. She is in tears.

She is not the only one who is sorrowful. Soon the door opens again, in fact, it flies open. A Sister comes briskly forth, leading the little girl who is crying lustily. Sister stands her on the pavement, and we hear her say:

"If you want to cry, cry in the street."

The tears cease at once. Sister Lucille takes the little one by the hand and leads her back into the orphanage.

This little girl is the subject of our story. She is three and a half years old, and her name is Mary Piguet. Later on, we shall know her as Mother Berchmans, but for the time being she is simply Mary Piguet.

And now we see her meeting her "guardian angel," a neat and pious little girl of twelve or thirteen, called Claudia. The two of them together disappear down the long corridor.

The nuns were to find that Mary was an intelligent and affectionate little thing, quick and lively, with many charming ways—and many others less charming. For her temper was as quick as her affections, and her repugnances as decisive and quick as her busy little mind. But, on the whole, she was a good child, and they determined not to be too hard on her; they would nurse her along and treat her with a certain amount of indulgence since she was also very frail. In fact, when the doctor examined her, he shook his head and condemned her to death.

"She will never live to be seven," he said.

Fortunately, he was wrong. During the next few years, although never well, Mary lived the happy life of a little child that was just opening the eyes of its soul, though still confusedly, upon a world that was full of God. It was a life, for one thing, full of processions. Everywhere the children went two by two, the littlest ones first. Two by two along the corridors, in a long parade, two by two to the playground, to the chapel, to the refectory. Two by two along the quays to the Rhone, and two by two up and down in the park, and often enough, two by two, to church.

Her greatest joy was on the feast of the Purification, when in all the churches there were processions for the children of the city, not the liturgical Candlemas procession only, but a special procession for the children which is a custom in Lyons. For that is the end of the Christmas season. And on that day, the little Jesus is taken from his straw in the crib, and the Magi and their gifts are put back in their boxes until next year, and the ox and the ass and the shepherds are wrapped up and put in a cupboard. So on this day, in all the churches of Lyons, there are processions of children accompanying little Jesus from the crib back to the sacristy. Mary liked this very much, liked it more than anything else in the world.

Back in the orphanage she held processions with her doll, Jeannette. They would go around and around the room together singing the *Ave Maris Stella*. Also, she would hear her doll's confession.

Confession! Yes, Jeannette was naughty enough, because, in fact, she was Mary's scapegoat. Mary was frequently in trouble. For instance, she had a pair of little earrings, of which she lost one. This loss led to another: that of her temper.

"Where's my earring?" she asked Claudia, with some heat.

"Suppose you look for it," said Claudia.

Now since she had already been looking for it without success, the studied unconcern of her "guardian angel" could only be construed as a gratuitous insult. So Mary took off the other earring, flung it on the floor, stamped on it, and then jumped up and down on it, screaming considerably at the same time.

Another time, for what crime we have forgotten, Mary was tethered to a plum tree like a rebellious nanny goat. So she worked off all her indignation on the tree, shaking all the fruit to the ground.

And yet she was sorry, and grieved for her sins: the whole of nature had the gift of tears on her behalf. When it rained, she would stare in awe and sadness at the drops running down the window, and soberly reflect upon the enormity of her faults that caused such weeping, for it was her belief that the rain was caused by the tears of her guardian angel for her great offenses.

We can see what a good and loving heart she had, too, by the fact that, where being locked up in rooms and tied to trees failed, she was really abashed and chastened, at least temporarily, by one device of Claudia's.

Claudia said: "If you are naughty again, I will take Korean vengeance upon you!"

"What's Korean vengeance?"

"Korean vengeance is like this: when we're walking along the Rhone, I'll take a knife and cut off my ear and throw it in the river, if you don't behave. That's Korean vengeance!"

Mary didn't even say "Oh!" to that one. Her mouth just made an "Oh!" shape, and the sound of amazement was not even breathed forth.

Soon she was naughty again, and then they walked along the Rhone, in a long procession, two by two, with the little ones going first, and Claudia far back with *les grandes* and Sister. All the time Mary was peeking back over her shoulder, looking for the knife and the slash and Claudia's ear flying through the air and floating away in the water. Maybe Sister would cry out and all the girls would faint, and poor Claudia, what about her? As long as they walked along the Rhone, Mary was as good as gold. And after that, not so good, for she began to breathe easier.

And yet, what a heart full of compassion! One of her favorite saints, from her earliest childhood, was St. Peter, whom she loved precisely because he had blundered into a sin and denied his Lord. She always prayed to him to console him for his sorrow and humiliation. The nuns told her that ever afterward he had wept so much for his sin that the tears had worn two furrows in his cheeks! Poor St. Peter, she would console him. She would make him smile!

Do you think this was all fancy, or that she failed? Have you forgotten that in the spiritual world time and space are without significance and souls travel to and speak to one another by thoughts and by desires, in the immense medium which is the infinite charity of God? Do you think that the great St. Peter's heart, in heaven, is not filled with yet more sweetness and gladness by the prayers and love of a simple child?

Finally, she had been told by the nuns, and by Claudia, that Jesus lived in everybody, especially the poor; everything that lived, but especially people, and the poor people, were holy, and we should love Jesus in them all. So Mary gave her hair ribbons to the little poor girls of the orphanage, and gifts of chocolate and sweets when she herself came by such luxuries. She would go away before the astonished little children could think of thanking her.

More than once, out in the streets, Mary was lost sight of, and had to be looked for, and was found in circumstances that would draw tears from a stone. For she had seen a poor beggar, in rags and weariness, lying down and sleeping on a newspaper in a doorway, and had gone over to where he was, gently and quietly and with awe, and begun to consider Jesus.

The little girl soon reached her seventh birthday—the doctor's prophecy of her death was not fulfilled, although she was still by no means strong. She began her classes with the other little ones of the same age and, what was more important, started her catechism in preparation for the immense grace of First Communion. In all these things, she showed herself diligent and attentive, careful and eager to do everything well. She was quick in her lessons and knew her catechism backward, applying herself with love to the learning of these holy truths, which are stated simply enough to mean at least something to a child, and yet which are of such depth and sublimity that no angelic spirit can exhaust them. It was as a reward for her love, not for the quickness of her intellect, that her First Communion was a true inception of a deep life of intimacy, in the secrecy of loving faith, with the Word of God, who is the truth and reality of all truths and all real things, and in the love of whose human heart lies the answer to our problems and our deliverance from death and sin.

The grace of her first Communion was, indeed, to operate a change in her somewhat tempestuous childhood; but meanwhile she continued to be carried away by sudden bursts of rather extravagant mischievousness, as well as fits of temper that made her quite a problem to the nuns and to Claudia. Because it was forbidden, more than for any other reason, she used to surreptitiously slip coins to her neighbor nearest to the fruit stands which they passed on their communal promenades, and the latter would buy apples or oranges which they would then eat.

She was, by now, a little past the age when Claudia's statement that she was "full of the devil" could prompt her to wash her whole forehead vigorously with holy water as a precaution against the visible growth of horns, but the metaphor was borne out by a certain perverse and rebellious tendency to persecute with practical jokes the most pious and holy little girls—the ones whose conduct was *always* exemplary and who always sat in the corner like holy pictures and were held up as models to the rest. One of the holiest of these little children had received a nice new copybook, and was just about to fill it with the most edifying holy sentiments in the most regular and beautiful handwriting, when she perceived that her inkpot had been filled with wax, no doubt by Mary.

The little angel was lucky to get off so lightly; for, another day, she would probably get some of the contents of the inkpot thrown at her.

The thing is, however, that Mary was always sorry, and resisted these movements of high spirits or bad temper, and gradually, as time went on, was overcoming them more and more. It was to be years before she could go without any exterior signs of impatience, much less any outbursts of crazy playfulness and dissipated mischief. These followed her not only to the convent, but also to her charge as mistress of novices, when even her poor bewildered Japanese postulants were not safe from her practical jokes.

But, the fullness of sacramental life, which she was to begin to enjoy in a few months, would help her to make great progress in overcoming all these movements of a passionate and vital nature. With what loving diligence she prepared to receive Jesus for the first time! How perfect, indeed, is the love with which such simple and faithful children as she respond to grace, without realizing that they are loving or knowing what supernatural love is. Many such children later on lose the simplicity and purity of a direct and unselfconscious desire of God, because they prefer an emotion which gives some satisfaction to their own selves, an emotion in which they can, so to speak, contemplate and taste their own excellence, instead of a love that goes so directly and unselfishly to its object, that it is all lost in God and leaves us no awareness of ourselves. But

Mary always belonged to the class of those who love without being aware that they love, and, indeed, lament that they don't love enough, while they love all the more because they are constantly begging God to make them love Him.

What was she thinking of? She knew that she would receive Jesus, and that she loved Him, and to receive Him was happiness, but perfect happiness was only in being with Him in heaven. Having heard from the nuns that little girls, who died right after receiving Holy Communion for the first time, went straight to heaven and were there with Jesus, never to be separated from Him, she spent the time of immediate preparation for this great grace with more and more fervent prayers to God that she might die the day of her first Communion. To her, this was the obvious thing to do. So simple was her faith that when night fell on the great day of April 26, 1888—that day in which she had been filled with a new and inexplicable happiness, so new and subtle and spiritual that she was hardly able to grasp the fact that it was a new experience, or even an experience at all—she lay down in her little bed and closed her eyes filled with perfect contentment and peace in the thought that she was going to wake up in heaven.

It was with genuine disappointment and surprise that she woke up the next morning in the little girls' dormitory of the Convent of the Redemption.

Still, she did not give up. The same favor, she was told, was shown to those who died right after receiving Confirmation. Since she was to be confirmed on the twenty-eighth of May, she renewed her prayers with equal fervor—and equal failure. Later on, she was to arrive at a deeper understanding of God's love and realize that, if He does not take us all at once into heaven, without labor or struggle, it is not for His benefit but for our happiness that He does so. No one was ever a saint without realizing the inseparable connection between the cross in this life and glory in the next: few have realized that connection more perfectly than Mother Berchmans.

But now that we are looking ahead to her life as Mother Berchmans, we must observe that it was at this time that Mary first began to desire that heaven on earth which the old Cistercian

Fathers called the *paradisus claustralis*, the "paradise of the cloister." And the beginning of her vocation was intimately connected with a deep and ardent and all-embracing devotion to the Mother of God.

The three great devotions that dominate the life of Mother Berchmans are the Holy Eucharist, the Sacred Heart (the two are practically the same), and Mary, the Virgin Mother of God. Around these three her life revolves, and they *are* her life.

Over and over again, she consecrates and reconsecrates herself to Mary, giving herself more and more fully each time, as her spirituality deepens and her love becomes more simple, more profound, and more heroic, until at last her whole life becomes one of perfect and total union with Mary, a union so close and so complete that it almost amounts to absorption in her.

All this began when, on the sixth of December, 1891, she climbed the hill to the famous basilica of Fourvières, from which shrine our Blessed Lady protects the city of Lyons with her miraculous influence, attracting pilgrims from all parts of France. There the little girl consecrated herself for the first time to a Mother who was to prove a sweet and generous protectress to her all her life long.

Now Mary is thirteen, and her education becomes more practical. She leaves the classroom for the sewing room, in which the Sisters prepare their charges for the struggle for a livelihood in the world outside. Indeed, after nine years of this apprenticeship, Mary, with all her inborn ability and good taste, was to become a skilled and perfect artist with the needle, able to produce the finest, most delicate, and most detailed work—work of a quality it would be hard to imitate in a world where men have ceased to learn such craftsmanship, and leave everything to the mediocrity of mass production by machinery.

Gradually, too, her lively and affectionate soul, open to the work of divine grace, and yielding more and more each day to the action of the Holy Spirit, was maturing in charity and joy. Her tantrums ceased, she far less frequently showed impatience, and her extravagant practical jokes and feats of mischievousness gave way to a milder and less animal form of humor. But she was always the joy and the life of the whole convent with her wit and good nature and her happy laughter.

It was now that deep and unselfish devotion to her companions and friends, that generous and instinctive love of others, though still so largely on the natural level, was beginning to develop into supernatural charity, through the secret, inward working of the leaven of grace.

She was developing a new seriousness and maturity, a new sense of responsibility, coupled with a dignity, good sense, and tact which commanded respect, so that, as the years of her adolescence went on, she was not infrequently left in charge of the workroom, and never failed to keep perfect order, nor to do so with sweetness, and charity. In a word, we see her, during these years, turning into a young woman of poise and grace, of gentle dignity and humble, chaste, and joyous charm; more than that, a young woman of great spiritual distinction, in whom one already sensed her vocation and future sanctification in a total sacrifice of herself to the Spouse and Life of souls.

She had become, as was natural, very attached to the kind Sisters who had been her first mistresses in the sewing room; it was under their care that she had first formed her lasting habits, her characteristic way of approaching her work. Now the mistresses were changed, and another came to replace them—one with an entirely different way of doing things and looking at things, and one, perhaps, less able or willing to understand Mary's own impulsive nature. No doubt, too, the new mistress was, by her very temperament, calculated to act as a hair shirt upon the sensibilities of the passionate girl. In Mary's soul there soon developed a great aversion to the person of this Sister, an aversion which she found it almost impossible to overcome, in spite of her good will. It was one of those situations, so common in community life, in which it seems that nothing either party can do to decrease the friction and embarrassment between them serves any purpose but to increase it. Every smile, every attempt at a friendly gesture, immediately goes awry, or is misinterpreted, or, in some completely unexpected way, fails, adds to the bitterness, deepens the wound.

Some of her companions took advantage of the situation to gratify their jealous spite and to calumniate Mary behind her back, by going to the mistress with their burden of petty and stupid falsehoods or exaggerations. What these tales were, everybody has forgotten, and they were probably never worth notice in any case; yet they managed to give Mary a taste of suffering, and an opportunity of acceptance of the trial and renunciation of her own will, which was, after all, what God wanted of her.

He did not leave her entirely without help or consolation. One of the other Sisters, who understood her better, soon realized what was happening, and was able to help and advise her.

She was received as a child of Mary—another thing, in itself apparently little and ordinary, which had a deeper effect on her soul that we can hope to realize. It represented another big step toward that union with Christ and His Mother, and brought her more closely than ever under the loving control and guidance of this most watchful and solicitous Mother of souls.

It will not be uninteresting to glance at the practical and external details of her spiritual life, at the time when Mary was growing to young womanhood in the Convent of the Redemption. We read, for instance, a page of resolutions to conquer her pride and sensitiveness. A resolution to be very respectful to her mistress, not to find fault with her instructions or commands, and to thank her for her criticisms and reprimands. A resolution not to give way to impatience—just what one would expect from a fervent child undergoing the difficulties that were hers. But then, too, we read that she resolves to die rather than commit a mortal sin; to say prayers attentively, realizing that she is talking to God, and keeping in His presence. After this medley of good and sincere desires, she sums them all up in one which is immeasurably more important and valuable, and which shows considerable spiritual maturity by the very fact that it is so simple and so fundamental.

"It seems to me," she writes, "that I am making quite a lot of resolutions. Am I going to keep them all? Yes, I hope I shall, for they can all be summed up in one word: Love. Yes, if I love God, I will say my prayers with more attention and piety, realizing that I am conversing with Him; I will behave better towards my companions, because I will see my crucified God in them; I will be more submissive to my mistresses because I will see them as the interpreters of God's will; I will be more severe with myself because I will remember that my heart is the temple of the Holy Ghost. O Jesus! Give me that love that can make virtue so easy, and which will give my life more merit in Your sight."

In this we see the difference between a soul that merely practices a lot of devotions, a soul that is merely "pious" in the bad sense that word has come to acquire in a secular parlance, and one that truly lives a life of Christian virtue—a life of love.

CHAPTER II

AN INTERVAL IN LYONS

In spite of all her little trials, Mary's life at the Convent of the Redemption was very happy, full of joy and love. That she had difficulties with only one mistress and one or two companions, and that only for a little while, serves to accentuate the universality and warmth of her affection for the Sisters and for her schoolmates in the convent. And so, when she had finally to leave them, in October, 1897, it was not without struggle and sacrifice.

After living surrounded for nineteen years (she was now twenty-one) by the care and affection of the Sisters, by the atmosphere of love and peace and quiet, she now had to live alone and almost friendless in a big and noisy, hostile and dangerous city, and try to earn her bread in it. The only remaining members of her family were her mother and sister, and they did not live in Lyons. Consequently, Mary boarded with an old maid who had once, like herself, graduated from the convent school. Each day the girl went out to work, turning to account the skill she had acquired in the Sisters' sewing room, by doing fine needlework for the rich and noble families of the city. She was also employed, for some time, as governess to a little child of one of these families, and, indeed, everywhere she went, she was treated with kindness and respect; but still, she had no real home, and her employers were still employers, rather than true friends. A year after she had left the Redemption, she made a retreat which only served to open the wound that was slow in closing. It reminded her of her last retreat at the convent, and filled her heart all over again with sadness and loneliness.

She wrote, in a little notebook, of that retreat:

"Sometimes I wonder if I will ever again be able to enjoy life and have pleasure, if I will ever again be happy." But then, immediately realizing the weakness implied by this statement, she goes on, not to try to deny her weakness, but to exploit it as an argument to induce Jesus to help her and deliver her from it: "Do not be angry with me, Jesus! For was it not You that gave me this heart of mine? And surely You know well enough how tender and affectionate a heart it is! Let this power, this great strength of love that beats in it, be raised up even to You, my Jesus! For only close to You will this passion of love find its full satisfaction."

This was to be the whole problem of her life, her greatest source of suffering and of merit: how to liberate her strong affections from attachment to creatures, to persons for their own sake, and set them free to fly as high as heaven and God Himself? The closer she came to God, the more the realization of her attachment to His creatures was to cause her pain.

Her love, insatiable in its desire for perfection, might have become just as insatiable in its appetite for tragedy and death. With her, it was all or nothing. Supposing she had drifted into the company of pleasure-loving people, careless of their souls' lives, and ready to sacrifice everybody else's happiness and salvation to their own desires? Where might she not have ended? There was no one to restrain her, no one to advise her should she start on such a course.

Fortunately, she had no taste for the world or its life or pleasures or ambitions. She did not even understand it. It meant nothing to her. She would have nothing to do with it. In spite of her natural good taste and love of pretty things, she was not even captivated with fine clothes. Her days were spent in the houses of those for whom she worked. In the morning, after Mass, a carriage would call for her, and the same would bring her back again at the fall of night. Then she would retire to her room to read a little or pray before going to bed. She had few friends, all of them girls she had known at the convent. She did not desire or seek any others.

Not only did she not understand the world, but she was completely ignorant of its ordinary dangers. She was surprised to find that a young girl could not always go about the streets of a big industrial city, alone and unescorted, when and as she pleased. She only learned this truth from the experience of being accosted and pursued by a profligate until she was forced to fly for refuge into the house of a friend! A good lady of her acquaintance was very upset to hear that Mary went through the empty streets to Mass, all by herself in the half-light of dawn, and thereafter saw her safely to the church door. On her return, however, especially after Communion, the young girl was glad to be alone, and even sought a roundabout way home, in order to avoid meeting acquaintances and getting into conversation.

There was another perplexing experience, caused again by her innocence and unsuspecting good nature. She was walking in the rain, and noticed a poor woman, soaking wet, to whom she offered the shelter of her umbrella. It was only after a little while that she realized from the woman's uncertain gait, her thick and confused speech, and the strong smell of alcohol, that her new-found friend was extremely drunk. To a young girl in France there is naturally something very shocking and painful about the sight of a drunken woman, because such a thing is rare enough in that country. But in any case, drunkards have an altogether embarrassing familiarity about them, and Mary was glad to escape from the tender regard her new companion suddenly developed for her.

However, she was not a Pharisee. When a childhood friend, who had grown up and fallen upon evil days, finally became involved in a public scandal, Mary did not despise or abandon her without consolation. The poor woman had figured in one of those *crimes passionels* that fill the back pages of the French newspapers, one of those outbursts of passion, that always end in violence and tragedy. What were the details? We do not need to know them; for there is a monotonous sameness about all these stupid crimes. Weakened by sin, and crazy with all the passions that crucify a jealous and sensual nature, someone had pulled out a revolver, or perhaps a knife: the woman was in the hospital, and the story in all the papers. And the other? Perhaps he was dead, having ended the business by placing the revolver against his own temple. That would be one variation of the familiar pattern.

The nuns of the Hôtel Dieu were affable to Mary, when she presented herself. Obviously a good and pious girl; they could see it written all over her. Yet when they heard her ask to see their notorious patient, their attitude was somewhat changed. Mary was not abashed by the evident suspicion on the part of the good Sisters; she went and visited and consoled her onetime friend.

When one of the girls she had known in the convent developed tuberculosis she was abandoned by most of her acquaintances, but not by Mary. She did not fear the sickness, nor hesitate to visit her often, to help and console her in every way she could.

Her charity was even attended with supernatural help and intervention. Another of her friends had diphtheria, and was given up for lost by the doctors. Mary, in a movement of strong and loving faith, took a silver medal of St. Philomena and put it around the girl's neck. During the course of the night the abscess burst, and the following day the astonished physician declared that the girl was out of danger.

It is no wonder that those who knew her thought she was a saint. Innocent, happy, affectionate, she was without a grain of envy or malice, generous, unselfish, and tender, yet reserved and recollected, seeing God in everything, prayerful, retiring, and quiet. Everywhere she went people were impressed with her simplicity and peace.

Later on, in the midst of trial and darkness, when as a Cistercian nun, she was to see herself apparently abandoned to every kind of temptation and imperfection, she was to cry out in dismay: "In the world, I was a saint, and in the cloister I have become a devil."

Mary's vocation to the cloister, vague and always present in the background of her consciousness since her first Communion, now began to be more clear and precise, more insistent in its appeals.

In the month of November, 1893, she made a retreat with a number of other girls of her own age—a retreat preached by a

Dominican friar, aimed especially at helping the girls to determine whether or not they had religious vocations. This was the question Mary had in her mind when she presented herself at the doors of the convent where the retreat was to be given.

"Oh my God!" she wrote in her notebook, "give me grace to profit by these days of recollection. I cast myself into Your arms. I abandon myself entirely to You. Do with me whatever You please, I desire nothing but Your will.... During these hours in which all will become silent within my soul, You will speak to me, Jesus; You will tell me what I am to do, what are Your plans for me. You will make known to me my vocation, and will sweep aside all that stands in the way of the accomplishment of Your will."

She was not to be disappointed. The preacher began his conferences. She spent hours in prayer and silence. The days went by. She listened; and by the time the retreat was over, God's answer had formed itself imperceptibly within her, in a manner that escaped all notice and attention, by a simple accumulation of desires and convictions arising out of the sermons and her conversations with God in her own heart. She was left with a great fear of growing cold in her faith, of losing the presence of God, of becoming weak and tepid. She felt a powerful desire to renew her faithful union with Him, to live more and more in His presence, to be always with Him alone: with a great and ardent desire of sacrifice, an undefined sense of pain and shame at not having given Him everything, a vague dissatisfaction and sorrow at the feeling that she was retaining too much for herself, a sense of embarrassment with the possession of anything other than God alone, for His own sake. There is no doubt that the retreat master was able to recognize in this hunger for God alone the true sign of a contemplative vocation, and he told her so.

Immediately after her retreat, she approached the Benedictine nuns of La Rochette, but they, too, were able to see in this intense and special hunger for solitude and sacrifice something that could only be satisfied by one of the most austere, the most enclosed, the most silent, the most penitential of all the orders in the Church: The Cistercians, La Trappe.

The Trappistines are the Sisters of the Trappists, and every bit as severe. But that does not mean that the strange legends that the world has applied to them and to the sons of De Rancé's reform were ever true. There is no need to explode the old jokes about the monks digging a shovel full of dirt out of their graves every day and never speaking except to say: *Memento mori!* The happy children of this enclosed order are beginning to be better known, now that books are getting to be written about them by people who have some idea of what the life is really like.

The truth is, the Cistercian life is a life of superabundant joy. It is hard, certainly. But the very function of the silence, the fasting, the hard labor, the long offices chanted in the night, and so on, is to liberate the souls of the monks and nuns from all the cares and burdens that make people unhappy. The Cistercian is joyful because he is free—delivered from the crushing anxieties that are bred of selfishness and passion. His heart belongs to God, and can fly to Him without fear and without impediment, and will always find Him there, even though He may be hidden in the deepest darkness by spiritual trials.

That was what Mary needed: a life that would concentrate all her energies on the one great activity for which she had been created: the love of God. It can be said, in fact, that God had made the Cistercian Order for her, and her for the Order. That is the way it is with religious vocations. Those who have the immense privilege of such a call can be fully convinced that God destined them from all eternity for this one particular function in His Church and fashioned them for nothing else.

He had made Mary's affectionate heart in order to plant her like a flower in the enclosed and hidden garden of the cloister to bloom for Him alone: yet at the same time He called her to be a Cistercian in order to unite her to Himself through the life of fraternal charity, so eminently characteristic of an order whose members are always in community and never live alone.

How happy Mary must have been when, in January, 1899, she received a reply to her first, tentative letter to the reverend mother abbess of the Trappistine nuns of Our Lady of the Immaculate Conception, at Laval.

The letter, it is true, was noncommittal and full of reservations, as the rule prescribes. It has never been the practice of the Cistercians to flatter or encourage postulants, since it is evident that if God is really calling them, they will be discouraged by no coldness; whereas if He is not, too much encouragement would only be cruelty.

Reverend Mother Marie Antoinette confined herself, in this first letter, to the mention of the ordinary hardships of the Cistercian rule, suggesting politely that Mary had better examine herself and study her vocation before attempting to embrace a life like that. But far from frightening the girl, this recital only fired her ardor to a still greater intensity, and strengthened her in her resolutions; yes, she could indeed see that this was the way God wanted her to go! For she could tell that here indeed she would find Him, and, giving up the world and herself, she would be able to rest at last in Him, and possess peace in union with her Beloved.

She continued to correspond with reverend mother abbess, and eventually her letters, so full of evident sincerity and generous faith, must have impressed Mère Marie Antoinette favorably, for presently practical steps began to be taken concerning her admission.

"Have courage, dear child," wrote the Cistercian abbess, "we hope that divine Providence will dispose all things so that you may make your first steps under the guidance of His Sacred Heart"—for Mary now hoped to enter Laval on that feast, which was the center of her own devotional life—"and may the Blessed herself lead you. Under such protection you may well expect to persevere—and we desire your perseverance as much as you do yourself."

Meanwhile, the spiritual director of the nuns at Laval happened to come to Lyons, to testify at the diocesan process of a saintly priest, Venerable Antoine Chevrier, whose cause was then in its initial stages. The good Cistercian, who went by the somewhat amusing name of Père Polycarpe Jaricot, had once worked under Ven. Chevrier as a secular priest in the slums of the great city, and had learned from him the secret of a deep interior life. Père Chevrier preached in season and out of season the necessity of a life of prayer, poverty, and sacrifice in the priesthood, and he had been

Father Jaricot's director for some fourteen years. Père Polycarpe had been present at his death.

This priest, who was now to become Mary's spiritual father, had entered the Cistercian Order at the ancient monastery of Tamié, high up in the Alps of Savoy, famous for the memory of its first abbot, St. Peter of Tarentaise. There he had become prior, and only left that charge and his monastery at the command of the abbot general of the Reformed Cistercians, Dom Sebastian Wyart, who appointed him confessor to the Trappistines of Laval. In doing so, Dom Sebastian had told the nuns: "I have given you the most pious, the most interior, and the most saintly monk that I know of."

This experienced priest now took advantage of the occasion to interview Mary in Lyons, questioning her about her desires and aspirations, and all her reasons for wanting to enter so strict an order. To him she opened her heart, with all her inborn sincerity and simplicity, and showed him there so true and fervent a love of Jesus, so complete and absolute a need to be with Him alone, live for Him alone, work, pray, fast, make sacrifices—yes, sacrifice everything, down to her last breath, for Him alone, that Father Polycarpe could not help but cry out, when she had finished:

"There is no doubt about it: you belong in La Trappe!"

CHAPTER III

THE CONVENT AT LAVAL

Under the soft brightness of the June sky, the countryside of Mayenne, in which lies the little city of Laval on the borders of Normandy and Brittany, lay steeped in warmth and fragrance and peace. All the fields and orchards were full of flowers. The quiet air, since it was late in the morning, was beginning to be heavy and sleepy with the luxury of summer sunshine; but the songs of birds still refreshed the ear, the songs of birds and of bells from the Trappistine convent, at which Mary was even now arriving, while the conventual Mass for the great feast of the Sacred Heart was nearing its close.

All her prayers were being answered; all the desires of her heart were being fulfilled. She was entering the convent as she had planned and hoped to do, on her favorite feast day. All the beauty of the woods and fields, the peaceful suburban houses that straggled out to the convent from the edge of the city, the sky, the birds, the bells, spoke to her of the love of the human Heart of Jesus for her and of His inexpressible tenderness and kindness to all men and all living things, whose life He cherishes and sustains in the hollow, so to speak, of His hand. But her own weariness and weakness of body after a journey and all the other experiences of the past few days, lay upon her like the burden of a great cross, a burden and a shadow upon her own heart, tempting her with fear and sorrow. Yet the fear and the sorrow were nothing at all, because of the courage that was poured into her heart from the Heart which is the center of all hearts, and the fountain of all consolation and strength.

When the extern Sisters at the convent gate looked out of the little barred peephole in the door to see who had rung the bell, they beheld a pale, sensitive, angelic, beautiful face, full of weariness and suffering, and yet of joy and hope and eagerness. Who was this tired girl, in her sober yet elegant clothes? Did she, perhaps, expect to enter the convent and face the hardships of their life? Look at her thin white hands, her delicate and slender frame, her sensitive face! But in the midst of that pale, expressive countenance two large eyes burned with courage and eagerness, love and simplicity. No matter what happened, she had not come to the convent *pour rire*—as a joke. And if she stayed, and if it cost her any price, she looked as though she were burning to pay that price, burning with courage and good will. If she stayed, she would become a saint. If she stayed—but would she even be admitted, so weak and frail?

The last few days had been harrowing for Mary. They had torn her body and her soul to pieces, and it would not have been surprising if she had collapsed on the threshold of the convent. She had needed all the help and strength she could gain from a pilgrimage to Lourdes, the month before, in preparation for the ordeal of separation from her family and the journey to Laval. It was true that she had lived all her life apart from her mother and sister, but she had spent her vacations with them, and was bound to them by ties of the closest affection, as were they to her: the whole family was filled with the same sensitiveness and affection and warmth of heart. But they were not, like Mary, prepared by a greater and more ardent love for God to stand such a separation. Nor were they even ready for her to announce her intention to enter so austere a cloistered order, although they must surely have suspected that she would eventually enter religion.

Her mother took the news as a great shock, and did not attempt to make it any the lighter by restraining her emotions. Friends and relatives gathered to hear the tidings, and were not much help either. Most of them were loud in their recriminations of such folly. Did the girl want to kill her mother by this suicidal act of hers, burying herself alive among the Trappistines? "*Et pourtant*," cried her aunts with monstrous shrugs, flinging out their arms in amazement and protest, "*et pourtant elle n'a tué ni père ni mère*," thereby subscribing to the belief current among the French middle class that, in order to become a Trappist, one must first have shot his father or stabbed his mother. But Mary had committed no murders. There was much clicking of the tongue and shaking of the head, and everyone had some kind of a suggestion for her. All knew of some order or other that would be more appropriate for her, if only she would not enter the Trappistines. Of course the whole thing was based on the obvious supposition that she shouldn't enter any order, but stay out of religion and get married like any sensible young girl.

Meanwhile mother wept and sobbed, and some of the others with her. The only one in the whole crowd who had really been calm and tearless through it all was Mary herself. "Mama," she finally said, gently, "are you going to weep because I am happy? *Tu pleures mon bonheur?*"

These tearful farewells were not prolonged. Mary left again as soon as she decently could, and hastened alone, in the dusk of evening, toward the station. It was only then, by herself, and seeking refuge for a few minutes in the peace and darkness of a church, that she allowed her own heart to overflow. The sanctuary lamp flickered in the shadows where her Beloved stood, tenderly considering her. She felt the peace of His sweet gaze fill, not her eyes or her imagination, but the root and depths of her will flooding her with strength and acquiescence, with consent and peace. The flow of warm tears eased her and she went on to the station more tranquil and freed of the nervousness and strain that had followed her from her mother's house.

The physical ordeal of the journey from Lyons to Laval was as great, in its own way, as had been the emotional crisis at home. For all the French railway systems converge upon Paris, and the way from Lyons to Laval does not lie through Paris; it cuts across several of these systems, so that Mary spent the whole night on second-rate trains, frequently changing at dark and smoky junctions, and, for the rest, sitting sleepless against the hard cushions, staring at the inevitable, yellowish photos of romantic spots along the line.

Now she was left alone in the cool, shuttered room in the convent guesthouse, listening to the hushed footsteps of the extern Sister hastening away down the corridor, outside, to get Father Polycarpe.

Even this good priest was shocked when he came into the room by the fatigue and pallor of Mary's face as she stood up to welcome him, and one of his first remarks was to question her again about her health. Did she really, seriously, think that she could stand the Trappist life?

Her answer reflects all that must have been going through her tired mind, and is filled with humble courage and determination to sacrifice everything for her Beloved, even though all she had to sacrifice might be practically nothing.

"Father," she said, "if I last long enough to receive the habit, it will be enough!"

She must indeed have been tired, tired and unwell.

The rule prescribes that, when a postulant presents herself, she is not to be encouraged, but rather tried and tested by a frank, if not brutal, presentation of the difficulties of the life. Apparently, Father Polycarpe did not have the heart to go about it with dogged seriousness; instead, his threats and menaces were touched with a certain irony.

"You know," he said presently, after considering her elegant clothes and delicate white hands, "one of your jobs will be to take a basin of hot water and give the pigs a bath." Trappist pigs, as everybody knows, are spotlessly clean—for pigs. Mary did not quail at the prospect.

"Another thing," he added, "if you make any useless signs, they will hang little bells on your fingers, so that if you repeat the fault, your disgrace will be known all over the convent."

After all these semiserious menaces, he brought their short interview to a close with a suggestion that really did arouse her opposition. It was almost noon, she was very tired, and so, perhaps it would be better for her to have something to eat right away.

But she had waited all this time for Communion; surely he would not disappoint her!

"It is late," he said. "You are exhausted. I dispense you from Communion. You had better get something to eat."

The notion of a "dispensation" from Communion, as though it were a duty and not the greatest joy in her life, had no place in the understanding of this fervent young postulant.

"Well I don't dispense myself," she said quickly. "Please, Father, please give me Communion!"

So earnest and sincere a desire was not to be denied, and, indeed, to have denied it would have been a great act of cruelty; so Father Polycarpe did not insist on his authority.

They passed down the corridor and soon found themselves in the vast, shadowy silence of the secular chapel adjoining the convent church, from which it was separated by the high grille that marked the inviolable enclosure of the cloistered Sisters. Facing the priest and the young girl as they came in was a statue of the immaculate Queen of heaven, welcoming her child with open arms to her new home; but the heart and eyes of the girl flew straight to the high altar, where, in the midst of a garden of flowerlike candles, Jesus in the Blessed Sacrament, solemnly exposed for the great feast, looked down upon her in silence and in peace, and blessed her with gladness and inward rest.

The whole church was empty, except for the two nuns watching behind the grille; the rest of the community had retired for the *meridienne*, or noonday rest, prescribed by St. Benedict in the summertime. The young girl sank to her knees, closed her eyes, bowed her head, emptied her heart of the noise of the world and of all that had pursued her across France in that miserable night, and waited in loving peace for the coming of her Christ.

She heard the furtive scratch of the tabernacle key, and the whispered words of Father Polycarpe; then she closed her eyes again and remained in perfect tranquility, speaking in the depths of her heart to Him who had come, less to be absorbed into her being than to absorb her into Himself.

That afternoon, writing in her little notebook, in her room in the guesthouse, she summed up everything that had happened that day with these words: "Even if it kills me: I am going to be a saint!"

Her life of sacrifices was not long in beginning. Right after she had finished the simple dinner provided for her in the guesthouse, the first demand was made upon her will and judgment. It was nothing very great—she was not asked to take the discipline, or put on a hair shirt, or go to the gatehouse and cast herself at the feet of all the passers-by, asking for their prayers. Such would not have been an appropriate beginning to the Trappist life, which, if hard, is nevertheless essentially undramatic, no matter what it may seem to be in the imaginations of those outside the monastery. The sacrifices demanded of a Cistercian are crushing, not by the weight of physical torture they impose, but by their relentless accumulation of trivialities and little monotonies which wear out our self-will by their own very insignificance. With so many and such petty sacrifices it becomes almost impossible for a sincere religious to dramatize himself as a hero, when his repugnance to such minute and colorless things only serves to remind him of his complete lack of heroism. They make him forget himself and think only of God, who alone is truly great. Greater and more showy sacrifices might easily serve to make us satisfied with ourselves.

When the contents of Mary's suitcase were examined, it was soon found that none of her dresses had the simplicity required of a postulant in a Trappistine convent. They were all in excellent taste, of course. In fact, they were in too good taste. They expressed an elegance and refinement that would arouse too much attention and comment. And so, something a little more monastic had to be found. The extern Sisters procured for the young girl a dress that had served, day and night, for the postulancy of someone of the nuns. Its colors were faded, its design was blurred. It was only an approximate fit. But Mary exchanged her stylish dresses for this shapeless garment and felt great interior satisfaction at being able to make this first sacrifice of her own taste and will. From then until her reception of the habit, she wore no other dress, even on Sundays.

She was no sooner fitted out in this new apparel than another and more pleasant surprise awaited her. Called once more to the guesthouse parlor, she was astonished to see the door open to admit a nun pushing a wheel chair in which sat a figure at once impressive in every way. For Mary now beheld one of those extraordinary persons who, even in sickness and weakness, inspire respect by a kind of tremendous inner dignity and strength. To such persons, even a wheel chair can become a throne. Not that Reverend Mother Mary Antoinette (for it was the abbess herself) was a domineering or overweening mistress. Her power was of a different kind. Her strength was a strength full of sweetness. Her authority was the authority of inward peace, profound inward peace which can only come from a life that is plunged and immersed in the Holy Ghost.

Mary loved this saintly abbess at once and accepted her as her new mother, and the abbess, in her turn, was very pleased with what she saw in the new postulant. For she, with a keener and deeper and more penetrating glance even than that of Father Polycarpe, saw straight into the fervent and courageous heart of this sincere and simple girl; unlike the nuns' confessor, she did not hesitate or wonder for a single moment about the pallor and exhaustion of the girl's face. All that was indifferent to her, since it could no longer cast a shadow of doubt upon the vocation which she clearly saw written in the frank and earnest eyes of her new daughter. Therefore she made no difficulty about accepting her at once, and she said:

"Well, child, tomorrow morning you will be at the cloister door, and Mother Dominic, our novice mistress, will come and let you in and show you where you are to sleep for the time being."

It was still only a transition from the guesthouse, not full participation in the life of the novices; but she would be within the cloister, and praying in choir, and eating in the refectory, and going to chapter with the others.

The next morning, Saturday, the tenth of June, 1899, under a statue of the Mother of God, this little postulant waited by the locked door of the cloister, impatient to hear the quiet footsteps and the sound of the key from within.

Such a moment is unforgettable. It is as great and moving and terrible as death. Indeed, it is a death, a true death, the death of a secular. A person, a young girl from the city of Lyons, a working girl, a certain unit of secular society, a citizeness of France, was to cease to exist as certainly as if she had been put to death. As soon as she placed her foot over the threshold, into the cool and absolutely silent cloister of these penitential nuns, she would die a legal and a moral death, and become a new person, a new unit in a different society, a postulant in a convent, and before her name would be the word *Sister*. It is astonishing and beyond comprehension how real and deep a change is operated in a person taking such a step—taking it, that is, with the full intention of never turning back.

Nor was there any fear or any hesitation in her heart. She stood alone, in the empty hallway, before this blank, barred door behind which lay a mystery capable of striking a girl's heart with the coldness of mortal terror: the mystery of complete separation from everything that appeals to natural affection, taste, and desire: the mystery of leaping into the dark, blindly and with total abandon, simply because the voice of a Lover you have never seen calls you to come to Him.

Mary faced all this with a sense of exultation and triumph, because already, by her love and faith and eager acceptance of His call, she was in close union with the God who loved her, and who had said: "Fear not, for I have overcome the world." Indeed, at that very moment, she was tasting the triumph of the everlasting, complete, and universal victory of Christ over death. At that very moment, her soul, mystically one, by faith and love, with the soul of Christ, was emerging like a thunderclap from a sealed sepulcher in Jerusalem that her bodily eyes had never seen and never would see in this life. For there is only one real joy for mortal men in the whole universe, and that is the supernatural joy of Christ's resurrection from the dead, of which all our own joys at conquest of sin, at overcoming the world and its ambitions, are a true participation.

If Mary now looked back upon the world, it was as one looking back on something that had suddenly become alien and strange, weird and already unbelievable, the way Jesus looked back on the sufferings before His death, once He had risen from the tomb.

Mary's only thought now, as far as she was concerned, was of joy that she had escaped from the temptations, errors, and confusion that were now behind her. But there was another thought that prevented her from being perfectly joyful, perfectly satisfied: the thought of her mother and sister, who had not escaped, and who were still out there, in the world, in the battle, in the whirlwind.

She had lifted up her eyes with prayers for them upon her lips when, to her surprise, the key was already rattling in the lock; the door was opened and she was welcomed by the young, round-faced nun, who was mistress of novices, into the silent cloister.

At a sign from Mother Dominic, Mary followed her down the cloister to a door that admitted them, first of all, into the convent church, where her first act as a Trappistine was to fall on her knees in great excitement and joy. No doubt it was hard to make an intelligible prayer of any sort, but surely Christ accepted her confusion and happiness as a most pleasing salutation and thanksgiving. Then, in a moment, she followed the good nun back into the cloister.

Every stone, every inch of this convent was spotless. The fragrance of cool cleanliness communicated a sense of refreshment and peace to the mind of the young postulant. But now her wide and earnest eyes were spelling out the pious inscriptions painted, in the Trappist tradition, all along the walls. "I look for no reward," she read, as they walked, "and no rest in this world. My hope is in heaven with God, the object of my love."

Mother Dominic had opened another door and they were in the chapter room, with its crucifix, its three severe thrones, and the long benches for the Sisters. Ever since De Rancé, the chapter room has been regarded as a peculiarly Trappist place of penance, for the great reformer of La Trappe was a zealous promoter of the chapter of faults, in which the Cistercian momentarily regains the power of speech, in order to accuse his brethren, in a few words and gently enough, of external faults against the rule or usages or the known will of the first superior; from that point on, the bitterness of the penance depends on the superior. The tradition of De Rancé indicated merciless humiliation as the most merciful and charitable form of correction. This is not the usual thing, by any means, nor is there any reason why it should be. But anyway, in a moment they were back again in the cloister, and Mary was reading another inscription: “Here is the place of my rest; here will I live, for I have chosen it.”

In the refectory, the mistress of novices led Mary along the spotless tables to the place that was to be hers. There was a simple water jug, a wooden spoon, fork, and knife, an earthenware mug, an enameled plate, and a large napkin folded and disposed over the mug and other implements in a special way. Looking up and down the table, one could see, in strict and martial array, a long line of similar jugs and napkins. Mother mistress explained the mystery of how to fold the napkin, and warned the postulant that after her meal which would consist of soup, bread, vegetables, and, perhaps, an apple, she would have to wash her knife and fork and spoon in her drinking mug and dry them on her napkin, empty the mug into the soup bowl and dry it also on the napkin, leaving everything as it now appeared on the table. Deep in her heart, the postulant felt the stirring of a certain worldly delicacy that began obscurely to resent these details, but she said nothing; and, anyway, everything was so confusing that she soon forgot her repugnance—until a few days later when it was to become one of those trivial crosses that God in His mercy gives to Trappists as a special favor, to keep from imagining that they are heroes of asceticism.

From there, they went up to the dormitory to see the cell that Mary would not immediately occupy. For a few days, she would be allowed a separate room to sleep in, to make the transition to this hard, new life more easy. Now she viewed the long, bare row of cells, separated by partitions. Inside on three planks, was a straw mattress and a straw pillow, under which she would hide the knotted cords of the discipline, brought forth for the scourging of her bare shoulders on Friday mornings, in the darkness just before dawn, right after the night office.

Leaving the bare dormitory, they descended to the cloister, and one more inscription struck Sister Berchmans even to the depths of her heart: “I weep to see Jesus abandoned and outraged. No one consoles Him.... No one loves Him. He is left alone.”

Filled with all these mixed impressions of wonder and joy, sadness and hope, the confused sense of the magnitude and glory of her vocation and the weight of the responsibilities it would put upon her soul, Mary entered upon her new life.

Like so many postulants—one might almost say, like the majority—she tasted in these first days in the cloister a happiness that she had never known before. Having entered the order in June, she probably avoided one small cross that is the usual lot of the secular trying to become acclimatized to a Trappist monastery; that is the worst cold in the head he has ever had in his life. At any other but the mildest seasons, the sudden change of life usually produces this effect, but it is not recorded that Sister Berchmans suffered from anything of the sort. We do not need to feel disappointed; there was plenty in store for her later on.

It seems that her first days in the community at Laval—indeed, all her days there—were days of unmixed joy, upon which the minute external trials of the Cistercian life did not even cast the smallest cloud. She did not find the life hard: on the contrary, all the observances were, with a few small exceptions, a joy to her. She was not so inhuman that she did not find at least a few things about the life, or the convent, repugnant to her, but like most fervent souls, she took these things in her stride: nor would it even be worth mentioning that she thought it a little idiotic to go through the ceremony known as "prostrating on the knuckles," or definitely repugnant to wipe one's hands on the same towel as all the others just before entering the refectory to eat, if such strange things were not often seriously offered as excuses by postulants who find the life unbearable.

There were only a handful of novices at Laval, when Sister Berchmans entered there; but here, even in the natural order, she was most fortunate in her new companions. All of them were young girls filled with her own spirit of joy and innocence, intelligence and ardent generosity. Most of them, too, shared her sensitiveness and delicacy and good taste. One of them was the aristocratic daughter of an ex-officer in the papal zouaves; another was a Polish girl, full of the fine and angelic ardor that is very often found in the people of her nation, and which expressed itself in irrepressible joy and gratitude for her vocation.

Sister Berchmans entered with her whole heart into this atmosphere of happy generosity. As one might expect from her impulsive nature, she was too often carried away, by her own gaiety, to extremes; but everyone has to have some natural weakness or other. Either one is inclined to be too affectionate or too cold and critical, too boisterous or too melancholy, too quick tempered or lifeless and lethargic, too energetic and bustling or lazy and too slow. If, from the point of view of a silent community, a person who is always bursting out laughing and making a lot of idiotic and incomprehensible signs may prove at times to be a real nuisance, that person's gaiety is a much better weakness than no gaiety at all.

When Mary became a novice, the dinners of the community would quite frequently have, as their prelude, a public penance in which she announced in a loud, clear voice, her failures in modesty and recollection, or read aloud St. Benedict's ninth and tenth degrees of humility, concerning monks who talk too much, or laugh too much, including the scriptural comment that "the fool lifteth up his voice in laughter."

Relations with her Sisters in the novitiate were not all on this more or less natural level; if they were, there would not be much point in remarking on them. Where is the special merit in being happy in the company of people who are gay and happy as yourself? "Do not even the gentiles so?" But Sister Berchmans poured out her heart in every possible act of charity, excelling all her sisters in ingenuity and zeal in finding out new favors and services to perform for others, new ways of giving up her own pleasure and comfort and satisfaction for others. In this she was a true Cistercian from the very start, for it is of the very essence of the Cistercian life to show, in all things, reverence and honor, solicitude and care for all of one's brethren in the cloister, "preventing one another in honor" and "obeying one another, knowing that by this path of obedience they shall come to God" (Rule of St. Benedict, Chap. 71).

Indeed, her love was as exuberant as her joy, and this exuberance made every sacrifice easy. More than that, she was impatient with what she feared was her own lack of generosity, and desired to miss no opportunity for giving up everything, down to the last detail. Therefore, she had not been many days in the novitiate when she determined to make the spoliation of herself even more complete than it had been before. She stripped herself of her smallest possessions; her own beloved rosary was exchanged for one more plain and indifferent to her, the little holy pictures she had brought with her were all given away, as well as a pious book or two. Everything went with them, down to the last medal and memento of her first Communion and even her sodality ribbon. She wrote in her diary: "Now there is no bond left to keep me back...."

Jesus, who was very close to her, even in her heart, said nothing, did not chide her, did not despise her sincerity, did not laugh at her, but from the depths of His infinite and silent wisdom loved her all the more. There was plenty of time for His love to take its wise course, and reveal to her so many bonds tying her to the earth that she would be tempted almost to despair, until she saw His secret love, in the darkness of her trials, cut them, forever, one by one.

More joy! She writes in her notebook, on the twenty-fifth of June, barely two weeks after her entrance into the convent: "I can hardly believe the joy that fills me to overflowing. My confessor agrees to let me go ahead with what I desire so much: he is going to allow me to make a vow of virginity before religious profession.... My God, You are too good! What can I do for You in return? I will immolate, sacrifice myself upon the Cross! Dear God, do whatever You please with me. I am Your little spouse. I love You, O my Beloved; I love You, my heavenly Spouse...."

This was only the beginning. Her whole three months' postulancy was to arrive at a crescendo of romantic fervor that was only increased by the delays and reserves imposed upon her ardor by Father Polycarpe. He agreed to allow her to consecrate herself to God by this vow on the sixteenth of July, which was still a month distant. And then, he permitted her to make the vow for only a month; she was to renew it in August. All this simply heightened her expectation and her desire.

At the end of June the nuns kept the feast of the Perpetual

Adoration by exposing the Blessed Sacrament for twenty-four hours, and the hour to watch before the altar, from eleven to midnight, was assigned to Sister Berchmans and a companion—probably the other postulant, Sister Mary Angela, who was to receive the habit on the same day as Mary.

Alone in the dark church, before the quiet blaze of the candles and the silence of their Spouse's inscrutable love, isolated in the midst of the profound quietness of the sleeping convent, the two young girls lifted up their faces in wonder and love to their Jesus, and drank into their souls full draughts of grace and consolation. It was one of those moments when God chooses, in His wise, kind mercy, to bend down to His little creatures and speak to them and console them in their own sensible language, moving their hearts with lights and ardors that they can perceive and comprehend, in order to strengthen and attract them, and lift them up to receive, in darkness and emptiness, the far greater graces which cannot be understood or felt, because they are infinitely above the level of our natural comprehension.

"O Jesus!" Sister Berchmans hastened to write the next day in her diary, "Is it not to You that I owe my selection of that particular time? To think that I was able to spend, before the Blessed Sacrament, the last hour of this month of June which has been so momentous for me, since it has determined my eternity! Oh, what delightful moments I spent there before the Tabernacle: I felt very near to my Beloved, and the dark, ugly curtains that usually hide from me the dwelling of my God were taken away. Jesus was all mine! Oh happy hour, oh heavenly moments in which the soul forgets all, in God: why are you so short? In this solemn hour, I felt myself animated with an ardor altogether new, and in the intoxication of my happiness, I asked my Beloved to deprive me, from now on, of all sensible graces."

It was not necessary for her to realize what she was asking, or what such a request might cost, any more than it is necessary for us to be established in sanctity before we can reasonably desire to become saints. God had really spoken in the depth of her heart, and some movement of the light that flooded her had made her realize, in some obscure manner, that all this sensible joy and pleasure and consolation was something far less perfect than the pure love that is liberated from the senses and imagination and the feelings, and therefore lifted above all mood and vicissitude and change, making us, by our oneness of intention and unswerving desire of God alone, like unto Him in His unchanging perfection. And so she added: "I want to love Him simply for Himself alone, and my love will be more pure, when stripped of all these celestial favors."

And yet, such a prayer as this can be the result of caprice, even of pride, in a soul which might utter it, for example, out of a conviction of its own superior sanctity and ability to bear any suffering. Mary evidently did not mean it in any such sense. It was the simple, sincere response of a truly loving heart that desired only to please her God, something probably not uncommon among novices and postulants in such an order as the Trappistines. Surely her Spouse was not displeased with her. He did not answer her prayer right away—unless we take a passing mood of dryness and loneliness, of a more or less natural order, for an immediate consequence of the prayer.

"Why are you troubled, O my soul!" she exclaims, only a few days later, not without the melodramatic overtones of a Chateaubriand or a Lamartine. "Why this vague sorrow? No, you are not alone! Is not God with you? You are appalled at the isolation that is all around you, and at the depth of solitude that meets your gaze! And your Jesus, your Beloved? Have you forgotten that He is near you? And that Divine Master, He suffers at your suffering. How can you believe that, after having taken you out of the crowd, and led you into solitude, He could leave you alone, all by yourself?"

It was not yet the dark night of the soul. By the next page of her journal, the cries of woe, the *vague tristesse* are forgotten. It was simply one of those inevitable movements of nature, a passing mood of sadness, which occur in everybody's life and not just in convents.

On the twelfth of July, she has received permission to make her vow of virginity on the sixteenth, and now her sincere and loving heart is overflowing with earnest resolutions.

The vow is only for a month, but she writes: "You know well, O my Saviour, that in the depths of my heart I am consecrating myself to You for life." Then she adds: "These few days that yet remain before this most important act, I shall spend them in silence and recollection. I shall avoid every useless word and sign. O Mary! My dear and tender Mother, bless your child and make haste to prepare my heart, which is about to become the treasure of your Divine Jesus!"

What need is there to go into details? The feast of Our Lady of Mount Carmel came, she made her vow, her heart was filled with joy—and so was her diary. Again, it is the romantic overflow of the heart of a pious young girl, but the grand phrases cannot conceal her deep sincerity: "What pure joy floods my soul! I seem to be back on that beautiful day of my First Communion. At last I am consecrated to Jesus.... He is my Bridegroom and I am His spouse. O earth, vanish out of my sight, I want only God. God alone is my portion.... O dear, sweet Mother, I am powerless to tell Jesus all my love. Be my interpreter, speak to Him of me, and to me of Him."

Mary always in the forefront of her mind, her ever-present help in all her needs, always there to lift her up to Jesus, when her incapacity to reach Him crushes her to the earth. But finally she ends on a note of sadness at her sense of exile, which betrays her inability to be content with the consolations that come with even the most generous acts of religion and charity possible to us on earth. "O my heavenly Lover! Why must I live far from You? When will You break these bonds that keep me on this earth? O Jesus, hasten to plait my crown, in order that Your little spouse may soon be united with You!"

Always, at the back of her mind, in the depths of her heart, is the restlessness of discontent with mere consolation and the eagerness to prove that her love is pure: although both these thoughts are colored by a generous admixture of natural feelings. The very next day, July 17, after all the joys of the feast of Mount Carmel and of her own consecration, she is asked to sacrifice what was always perhaps her greatest consolation: that of receiving Communion. For, although she was now in religion, she still could not go to the holy table every day of the week. Daily Communion was still uncommon at that time. Her diary laments the sacrifice, and her pen is quickly led, once more, to thoughts of eternity where all these changes and vicissitudes will be over: "Do not make me pine away long years far from You, Jesus. O, you must make it possible for me to cover a great distance in a short time.... O my God! Make haste, come quickly! I must hurry to gain my crown, in order to be with Jesus as quickly as possible. Yes, from now on, I don't want anything but Jesus and His Cross: the naked Cross, without sweetness, without consolation; I must drink my chalice to the dregs."

Words from the diary of a Trappistine postulant! They are the sort of words that a spiritual director would not encourage everyone to utter. But, Père Polycarpe was to prove favorable to such aspirations in his generous penitent.

These prayers were someday to be answered, in the life of Sister Berchmans—and sooner than she thought. Certainly, the answer was the one she least expected. And this is one of the commonest truths of the spiritual life. Whether we ask for a cross or not, if we correspond with God's grace, with His loving desire to purify us and restore in us the integrity of His divine likeness, deformed by sin, we will inevitably get not merely the cross, but precisely the cross that we least want, the one that will most humiliate and confuse and annihilate us, the one that will give us the most trouble and anguish.

Meanwhile the time came for Sister Berchmans to receive the habit of novice. August had passed, with the great feasts of the Assumption and of St. Bernard, and now September 7, the eve of the Nativity of the Blessed Virgin, was set for the admission of two postulants to their canonical novitiate. The other was Sister Mary Angela, who had presented herself at the convent gate a fortnight or so before Sister Berchmans. The two would make a pretty pair in the choir on that solemn day! They had so much in common, anyway. Both had the same nobility, sincerity, and generosity of soul. Both were full of gaiety and joy. Both had the beautiful candor of complete and perfect innocence about them. They had no notion of mortal sin, no notion of any real evil.

Often, in those days, reverend mother abbess would be seen proceeding majestically through the large convent garden, in a solemn progress along the winding gravel paths, in and out of the trees and clumps of laurel and the flower beds soon to be rich with gold and rust and the heady, peppery fragrance of chrysanthemums. Her wheel chair would be drawn by the charming pair: Sister Mary Angela and Sister Mary Berchmans. Drawing up, they would stop, and reverend mother would point to the two and say: "There are my Angel and my Archangel."

Sister Berchmans' diary is silent, as she goes on retreat for her reception of the habit, but we have a good enough idea, now, of what was going on in her soul. Lest her ardor become embarrassing by its own exuberance and lead her into a welter of ambitions and resolutions impossible to keep, Father Polycarpe stepped in and simplified everything by giving her one, and only one, resolution to keep. But she was to keep it all her life. It was the resolution, never to let a day go by without recalling to mind and reflecting upon the words of our Lord: "If any man would be My disciple, let him deny himself, take up his cross, and follow Me."

The ceremony of reception in our Trappistine convents is a very elaborate and beautiful one, full of symbolism and ritual. But it is not for us to go into all the details of how the postulant, dressed as a bride, goes to the front gate of the convent, is ceremoniously admitted, led in procession to the sanctuary, and so on. In 1899, at Laval, as well as at several other convents, all this was very much simplified. Sister Berchmans and Sister Angela received the habit quietly, in a plain but dignified ceremony, at the grille of the choir.

The relative simplicity of the ceremonial, and the silence of her journal on the subject, do nothing to lessen the importance of this step in the life of Sister Berchmans; for this was the official beginning of her religious life. Clad in a white veil and cloak, she had become, more truly than ever, a *nova creatura*, clad and enveloped in the grace of the special love and protection of Jesus, dressed in the beautiful garments of His election, and clothed, as it were, in the mercy of His everlasting choice of her to be His spouse. Now, indeed, her time was all fruitful and full of hope, whereas, as a postulant, it had been, relatively speaking, only a period of unavoidable delay. The canonical novitiate, that would necessarily have to elapse before she could complete her sacrifice and make profession, was at last beginning. Now every minute that ticked by meant something immeasurably great, for it was the passing of a definite and ordained time, bringing closer and closer the day, fixed in the explicit will of God, that would most truly unite her to Him.

Her first Confession after the reception of the habit left her with a new and deeper conviction of the greatness and reality of her vocation, not only her vocation, in general, as a Cistercian, but her own special vocation to the very highest perfection of love and sacrifice.

"You are called," Father Polycarpe said to her, with the deepest seriousness, "you are called to love much, and you have power to accomplish great things. God is expecting very much of you. O, my child, be very, very faithful to grace. Promise me that you will never refuse the good God anything."

But before she could even begin to reply, the quiet and earnest voice of the saintly priest continued: "I understand far better than you do what graces God is giving you: and you will never be able to thank Him adequately for them."

And then, with even greater emphasis: "Listen carefully, and do not be afraid. God has great sufferings in store for you. Your heart will become the prey of the most profound sorrow. You will find yourself surrounded by a great void, an abyss that will separate you not only from your sisters and mothers in religion, but even from those on whom you should and must count, that is, your Superiors, and perhaps even your Confessor. All these will fail you. You will be left absolutely alone, unable to find support in any creature, in order that you may go to God alone. Oh! Do not refuse the cross that Jesus is preparing for you. Tell Him that you abandon yourself to His holy will. Once more, child, promise me, please, never to refuse Our Lord anything whatever."

Grasping, by a kind of intuition, all the depth and all the implications of these momentous words, which she yet was unable to understand completely, Sister Berchmans remained breathless with exaltation and a kind of fear. She was swept off her feet, both by the vehemence of her desire to live up to her vocation, and the sense of her complete nothingness and inability to do so.

Leaving the confessional, she threw herself into the arms of her Spouse, abandoned everything into His hands, plunged into the abysses of His infinite mercy and love, in which alone she could find strength to follow Him through the dark void of the future, and cried out in the exaltation of her total renunciation: "At last You are going to satisfy my thirst for suffering."

CHAPTER IV

THE NOVICE

Sister Berchmans had been a girl of very pronounced tastes, ideas, judgments, desires, and opinions; but she started out at once by sacrificing them all—so she sincerely thought—to regularity. From the very first, she was so studious an observer of the will of God in the usages and the requirements laid down by her superiors, that one of her companions said of her: "If you want to know where Sister Berchmans is to be found, in the intervals, just consult the novitiate schedule."

Add to this that she did more than simply obey her superiors: she had that truly Cistercian virtue, so vitally important in our life of reverential love for her superiors. This love, in her, was truly supernatural. It made no distinction of persons, and did not stop at the human or exterior accidents of the person placed over her by God. It was not merely that she liked her abbess, or novice mistress, and found in them a sort of natural substitute for her mother and relatives. When Mother Marie Antoinette was replaced by Mother Lutgarde as abbess, Sister Berchmans showed her the same obedience, reverence, and affection, and the childlike submission that is one of the most beautiful characteristics of a true Cistercian, and one of the principal fruits of his rule. This submission is one form of perfect charity, because by it we reverence, not ordinary persons, but the divine Person of Christ, in our superiors.

Another thing that the rule is careful to demand of novices is that they be zealous for humiliations: *sollicitus sit ad opprobia*. We have seen, and shall see, how often Sister Berchmans' little journal was to voice her ardent desire to suffer and be humiliated for Jesus Christ. But in practice, too, she was prompt and eager to accept the small and trifling humiliations that come the way of a Trappistine novice.

In a word, she generously embraced all the regular austerities of the Cistercian life: the hard couch in the dormitory, the manual labor, the simple and often completely tasteless food, and the comparative lack of it in time of fasting, the heat and cold, which, because of the simplicity and unvarying make-up of the Cistercian wardrobe, are one of our greatest penances—all these she welcomed with an ardent and supernatural enthusiasm. She so successfully concealed the fact that they cost her considerable sacrifice, that, at the end of one of her Lents as a novice, having followed the strict fast up to the end, including the last three Fridays on bread and water, and not having missed a moment of the long hours in church, she finally collapsed in choir. Yet, as soon as she came to herself, and realized that the Sisters were trying to take her up to carry her out, she struggled to her feet, as pale as a ghost, and walked out of the church by herself.

External penances did not frighten her, but when the mistress of novices issued orders that the letters which the novices were allowed to write, at long intervals, to their parents, were to be cut down to two pages, Sister Berchmans' tender heart nearly broke. She could not restrain her tears when she told Father Polycarpe about it. What would they think at home? Mother and sister would imagine that she did not love them any more, that she had grown cold and heartless, that she was indifferent, that she hated them, perhaps. It was too much! The good confessor was touched by her pleading and managed to effect a compromise with the novice mistress, which resulted in Sister Berchmans being allowed to write three pages, in honor of the Most Holy Trinity.

Considering the life in its entirety and her own great desires, she felt, as many fervent novices have felt, that she wanted to give more than she was asked to give. And it is right that one should feel this way. St. Benedict allows for it in his rule, in which all things are so ordered that the weak may not be overwhelmed, and the strong may desire to offer more. But the question is: How are we to offer more, and in what does this "more" consist? Sister Berchmans, it seems, never tried to force her superiors to allow her to starve herself on bread and water in the refectory, nor to let her stay up all night praying. Nor does it appear that she tried to get permission for any extraordinary austerities, like iron chains or disciplines decorated with small pointed pieces of metal. All these things, although at one time favored by a few of our saints in the thirteenth century, are really foreign to the spirit of Cistercian simplicity, and are very rarely found in the earliest days, the time of the great patriarchs of the twelfth century.

But Sister Berchmans was burning with a desire of sacrifice—a desire to be a victim with Jesus for the expiation of sin, and to fill up in her body what was wanting of the passion of Christ for His Body, the Church. This desire in her was most ardent and sincere, and was encouraged wholeheartedly by her confessor, who had visions of her becoming a second St. Margaret Mary. There was no difficulty in getting her to share this desire! But we find her, on the threshold of a life of sacrifice, full of a generous longing to suffer all things for God, and, at the same time, a sense of diffidence and confusion which she found hard to express. Perhaps she did not too clearly realize it herself, but we may observe it in the following passage from her journal.

"O My Beloved, this assurance that I am called to be a victim stirs and troubles my heart. Am I pure enough? Am I worthy to be offered as a holocaust to You? Alas, Jesus! You know the depths of my heart, and I cannot hide it from You. I am a sinner, and I do not fear to add that there is not one single soul that ever so greatly abused grace as I have, nor any one that has offended You as much as I. And when I say this, I do not do so in the holy exaltation of Your faithful servants; You know, O Jesus, that it is the truth, and You needed all Your infinite mercy in order to tolerate me...."

Is any comment necessary? Her own qualification of the statement that she was the worst sinner in the world shows us at the same time the sincerity of her desire to say this and really believe it, and her fear that she does not yet believe it with the deep conviction which the saints had. Her realization of the fact that she has abused grace is still rather an academic matter, as one gathers from her tone. She is trying hard to make herself believe it, but God does not despise such desires.

She goes on in her journal: "I answer Your call. Here I am: I desire nothing, from now on, but Your holy Will, and Your Divine Heart will be the altar of my immolation. Yes, it is in the furnace of love that I desire to see consumed all that remains of myself, in order that I may no longer be myself but You, O Jesus. Continue in this heart, which belongs to You, the tortures of Calvary, for as long as this new victim is not immolated, Your Sacrifice will be unfinished. Your work of redemption incomplete."

It is easy to see that her spiritual life was receiving a sound intellectual and dogmatic foundation, probably from Father Polycarpe, in these notions of incorporation with Christ, and the participation in His sufferings for the salvation of souls—having in view not merely the Person of the Incarnate Word, but also the great Mystical Person of the Whole Christ, *Caput et Corpus*. Unless we love the Whole Christ, Head and Members too, can we be said to love Jesus?

Equally fundamental was the emphasis on His will above everything else. He was to do everything, He was to make all the choices, as indeed He must. No matter how bloody a cross we choose for ourselves, it will probably never kill our self-love, but only increase its power. Jesus must even choose our crosses, and nail us to them, and kill us on them with the cruel contrast between His love and our ingratitude, a light that will never shine in the twilight of our senses or imagination, but only in the midnight of emptiness and desolation where faith alone can guide us and unite us to Him.

But the first of His crosses may even be to counteract our very desire for crosses by making everything easy just when we want it to be hard; this is a contradiction that soon eliminates many souls whose spirituality is superficial and imaginary. They refuse to obey. They wear the hair shirts that Jesus wants them to throw away, and refuse a far subtler and more interior trial which they are, perhaps, too carnal to recognize.

"If it pleases my Divine Master," writes the generous novice, "to lead me on a road all covered with roses or lilies, I will have to follow Him without astonishment. If He prefers the way to be strewn with brambles and thorns, and if He prefers that I be laden with a heavy Cross, and fall beneath its weight, incapable of making the slightest movement, I will have to remain in that position, without ever doing the slightest thing to thrust far from me the object of my torment."

These are deep and beautiful words, expressed with a sincerity and power that show she already realized something of what they meant. Grace had indeed been working in her heart, and had filled it with a generosity of love that could come only from the Holy Spirit. Now all that remained was for her to find out what this all meant in practice.

She had said all that needed to be said. Jesus was to choose the path for her to follow. She must not be surprised at any of His decisions. Inevitably they would be just what she did not expect. She must not resist His will, or put the slightest obstacle in His way by questioning His intentions in her regard, or trying to change His dispositions for her purification. All that remained was for Him to present her with her first, unexpected trial.

The curious thing is that that trial was already upon her, as she was writing those very words, and she did not recognize it. So subtle is the work of the Holy Spirit, of whom there was never anything more truly said than that no man knows whence He cometh or whither He goeth. He is here and gone before we realize what has happened.

What was this trial, this cross? Was she sick? Was she despised and misjudged by her superiors or her sisters? Was she attacked by visible devils? Or was she disfigured and made hideous by some terrible accident? Was she asked to fast seven years, like St. Lutgarde, on bread and small beer? It was none of these things, but a temptation so ordinary that she was unable to recognize it for what it was; and she rebelled, and it became in every sense a real temptation.

It was the liturgical life, the divine office, choir, the psalms. In the first place, she did not understand Latin. In the second place, she could not sing. Her voice was toneless and very weak. She had no ear for music, and not much appreciation for it—least of all for Gregorian chant. In later years, she was to be so weakened by sickness that she could not produce the slightest sound during the night office. But even at her best, she did not contribute much more than a toneless and somewhat harsh and flat series of noises that roughly approximated the melody sung by the rest of the choir. Not that she resented her inferiority in this respect. She was never to complain of the fact that she was no nightingale, nor lament her inability to praise God as sweetly and harmoniously as her sisters. But undoubtedly if she had been a singer the real temptation would have been less great.

She resented having to spend so much time singing a series of words that were completely meaningless to her, without sense or charm to her ear, mind, or heart. Yet even this would have been bearable if the translation and study of the psalms had brought any new light to her understanding, or offered any appeal to her will. But it was quite the opposite. Even when the psalms were put into French, they were still largely incomprehensible to her. What were these strange metaphors? What was this weird sequence of apparently disconnected and outlandish images? Why did the psalms never seem to say anything definite? What were they all about? Why did they all appear to be without beginning, middle, or end? What were they driving at, anyway?

Sister Berchmans was a child of the nineteenth century, a child of the modem bourgeoisie, with all its love of everything that makes a plain, direct, and frank appeal to the senses and imagination, without putting too much burden on the intellect, except in the most obvious and experimental sort of things—matters capable of being dealt with either by empirical reasoning or common sense. But when it became a matter of mystical meaning largely divorced from any superficial appeal to the senses or emotions, striking directly at the very roots of the intellect and will, where they are joined in the substance of the soul—all this she had neither the training nor the type of mind to grasp at first sight.

For her, to pray meant to pour out her heart, as we have seen her doing, in simple, dramatic, and fervent acts of love to the Sacred Heart, acts of love that were fraught with plenty of emotion and sprang from the heat of the imagination and feelings, to spread thence, thanks to God's grace, into the depths of the intellect and will. Hers was the piety that would easily burst into flame before a life-size statue of a Jesus with brown and flowing locks and large tender eyes and a most natural seeming red-and-white complexion; and the plaintive, rather sentimental hymns that congregations of the faithful usually sing to Jesus at Benediction, in the present day, were all that was needed to stir up her feelings to a great warmth of love.

To such a soul, unless it has some special natural aptitude, an appreciation of Gregorian chant and the wonderful depths of the language of Scripture must necessarily be an acquired taste, just as meat and the solid food of grown-up men has to become an acquired taste for babies at the breast. They cannot go from one to the other all at once. The truth is that modern devotions are very much like baby food compared to the solid nourishment of the ancient liturgy, which is so poorly understood. But once one has come to thrive on this solid food, one no longer has any particular desire to return to the carefully warmed and sweetened milk that fills the baby's bottle. Now all this weaning evoked a loud protest from Sister Berchmans.

One day as she was kneeling by the desk of reverend mother abbess, Sister Berchmans began, as a good novice should, to unburden herself of her repugnances and difficulties. And it turned out that she could not understand why the obligation to say the office should be imposed upon certain members of the Church under pain of mortal sin. Certain members—that is, religious under solemn vows and clerics in major orders; but Sister Berchmans herself came under neither of these categories, nor was she (according to the legislation of the time) preparing for any but simple vows.

Yet, with all the pent-up feeling of one crushed under an unjust burden, she exclaimed: "How can I believe that Our Lord will make it a grave sin for me to pass over my Office just once? Really, that seems to me to be too severe. I can't believe that of Our Lord."

She was very definite indeed on this point, which simply did not fit in with any of the roles under which Jesus figured in her young girl's imagination. It was the Jesus of the pretty statues, with the tender brown eyes and the flowing locks, that she was thinking of. Where were her notions of the whole Christ now, and of filling up in time not only the sufferings but the praises and love of Jesus for His Father, singing with the voice of Jesus His songs and His poems? For the magnificent and holy plain chant is the voice of Christ, and the psalms are His songs of love and praise.

But, no, Sister Berchmans did not see this. "He is far too good for that," she said, firmly. "I assure you, I can't see my Divine Spouse in that severe light at all!" It did not make sense to her because she was looking only at the disproportion existing in the purely natural order between the omission of a few lines of Latin that she could not understand, and the eternal damnation with which that omission would be punished, if it were deliberate and unrepented. Her final reason was enough to establish quite definitely that her thoughts were running on a purely natural level, and did not have very much of faith about them. "Besides," she then said, "I *like* to say prayers that I understand. I *like* to feel what I am saying."

There is something rather charming about the complete ingenuousness with which she gives herself away. It takes nothing away from the sincerity of all the grandiose claims of her diary, although it does show us that she was, as all the greatest saints (except our Blessed Mother) once were, a novice in the spiritual life and apt to make mistakes. Reverend Mother Marie Antoinette was no doubt quick enough to make capital of these simple words, "*I* like to say prayers.... *I* like to feel.... " Poor Sister Berchmans! But what does it prove? Nothing, except that she was truly tempted, as we must all be in one way or another, and with a particularly human temptation, at that.

Nor was she persuaded to drop all her objections to the liturgy at the first encounter with the other view. On the contrary, she proceeded to criticize the one psalm that especially displeased her. By a strange irony, it was the psalm that praises the fraternal charity which was to be one of the most beautiful ornaments of her soul. *Ecce quam bonum et quam jucundum*...(Ps. 133).

"Behold how good and how pleasant it is for brethren to live together in unity.

"Like the precious ointment on the head that ran down the beard, the beard of Aaron,

"Which ran down to the skirt of his garment, as the dew of Hermon which descendeth upon mount Sion.

"For there the Lord hath commanded blessing, and life for evermore."

That is the whole psalm.

Surely this is a perfect poem and a perfect tribute to the intense bliss that comes of disinterested love of other people in God. What hyperbole, what images, what dramatic amplitude could ever have told us so effectively of the sweetness of that joy? Yet here it is all given to us in a simple and funny image of old Aaron dazed with happiness, with ointment running down his beard—and then, the fundamentally humorous comparison with Mount Sion's dews!

Sister Berchmans did not miss the fact that it was funny. She had a very good sense of humor. But to think that we could say such things to God! And solemnly sing them to Him in church! It was beyond her. Which all goes to show that she had far less simplicity, as yet, than the early Christians or the prophet David.

So here she found an early opportunity of carrying out her generous desire for sacrifice. "I desire nothing," she had written, "but Your Holy Will, and Your Divine Heart will be the altar of my immolation." With this small and trivial sacrifice of her private tastes and opinions her long immolation was to begin.

It was not an easy sacrifice, nor did it soon give way before her desire to comply with what God so evidently wanted of her. For a long time she wondered if perhaps her vocation were not rather to the lay sisters than to the choir. Yet that was manifestly not so, and her superiors soon recognized this as an illusion of self-love in her.

By the time of her profession she was to write: "I wish to impose upon myself the obligation never to desire anything but what the good God desires for me: that is, to cease casting envious looks toward our good lay-sisters, and to make it a duty to love the Divine Office."

But the upshot of these struggles was that she learned, early in her novitiate, what kind of crosses she must die on. Not by the firing squad or the guillotine, like the Cistercian nuns martyred at Orange during the French Revolution; not by the hangman's rope, like our martyrs of England and Ireland; not by the knives and clubs of heretics, or the swords of invading Tartars, like so many Cistercians of Germany, Bohemia, Poland, and Denmark. Hers was to be the more Cistercian martyrdom, the bloodless martyrdom of a St. Bernard or a St. Lutgarde: obedience to the rule, to superiors, and to God's good pleasure in all the events of her ordinary life.

A good retreat, preached by a Benedictine Father to the nuns in January, 1900, made this all clear in her mind. The first thing she did was to obey the retreat master himself in his suggestion that they should not take notes on his retreat; we have no record of what went on in her mind, except a couple of sentences and a resolution.

Dom Eugene, abbot of Port-du-Salut and Father Immediate of the convent at Laval, soon afterward made his visitation and had an interview with the novice, during the course of which he asked her what had been her resolution at the end of the retreat.

"To be really obedient, Reverend Father," was her answer.

Dom Eugene must have been impressed by the little Sister, and by her sincerity. For when he returned again, sometime later, he had not forgotten their previous interview, nor what she had told him. And he asked her if she were still making the same resolution.

"Yes, Reverend Father," was her ingenuous answer, "once was not enough." Nor was twice. She stuck to this resolution after her profession, and all the rest of her religious life. Nor were her efforts to correspond with this great grace without effect, for her mother mistress was to say afterward that her great virtue was *obedience*. It was so in the novitiate, and we shall see that it was so in her days as a professed nun.

Other crosses were not slow in coming.

On February 1, 1900, she wrote something in her journal that gives us only a vague indication of what was to be one of her gravest trials, not only for the rest of her novitiate, but for several years to come.

What was this cross? It was something strictly interior, a temptation deep in the soul, a profoundly humiliating and bitterly difficult tribulation within her heart, one of those intangible and torturing crosses that crush and pain and purify us more than any other because they crucify our self-love in its very roots, striking at the very foundations of our self-respect.

Precisely what was this temptation? We do not know. Our only source of information is the Cistercian monk and priest, Father Robert, who was to be her confessor and spiritual director in Japan. Since this trial was still going on in the years when she was his penitent, he cannot tell us anything about it. If her journal shrinks from talking about the trial in its details, it still gives a good and perfect picture of the exemplary meekness and love with which she accepted this cruel humiliation, whatever it may have been.

"How heavy," she writes, "is the Cross which Your tender love has reserved for me, O Jesus! Ah, my Beloved, You alone know the bitterness of my chalice; my nature is in revolt, and I feel everything storming within me. My heart alone is calm, for it understands that now, alone, it is truly united to You, Jesus. But I cannot believe this thing. What! Is Your little spouse, the lover of Your Sacred Heart is she....

"But no, I must keep silence, and never pronounce that word that is like a sword through my heart. Oh my Beloved, forgive these tears that anguish wrings from me. You well know that they take nothing away from my resignation. Yes, I accept the Cross, I press it to my poor mangled heart, I kiss it with love. It is wet with my tears, this Cross of Your good pleasure, and in this kiss of love I gain the strength to murmur: More, more still! Lord, do not spare me, I am your victim. O Jesus, the thing that sustains me in my suffering is that You suffered it before it came to me to be endured....

"Your fatherly tenderness, in the past, had cast a veil over everything that might trouble my soul: but the day has come when I must share Your chalice, and bear my part of Your Cross. O Jesus, I bless You in all things and at all times, and may Your will be always mine. To carry my Cross humbly, to let myself be nailed to it in silence, in spite of all the pain, to die upon it as a victim, but a victim of Your love, that is what I aspire to. Mother, dearest Mother, You are close to me, are you not, to sustain and encourage me, and to show me Jesus dying on the Cross? Ah, what strength I find, in that sight, to keep me from weakening before the sacrifice."

The rest is a secret buried with Father Polycarpe, Father Robert, and Mère Berchmans herself. All we can do is admire the sincerity and perfection of the dispositions with which she accepted this suffering, which was apparently nothing small or insignificant to endure.

Meanwhile, the days of her novitiate were slipping by with that astounding rapidity with which time passes in a Cistercian monastery. Spring turned to summer, and already September was in sight, when, on the feast of the Nativity of the Blessed Virgin, she would make her simple vows.

There were the consolations of long hours of contemplation of Jesus in the Sacrament of His love, and the joys of silent but loving companionship in the novitiate. There were the warm and beautiful afternoons when the Sisters, with books or rosaries, walked among the flower beds of the vast convent garden, or stopped to pray at shrines hidden in the leafy groves. Then there was hard manual work, which, for all its difficulty, and for all the weariness and pain it sometimes causes, never fails to bring a special peace and liberty to the spirit of the true contemplative. Finally, as a remote preparation for her profession, she made a little retreat sometime during the summer, of which we still retain a record in the resolutions she made at its close.

They all bear on the same, principal effort of her spiritual life: the submission of her own will and judgment to God's will and to

His good pleasure, in the commands of her superiors, and in all the dispositions He makes for her in her daily life.

"I will never," she wrote, "stop to examine anything that may be given me for my use." A good enough resolution: for many religious vowed to poverty take back their vow in the practical details of their life, by complaining and being discontented with everything that happens in consequence of it. Sister Berchmans' second resolution dealt with obedience. "I will never see anyone but God in those who have authority over me, and I shall obey them as God Himself." Then she goes on to resolve upon greater recollection and purity of heart. "Total sacrifice of my heart! I shall shut the door not only upon my senses, but above all on my heart, keeping it in captivity close to the Tabernacle." The last resolution is the one we have already considered: "I shall make it my obligation never to desire anything but what the good God wills, that is, to cease casting looks of envy upon our good lay-sisters, and to love the Divine Office as a duty."

All these resolutions were practical and sincere; and she was to enter upon a real battle to keep them. Nor was she looking for peace, in the service of Him who came bringing not peace but the sword, and casting the fire of the Holy Spirit upon the earth, to consume our hearts and minds and wills as victims of sacrifice to His infinite love.

She knew what to expect. Father Polycarpe had not been wrong. God was going to ask much of her, for He loved her with a special love, and had chosen her for a greater sacrifice than her sisters. The time was drawing close when He would suddenly ask that sacrifice of her. Then would follow the test of her sincerity and love; and there would be months and years in which all her resolutions would seem to lie in ruins all around her, when she would cry out in terror, "In the world, I was a saint, and in the cloister I have become a devil." Meanwhile, she faced the future with the one desire: "To do, everywhere and in all things, the Holy Will of God, immolating my own unto death."

With these good dispositions she made her first vows, for three years, promising poverty, chastity, and obedience, together with stability and conversion of manners, and received the white Cistercian cowl, the beautiful garment of contemplation that envelops and encloses the body in its ample folds like the cloud that protected the children of Israel in their escape through the desert. She became, in truth and in fact, a Cistercian, a contemplative, and as she knelt in the middle of the choir after being clothed in this lovely vesture, and tried to raise up her hands in the immense, ungainly sleeves, she could reflect that this very ungainliness, which made any but the simplest activities all but impossible, was the symbol of her contemplation, which made her, by her sacrifice, useless and alien to the works of this world, and fit only for the liberty and rest of the pure love of God.

CHAPTER V

SENTENCE OF EXILE

Absorbed in her thanksgiving for so many graces, the newly professed nun had no idea of the affairs that were carried on behind the doors of mother abbess' room, nor did she dream that a problem that had exercised both reverend mother and Father Polycarpe for some months was going to result in a tremendous change in her own life. All the while she was struggling with her little repugnance to the office and other tiny difficulties, and at the same time tasting her meed of consolations and sensible fervor, the will of God, working peacefully, quietly, and imperceptibly in the office of her superior, was bringing to maturity a project that would really give her a cross. There was question of a most difficult and important step: one that involved, first of all, the existence of a young Cistercian foundation in a distant country, and might even affect the security of their own monastery at Laval.

In the old days of the Cistercian Order, when literally hundreds of new foundations were being made, the monks might come to choir, as usual, for one of the canonical hours, and suddenly look up to realize that the abbot was making a sign for certain ones to leave their places and come to the presbytery step. Thirteen in all, one to lead the others, would obey the summons. These would soon find themselves bowing before the high altar and hearing, behind their backs, the voices of their brothers whom they dearly loved, chanting the prayers for those going on a journey. And they would realize that they were now to be separated from their monastery and these brothers, and most probably never see them again in this life. By tierce of this day, which had begun like any other day, they would find themselves on the high road, some walking, some riding, and some leading the mules that carried the choir books, their only baggage, heading for an unknown place, perhaps at the other end of Europe.

Nowadays, the same process is less frequent, but it is not much less sudden. Not many years before Sister Berchmans entered as a Cistercian nun at Laval, in another convent of the order, poor and unfrequented, hidden in the Vosges mountains of Ubexy, the superioress had one morning announced in chapter that a new foundation was called for in Japan, and that she wanted volunteers to go there. Without any more ado, the entire community, from the youngest to the oldest, the strongest to the most infirm, stood up in a body and offered to go. And that had been the beginning of Our Lady of the Angels, near Hakodate, in the north of Japan.

Since that time, Ubexy had become too poor to support this filiation, and the abbot of the Trappist monastery at Bricquebec in Normandy, Dom Vital Lehodey, had assumed charge of the spiritual and material needs of the distant little nunnery. Once more there was a call for nuns to go there. As yet there were no vocations and several of the pioneers had died; now, if the convent was not to close its doors altogether, some new life from France must be infused into it. Ubexy was still too poor and too small a community to send all the reinforcements that were needed, and Dom Vital Lehodey had been forced to seek others elsewhere.

This was what had preoccupied Mère Lutgarde and Father Polycarpe for so many months. At first, Father Polycarpe resisted the proposals from Bricquebec with all his might, because he considered them dangerous to the Laval community. But Dom Eugene, the Father Immediate, and Mère Lutgarde, favored them with great enthusiasm. As the months went by and spring turned into summer, the good confessor began to lose his fears, since it would mean giving up only two or three of the Sisters at Laval. Finally he gave his consent. The plan could go into effect.

The early sun was beginning to filter through the windows of the church when the Sisters filed out of choir and along the cloister to the chapter room, after prime. Cistercians have no feast for St. Margaret Mary; much less was there one in those days, before the canonization of that fervent lover of the Sacred Heart. But undoubtedly Sister Berchmans' heart was full of love for her spiritual sister, on that October day. Devotion to the Sacred Heart carried with it an equally great devotion to the ardent mystic of Paray-le-Monial; and this was the day of her commemoration.

We can imagine her taking her usual seat in chapter, in that vague state of general peace and recollection that is inevitable after several hours of continuous prayer, and which the Cistercian always brings with him to chapter in the morning: a state in which one would be hard put to say whether he was recollected or distracted, but in which, in actual fact, the soul is pretty much at peace and no longer too much concerned with itself or with anything disturbing.

The martyrology was read, the remaining prayers of prime were recited, and a chapter of the Rule was read in French. Sister Berchmans listened intently to the words of St. Benedict, as well as to the explanation of them by the reverend mother. The voice of the superior is the voice of God, and a good Cistercian gets used to paying attention to the daily commentary of the rule as to a source of information about little ways of pleasing God during the day.

After the explanation of the rule, Mère Lutgarde adopted the more businesslike tone that usually indicated some important special announcement, and began to talk about the little community of Trappistine nuns, Our Lady of the Angels, on the other side of the world. Everyone began to listen very eagerly to this, for the Cistercian is very unsophisticated when it comes to news. The wars and revolutions of the world do not penetrate the cloister until they are actually introduced in violent and tangible form by the bayonet and bomb of the invader; so the smallest piece of information about another convent, another monastery, about their good or poor crops, their lack or plenty of vocations, their graces and their trials, can arouse a certain subdued excitement in a chapter room full of peaceful nuns.

On this day, however, there was more than common excitement at Laval. For Mère Lutgarde did not delay in coming to the point. Dom Vital Lehodey wanted nuns for the house in Japan. Dom Eugene had given his enthusiastic consent to the idea. Père Polycarpe had also given his wholehearted approval. Dom Eugene was even now on his way to Laval to help settle the affair.

The first thing that flashed into Sister Berchmans' mind, besides surprise and excitement at the news, was the certitude that it could not affect her. She was only a young, inexperienced girl, still in the cradle of her religious life, and as yet barely half formed to the service of God. And then there was her health. Obviously she would be the last one to be sent on such an expedition. And so, when, after having urged them on to a spirit of loving sacrifice, the mother abbess announced tentatively the names of two nuns who would be Laval's contribution to the little group of Sisters that would leave France within a few months, Sister Berchmans felt neither surprise nor disappointment that she was not one of them.

Leaving the chapter room—and probably not succeeding in resisting the temptation to make signs about the news to those next to her in line—she accepted the whole affair as settled, as far as she was concerned. The notion of offering herself probably never seriously occurred to her. The whole thing was completely new and foreign to her. She had never yet thought about it. All her notions of the religious life had involved nothing but living and dying at Laval, suffering there whatever trials it should please God to send her, but staying in her own beloved cloister. After all, stability is one of the Cistercian vows, one of the cornerstones of the Cistercian life.

The day went on: interval, tierce, High Mass, sext, work, none, dinner, and so on into the afternoon. Sometime in the afternoon one of the Sisters told her by a sign that Father Polycarpe wanted to see her in the confessional. She hastened to the church and knelt a few moments in adoration of her Lord.

"My child," said Père Polycarpe, when she entered the confessional, "did Reverend Mother not ask of you a great sacrifice, today?"

"A sacrifice? Me? No, father. But of course you know that this morning in Chapter she spoke about volunteers to go to Japan."

Father Polycarpe did not suffer her to say any more. He broke in on her sentence with the single imperative, that struck her heart like a thunderbolt: "Go!"

Sister Berchmans came out of the confessional so dazed that she hardly knew what she was looking at when she knelt again, in the middle of the choir, and lifted up her face to the grille, beyond which, in the shadows of the presbytery, flickered the light before the tabernacle of her Spouse, who viewed her quietly and peacefully out of the depths of His hiddenness. She did not stay long on her knees, but hastened, dizzy with the too much wine of God's command, along the cloister to the room of mother abbess and there, throwing herself on her knees, offered herself as a volunteer for Japan.

The matter was not long in being settled. Dom Eugene had arrived. He knew the fervent young nun and recognized her at once when she was ushered into his presence in the parlor. The consultations were not long. In a few minutes she had left the parlor and rushed into the novitiate, practically colliding with the mother undermistress, whom she astonished with a flurry of excited signs that said: "They are taking me: I am going to Japan," and then, bursting into tears, she threw herself into the good Sister's arms.

It was about time for tears. For this was a real cross. She had done well in not stopping to reflect too much on how great a cross it was. Only now that the offering was made and accepted did she feel the full weight of the burden.

Her prayers had been answered, with a mercifully cruel directness and simplicity. It was just what she least expected, just what she was least prepared to bear. The departure was several months away, and she was to have plenty of time to reflect on the weaknesses and imperfections of her soul which the very presence of this cross would throw into alarming relief.

The first and biggest thing of all was something she had long since realized, and yet, since entering the order, had seemed to forget. It was her loving human heart, so tender, so attracted to creatures, and so prone to rest in them and their affection. Now that she was to be separated from her sisters and mothers, from the novices and nuns she loved so dearly, and from the convent to which she had formed such an attachment, it seemed that the breaking of all these natural bonds could not be accomplished without the breaking of her heart itself.

God demands our whole heart when we are consecrated to Him in religion and will accept nothing less from us. And any attempt to bargain with Him, to reserve anything, however innocent, for ourselves without reference to Him, can only end in misery.

But now there was not a stone of her dear monastery, not a corner of the cloister or the quiet church, not a tree or flower in the garden that did not tear her heart with the thought of the coming separation. There was not a smile, not a happy expression, nor a loving glance of her sisters that did not pierce her, like a sword, with the thought that she would soon lose all this sweet companionship. More than that, as she looked at the October clouds flying across the gay, mild sky of France, she reflected with a deep and inexpressible anguish that she was about to be exiled into a fierce and strange country: a land of paganism inhabited by a curiously different race, hostile, perhaps, to her own race and nation, and to her faith.

Now the spoliation of her soul was to become complete indeed. Now it was a holocaust of more than trinkets and holy cards. She was giving away more than a rosary or a couple of medals. She was giving away her land of France, her people and her language, her blood and her kin, and all loves that nature drives to take the deepest root in our heart. She was giving away the security of a well-established, regular convent, in which there were no worries to speak of, no dangers, no constant threat of dying of hunger and want. She was giving away even that moral security which is one of the greatest blessings of a fervent community: security of conscience that springs from the fact that the regularity of everybody else makes it almost automatic for us to keep the rule well.

The very news of this change, and the mere prospect of the sacrifice that would be consummated, probably, at the year's end, did more to mature her in three or four days than all the trials and experiences of a year's novitiate. We have seen what she wrote in her journal as she ended a little retreat in preparation for simple profession. Let us now compare her thoughts on this situation, with the resolutions she made before simple profession, and with all the fervent pages of her journal as a postulant and novice.

We are suddenly confronted with a very different style and tone, and a completely new way of looking at life. No longer does she pour out her young girl's heart in dramatic and, perhaps, sentimental aspirations. The romantic ardor for sacrifice, the fervent idealism of the novice, have given way to a surprisingly sober, reflective, and analytic series of argumentations about her state and all that it involves. Nowhere so much as in this contrast do we feel how great was the impact of this shock to her sensitive nature. She has been jolted out of all possibility of relying on emotion or feeling to reestablish her balance, and now she is fighting for a foothold with a more desperate and argumentative seriousness. She needs, now, new convictions, solid reasons, explanations; she wants to understand. She wants to see where she is going. She wants to adjust her mind to this immense and strange and frightening set of problems.

"It is quite seldom," she writes (and note that now her reflections have become impersonal and general), "that a person who embraces the Trappist life is prepared for all the sacrifices that it calls for, and can demand of us, with a full knowledge of all they involve, and, consequently, with a heart generously disposed to receive them. And so, one may sometimes be surprised, and may be lacking in generosity before those that come upon one without warning: for instance, changing from one monastery to another."

The impersonal and apparently calm and speculative tone of her words, contrasted with the impassioned ardor with which she wrote as a postulant, is so impressive a change that we can begin to realize, from it, just how much this sacrifice was costing her, and how weak she felt in its presence.

"There is," she continues, "in the heart of man, a most natural love for the place in which he was born. This same love is found in the soul of a religious for the monastery which has received her, and for the persons who dwell there; the very stones seem to possess a kind of life. Habit, and what not, create around about her an atmosphere in which she breathes easy and takes her repose. But she is not aware of this; she even clings to the memory of her first sorrows and her first sacrifices. The places where she pours out her afflicted heart before God, in the secrecy of solitude, have charms for her; she loves to recall to mind her moments of anguish, and the help she has received in them. Everything that brings to mind anything that has moved her deeply, possesses a certain delightfulness for her sensibilities, and, let us admit it, at times even for her self-love.

"True, God can, if He wills, leave these souls always in this ignorance, but sometimes His holy jealousy goes further, and, in the various dispositions of His Providence, when He seems to be directing events only for the general good of a community, He is also working for the good of a soul, in a more complete sacrifice, as the term of perfection to which she is called. And the fact is that the soul that is thus torn asunder discovers in herself a host of hitherto unknown attachments."

"There are," she continues (and here we recognize the voice of Father Polycarpe), "certain more privileged souls, and God is still more jealous yet of these. Never will they be able to show enough fidelity and devotion to a single one of His special graces, which would be poured out upon them in superabundance if they correspond with God's designs upon them. Destined to live His life alone, and to concern themselves only with Him, to find Him in the depths of their hearts, and to begin their eternity even here below, can they, without a blush of shame, cheat their Master of one single thought, one single desire, in order to give it to a creature?

"...The religious soul, if it is to be worthy of the great title it bears, must die even to the way and place in which it is to be detached, just as it must die to every other thing. And for this, it must allow Him to tear out of its heart everything that is not God. If she is told, one day, to pack up and leave, let her go, not only physically but in her judgment and will as well. Let her set at nought her own pain, provided only that God's will be done. Nor does she have to believe that, in order to conform herself to God's will, she must feel no rebellion or repugnance: good will overcomes these things, but does not altogether shut them out.

"It is precisely at the moment when her sensibilities are thus awakened, that she must bow before the blows with which she is stricken by the love of God. He breaks this heart of flesh only in order to supernaturalize our affections. And it is a happy day, when the soul, in desolation, runs to cast herself upon the bosom of Him Whom alone she must love, and yet Whom she has, nevertheless, tried to share with creatures!"

Now Mother Berchmans is about to state, without realizing how much she is saying, the crux of the whole problem, and the explanation of all her sufferings for the next few years. The explanation is, in itself, perfect and the only true one, which goes right to the root of all her temptations, and which, it is important to note, she was so often to *seem to forget*. For when God tries us, and means us to have a real, inescapable, and empirical knowledge of our own nothingness, He even teaches us, beforehand, all the truths we might need to think our way out of our temptations, if thinking could possibly save us: and then He allows us to suffer all the more from our complete inability to put into effect what we have seemed to know and understand. So it was with Sister Berchmans. And here is what she says. It is very good and very important. It is the secret of all temptations.

"This soul must not draw back from the Cross, *or shrink from her own weakness, which is even more difficult to bear than the Cross itself, because it humiliates her, and it is humiliation that she is trying to escape*. Sacrifice pierces the heart, but strengthens it: and creatures vanish from the heart thenceforth."

Temptations are given us, not that we may overcome them by our own powers, but only that, realizing and loving our own weakness, we may glory, like St. Paul, in our infirmities, because they drive us to throw ourselves into the arms of God, who alone can deliver us from evil. As Sister Berchmans herself has just said, and we repeat it because of its importance: "It is a happy day, when the soul, in desolation, runs to cast herself upon the bosom of Him whom alone she must love, and yet whom she has, nevertheless, tried to share with creatures."

The whole doctrine is admirably summed up in the journal of one of our great modern Cistercians, Dom Symphorien, a definitor of the order, and confessor to the nuns at Ubexy. He writes: "*Where God is leading us is not to sanctity as it is too commonly understood, that is to say, the embellishment of ourselves: but to the annihilation and destruction of ourselves*. But, if we are to attain this end, God will have to do everything: select our crosses, place them on our shoulders, pick us up after our falls, strip us, nail us, make us die on the cross: the hand of the Lord alone can do all this!"

And he adds one shatteringly powerful sentence that ought to be branded in every Trappist heart: "*God must triumph upon the ruins of all our plans. Only His ends have reality. All else is nothing.*"

God must triumph upon the ruins of all our plans! The ruin of Sister Berchmans and the triumph of God in her had already begun.

It was fitting that this sudden maturing of her spiritual life should be sealed by her perpetual profession on the feast of a great Cistercian mystic, to whom Sister Berchmans had a special devotion. For the date of her vows was set at the fifteenth of November, which was then the feast of St. Gertrude the Great, one of the originators of the cult of the Sacred Heart of Jesus—a cult which had its roots so deep in the Cistercian mysticism of the thirteenth century, and goes back directly to St. Bernard in the twelfth.

On that day she forever offered herself as a sacrifice to God before His high altar—a double sacrifice, the character of which was clearly brought out by the presence, before the presbytery, of the two abbots who were, so to speak, the priests who had arranged and were to celebrate her immolation by exile to Japan, Dom Eugene and Dom Vital Lehodey.

With great emotion the Sisters sat in their stalls, beholding the frail little nun, standing alone in the middle of the choir, hands folded under huge sleeves, and head slightly bowed, listening, motionless, to the sonorous words of the sermon of the bishop of Laval. Poor little nun, isolated, before a bishop and two mitered abbots, and under the gaze of all her sisters! How small and frail she looked!

The rich harmonious sentences of the prelate followed one another to a grand and stirring conclusion. The echoes of his voice died away along the stones and arches of the choir. There was a rustle of parchment. Sister Berchmans held, in her hands, the formula of her profession.

And then, in her small voice without music or sweetness, she sang tonelessly, but clear enough to be heard, her vows, her sacrifice. "*Ego, Soror Maria Joannes Berchmans....*" Her voice dropped flatly on the flexes and puncta, and fell and rose with a strange, inharmonious little melody all her own as she promised her life to God in medieval Latin. Finally, on the last syllable of the last word, her voice trailed away on the ending reserved for lessons in the office of the dead, or prophecies on fast days, or lessons of the night office in Holy Week, when the Church mourns the passion of our Saviour.

Surely the vow of stability must have torn her heart with a special poignancy. She was to spend her first years in Japan, still considered as a member of the community of Laval. She had made her stability in such a way that it was nothing but a weird and paradoxical responsibility, bearing with it none of the benefits or privileges or peace which it should have had.

The choir of Sisters had begun to fill the church with the long, sweet, sad cadences of the *Miserere*, and Sister Berchmans had fallen to her knees before her mother abbess, to ask her prayers and receive her embrace. Nor were her eyes the only ones that filled with tears as she passed along the stalls, kneeling at the feet of her sisters, one by one, and embraced by each one in turn, with a whispered blessing.

The day of her departure had now been decided too: she was to leave for Japan on the feast of Epiphany.

Nevertheless, the dark, cloudy days of November were days of joy. The waning year, the bare trees, the onset of winter, and the gradual approach of her own separation from her convent and her own dear land of France, could not quench in her the peace and inward strength of her union with Christ, her Spouse, in the depths of her being. Nor could the impending sacrifice prevent her often overflowing with that same ebullient, natural joy and vivacity which had always characterized her, and which now seemed, at times, more vigorous and irrepressible than ever.

Perhaps it was the very notion of the coming separation that made her gaiety more unrestrained, as a sort of nervous reaction. It was not seldom that the whole novitiate would explode in a burst of laughter that set the mother abbess, their next-door neighbor, banging vigorously on the wall for silence and order! She probably had no difficulty guessing who was the cause of the outburst.

November ended, and with it the liturgical year. The penitential season of Advent began, ushering in the winter. Sister Berchmans, still not attuned to the deep meanings of the liturgy, derived little comfort from the underlying joy of the Church's Advent. Rather her interior repugnance, her sorrow, tended only to increase. There was less and less prospect of anything but gloom in her approaching departure. She multiplied her acts of love and resignation to God's will, and each act was purer than the last because each was made in the teeth of greater helplessness and desolation.

There was some small comfort, however, in a short retreat given to the Sisters by a Benedictine monk, which served to help her prepare for her exile. As for her Christmas, we do not know how it was that year: her journal has nothing important to say.

The first week of the new year was the last at the convent of Laval for Mère Berchmans and her companion in exile, who was to be none other than her former novice mistress, Mother Dominic. There were not many preparations to be made. A Cistercian, even when making a change of stability from one side of the world to the other, never has much baggage. A breviary, a discipline, a few plain garments, perhaps a grammar-school copybook full of personal notes, and that is all. It did not take Mother Berchmans long to do her packing.

The vigil of the Epiphany was a series of long drawn-out scenes of leave-taking that were enough to break anybody's heart. And yet they had an official character about them that made them more bearable. The last, purely personal, and most agonizing farewells were to come just before their actual departure, the following day.

On the vigil, however, the two Sisters knelt in the refectory, and publically begged the pardon of the community for the disedification they had given by all their "faults," during the past years. Afterward, they took leave of all their sisters by exchanging with each one a silent embrace, the silence of which was more eloquent than speech. All this took place under a certain decorous restraint which did not break down, in poor Mother Berchmans' heart, until bedtime. Then, however, when she had pulled down the curtain of her cell behind her, and lain down in her clothes upon her straw mattress, and pulled her blanket over her, her grief could no longer be contained. She spent the rest of the night sleepless in her sorrow, and the next morning appeared in church for the night office of the great feast, looking like a ghost.

In the majesty of the liturgy, before the throne of the incarnate Son of God, truly present under the sacramental veils of the Host hidden in the tabernacle, the gold, frankincense, and myrrh of the three wise kings were again offered for His glory. The gold of love, the frankincense of praising prayer were brought to Jesus by the heart of every nun. But more especially from the sorrowing soul of one there came to Him the precious myrrh of suffering, distilled, in slow tears, to embalm the Saviour's burying.

With what special love the glorious and hidden Christ looked into the heart of this poor little Sister who could not even sing, who could not even force from her sad heart one feeling of pleasure or joy in sacrifice, but who stood before Him with her head bowed, her hands full of the ruins of all her dreams and notions of the religious life, full of the fragments of every natural friendship and every human affection, too humbled and too weak to do anything but admit that it half killed her to give up all these things.

He did not tell her anything. He did not speak to her. He looked at her in silent love, watching her sorrow merging into the immense sorrow that He had once felt, receiving her union with Him as a gift of precious myrrh. He was looking at her out of the depths of eternity, where her gift, the King's gift, and His own sacrifice had all been one from the beginning.

Oh, if Mother Berchmans could have known it then! When she stood there in that cold ,choir, lost in so much misery that she could scarcely even see, drowning in the depths of her own weakness, she was saving the world!

After the High Mass, more embraces. This time, it was the novitiate: all her closest friends. All those to whom she was most attached. It was calm enough, but there were tears. Then the two exiles, instead of taking their dinner in the refectory, ate apart with Reverend Mother Lutgarde, and the old abbess, Mère Marie Antoinette, who had received Sister Berchmans into the convent.

The last scene of all followed this dinner. It was their departure. There were about twenty Sisters gathered in the front court to see them off. This time the embraces were more desperate and more fervent, for it was the end. Mother Berchmans no longer stifled her sobs, nor tried to hide the breaking of her heart. She could not. What were they saying to her? She hardly made it out. "We will meet again in heaven." And that was all.

One last, despairing look over her shoulder and the immense, heavy door swung shut, locking the two nuns out into the hostile world.

CHAPTER VI

THE JOURNEY

In the days when she had been deciding her vocation—how long ago it all seemed now!—Mère Berchmans had been offered a choice between two Trappistine convents: the one at Laval, and another, Our Lady of the Sacred Heart, at Macon, close to Lyons. She had not even hesitated in choosing the one at the other end of France. It had been her intention to get as far away as possible from all ties of this world, and at Macon she would still have been too close to her parents and friends.

There is something astounding in the directness and abruptness with which God had taken her intention more literally and with a more drastic completeness than she had ever envisaged herself. To increase the dramatic irony of it all, it was at Our Lady of the Sacred Heart that the party of nuns for Japan was to assemble. In all, there were to be seven Sisters in the group: two from Laval, two from Macon, and three lay sisters from Ubexy.

Supposing she had considered her own human weakness, and entered at Macon in order to be closer to her parents? There is no point in wondering whether she thought about all this, and how much more difficult, under such circumstances would have been her choice for Japan. There was one thing she did not know then: within a few years, the whole community of Our Lady of the Sacred Heart was to be transported bodily to Brazil, in an unsuccessful attempt at starting a new colony there. They eventually returned to

Chambarand, southeast of Lyons, in the foothills of the Alps—but that was long after Mother Berchmans was dead. If she had chosen Macon, her exile would have been only more certain.

The kindness of the welcome among their sisters at Our Lady of the Sacred Heart would have been enough to soften the anguish of her departure, but there were many other things that helped her, for the moment, to forget her sorrow.

To begin with, Dom Jean Baptiste Chautard, abbot of Sept-Fons and almost as great a Cistercian traveler in our century as St. Bernard in the twelfth, came to give the Sisters the benefit of his deep wisdom and prudence in all matters, both temporal and spiritual, that concerned their journey. This truly great man, the magnitude of whose work and character is best measured by his *Soul of the Apostolate*, which was the bedside book of Pope Pius X and of countless other priests in every part of the world, had a special interest in the young Japanese foundation of Our Lady of the Angels, and was to make many visits to that convent in his travels around the world.

At this time, he gave the Sisters who were about to leave various offices to take charge of in their group, and Mother Berchmans was made treasurer. Father Robert, in his manuscript, views this choice with a rather rueful eye, and remarks that all the valuable practical advice that was given to the Sisters by Dom Chautard simply went in one ear and out the other as far as Mother Berchmans was concerned. But there are no more details, and we may assume that the nuns suffered no financial disaster before reaching Japan.

Another surprise was the unexpected appearance of two nuns and no less than sixteen former students of the Convent of the Redemption at Lyons. Somehow the news had reached them, and they came to give Mother Berchmans a comparatively noisy send-off. Even she, after two years of silence, seems to have found it hard to handle so many affectionate and talkative friends all at once; she finally put an end to the visit by asking the mother prioress to intone a *Magnificat* and give them all her blessing. Thus effectively silenced, the eighteen visitors filed out with sighs of love and admiration.

It was after the relief of this interlude that the journey began. On January 12, the seven nuns left Macon by train for Marseilles.

The first important stop after Macon was Lyons, where there was a fairly long wait; long enough, had Mother Berchmans desired it, for a little talk with her parents. But she had made a special point of telling them nothing about her journey or her passing through Lyons. Even then, all the while the train was at the Gare de Perrache, she kept well out of sight in a corner of the compartment, just in case some relative or friend might chance to be walking about on the platform.

But when the long shrill whistle echoed in the gloom of the station, the cries of the trainmen mingled with the first roaring burst of steam from the locomotive, and the long express began to move out into the light of day. Mother Berchmans looked, with a peculiar tenseness and emptiness of heart, at the crowded buildings, the dark towers, and the hills of this city she was seeing for the last time in her life, and which had once been her home. One last glance at shrine of Fourvières, where she had first consecrated herself to the Mother of God; and then she returned, within her heart, to the Spouse who had called her and was leading her, by the hand, on this way that she did not yet fully understand, but in which she acquiesced with all her will, in spite of the rebellion of her feelings.

The train sped southward along the banks of the Rhone. Mile after mile of bare, rocky, sunny hills, and France fled away from her, forever. Mother Berchmans did not look. Peacefully, she prayed, and sacrificed her country, mile by mile, to God.

Night was falling when they reached Marseilles, and came out on to the great platform before the Gare St. Charles dominating the vast blue amphitheater of the city. At the corners of the balustrade, huge and shadowy, the monumental, allegorical statues of the five continents greeted them. Beyond the city was the sea; and through the obscure and rumorous sound of a thousand crowded streets, came the low, sad call of a ship in the harbor mouth, deep and strange, utterly alien from the things of the land. For the first time Mother Berchmans' heart became acquainted with the sea and its own immense and peculiar loneliness. It harmonized with hers;

it was the sadness of her own exile, with which it had a kind of causal relation.

They descended into the city, innocent of the terrors that fill that labyrinth of narrow streets, and were soon safe behind the walls of a friendly convent.

The next morning, still fasting, they hastened all together, as the dawn was breaking over the already busy thoroughfares, over the cobbles, and past the fishing boats of the Vieux Port to the foot of the steep, bare hill that is crowned by the shrine of the Protectress of that vast and violent city. From the high tower of Notre Dame de la Garde, the statue of the Mother of God looks out in mercy and pity to the bright sea, where go the ships that carry her children to the far corners of the unfriendly earth.

How pervasive is the influence of the Queen of heaven, on this bare rock, above one of the most terrible and sinful cities of the world! How real, how present is her mercy, her pity, and her help, hovering over these quays and slums and docks, these tenements heavy with the threat of murder and of vice! Nor does the power of her special intercession ever cease to penetrate, with a purer and more irresistible strength, even into the darkest corners of this labyrinth, where she alone does not abhor the murdering lascar or the dying harlot.

The seven little nuns, destined for Japan, who knew nothing of the city they were in, came up the street that ended at the foot of the rock. Already their eyes ascended the hundreds of stone steps to the Basilica, when suddenly they noticed two figures at the bottom of the long flight. They were monks. Under their dark overcoats, was the white Cistercian robe. These were the two Trappist priests who were to accompany them on their long journey. All together they climbed the steps, turning now and again to watch the city spread itself out, white in the rising sun, beautiful in its amphitheater of hills sloping down to the blue sea.

They paused a moment at the top, with the whole harbor spread out at their feet. But they did not stay to gaze at this sight that made them all sad. Through the darkness of the doorway, they already saw the garden of bright candles at the shrine. They knelt. The two monks silently went to vest for Mass.

Mother Berchmans lifted up her eyes to Mary, her Mother, her Protectress, her Queen, to whom she belonged, body and soul. The two priests, bowed heads circled with the monastic crown, began, in intense recollection, each one to say his Mass.

It was here, on top of the rock over the harbor, and at the feet of His Mother, that the Lord Jesus came into the soul of Mother Berchmans and her companions for the last time on the soil of France.

That evening, at five o'clock, the great hawsers splashed into the dirty water of the docks, and the black hull of the liner *Sidney* began slowly to fall away from the quay. The clangor of winch and chain, the rushing of steam, the deep roar of the whistle that shook them to the soles of their feet and left them filled with a ringing din that deafened their whole minds; then they realized that they were on their way, the land was separated from them by an ever-widening gap, the ship was slowly turning, nosing out of the harbor, and setting her bow for the open sea.

They stood at the rail, devouring with their eyes this land of France that they would never see again, and, in one unspeakable rush of anguish that choked their very hearts, they offered up to God this total sacrifice of everything their nature loved: their quiet homes, their fathers and mothers under the trellises of peaceful French gardens, or working in their vineyards or shops. They offered up the lovely villages that were now lost to them forever, the mansard roofs, or the boulevards lined with plane trees, the market squares where the children play in the white dust, the little churches, or the great quiet cathedrals, the clean cloisters of their convents, the smiles of their own dear sisters, their kindness, their little attentions, even their little faults and peculiarities; all these were things well loved and matter for sacrifice.

Dusk was beginning to gather once again; Marseilles was falling into the sea; Mary, on top of her tower, looked after them and never averted her eyes, when the nuns and the Trappists, their companions, drawing into their aching lungs deep draughts of the air of the sea, began from the fullness of their anguished hearts to thank God for their sacrifice: *Magnificat anima mea Dominum....*

Mother Berchmans raised her eyes to the shrine on the rock, joined her poor voice to the others, and joined her heart's sorrow to the eternal joy of the Mother of God in the canticle of the thanksgiving for her glory and our salvation: "My soul doth magnify the Lord: and my spirit hath rejoiced in God my Saviour...."

Rejoiced? Yes, rejoiced; for in spite of all her tears, she had in her heart more joy than she realized in the pain of this sacrifice, for she was uttering once again that same *Fiat* which was the salvation of us all.

When they arose next morning to find themselves off the coast of Corsica and entering the straits of Bonifacio, all Mother Berchmans' sadness was swept away, at least for a time, by the beauty of the mountains and the sea, and her heart filled with exultation and joy, to see God magnified in His works; later, when they came to the even more beautiful straits of Messina, between Sicily and the Italian mainland, she was to write to those she had left behind at Laval: "How all this speaks to the heart, and lifts it up to God, making it forget, for the moment, the sorrows of exile, and the rocky path that leads to our true home...."

But as the course brought them closer and closer to the eastern end of the Mediterranean, her thoughts turned to the Holy Land. They would pass so close to it, and yet see none of it! This made her sad. From Port Said she wrote: "We are only twelve hours away from Jerusalem...."

Standing at the rail, she looked beyond the dock and the dusky stevedores filing interminably up the gangplank laden with coal, out beyond the low roofs of the city burning in the sun, to the desert, and saw there, in her imagination, the obscure St. Joseph and his Spouse, whom no one knew was the Mother of God but he himself and one or two others back in Palestine, coming through the rocks from the desert, down into Egypt along the road of the caravans, bearing with them, hidden and protected from the sun and from the eyes of men, the Sun of Justice and the Glory of the

Universe, emptied of His visible glory and power to become a weak and helpless Child for our sakes.

All this time, as one of the other nuns wrote to Laval, Mother Berchmans was remarkable, outwardly, only for her extraordinary cheerfulness. More than ever, she was full of good humor and wit and high spirits so that it could be said of her: "Sister Berchmans gets first prize for gaiety. By her good humor, she helps very much to keep up the spirit of charity...." And it may also be added that it helped not a little when some of the Sisters were overcome by rough weather, and succumbed to the harmless but humiliating affliction of seasickness; but there it was her tact as much as her cheerfulness that produced its good effects for no one who is seasick is in any mood to enjoy jokes.

Interiorly, however, her natural unhappiness at being exiled from the convent of her choice, and where she had been so happy, instead of growing less, was only intensified by the monotony of the long voyage. The endless sameness of the Indian Ocean, with day succeeding day, bringing no change or relief from the blinding heat and the dreary emptiness of the horizon, favored the work of the enemy of souls. She began to be tortured with doubts—doubts which she hardly knew whether she was admitting to her consideration or not. And her mind was not at peace. There was a constant fear and anxiety, in her soul, that all was not well, that this journey had something wrong with it.

To be more precise, she began to wonder if there were not something wrong with her own soul. Surely this exile must be some sort of a punishment: there was every reason for her to think so, when she considered herself and found so many imperfections, such selfishness and pride. Now one of the things that most distressed her was the fact that no amount of praying and trying and good will on her part was able to make her exile more agreeable to her.

Had she not realized and written in her journal, months before, that we need not believe we are not accomplishing God's will, merely because the lower part of our soul is filled with feelings of repugnance? "Good will," as she had said, "overcomes these things but does not shut them out."

If she had only known how much she was learning, and how much progress she was making, merely by being confronted, day after day, with the inescapable truth of her own helplessness! But a sentence from a letter will show what confusion was in her mind: "It is my belief that when the good God truly loves a soul, He seeks to keep her unobserved, and hides her as completely as possible in the little place to which His love has led her. He is jealous of her slightest look. And yet in my case it is just the opposite. One would think He was in a hurry to cast me out into the world, since after barely two years of the hidden life, He hurls me back into the whirlwind."

And then she adds: "I have not enough virtue to overcome myself, and instead of working for the glory of the Divine Master, I only sadden His Heart."

All this confusion and imperfection was not without its good reaction. It was not long after her arrival in Japan that she could write, in spite of the continuance of all the same repugnances, and even their aggravation: "Oh, how well the Good Master knows what He is doing! I had great need of this separation, this shattering of my heart, to detach me from creatures and bring me closer to God."

Ceylon was her first experience of the Far East, and there the luxuriance of the vegetation, the myriads of birds, the thousand new and wonderful kinds of flowers, the sounds, the strange, harsh, exotic cries of the jungle all stirred her heart and lifted it again to God in wonder, adoration, and love, but with an added sense of the tragic contrast between all this natural manifestation of His glory, and the hopeless labyrinths of error, the caverns of fantastic natural mysticisms, in which the souls of the millions of men living in all these lands, were imprisoned.

Burma, Indo-China, and then the China Sea, notorious for its treacherous winds and sudden, terrible storms. They had rough weather for many days, but Sister Berchmans was more fortunate than most of her sisters in not suffering from seasickness, and only the more exultant at the wonders and violence of the heavy seas. She took a childish joy in fighting her way up and down the reeling decks, flattened to the side of the ship by the strong wind, or at times, nearly carried off her feet by sudden gusts of it, and almost always soaked to the skin by the stinging clouds of spray that lashed and covered the ship with their blinding force. And all the while her heart was drunk with joy at the sight of the huge seas that bore down on them like mountains, as if to swallow them up, but on whose surging mass the ship would lift and roll and finally poise and shudder for a dizzy second before plunging straight down, in a sickening dive, into the depths that suddenly yawned before her bows.

There was only one drawback to all this: it was impossible for them to have Mass all the while they were in the China Sea. Every piece of furniture on the ship that was not already permanently screwed to the floor was now lashed together against the walls, and it was almost impossible for the few who cared to visit the dining saloon to keep the dishes safely within the confines of the clumsy wooden "violins" erected upon the tables. Under these conditions, it would not have been proper to try and offer the Holy Sacrifice; the dangers were far too great.

Finally, however, they sighted the southernmost extremity of the island of Kiushu, after which they soon landed at Nagasaki. From there to Yokahama, and from Yokahama to Aomori, they traversed almost the full length of the Japanese empire. It remained for them only to cross the Sangar Strait to the Island of Yesso, and they would be "home."

The thought strangely chilled the heart of Mother Berchmans, as she looked out at the bleak, steel-gray waters of the bay. Somewhere in those mountains was a poor convent that was her home. The rest of her life on earth was to be Japanese, like the strange people all around her, who viewed her without comprehension or sympathy. This was her nation, now. She was one of them.

They had to wait at Aomori until the following morning for a boat, and this was the cause of a rather cheerful interlude, in which they became the guest of a missionary who was famous in all Japan for his sanctity.

The simplicity of Père Faurie won Mother Berchmans' heart and did much to keep her gaiety alive right to the end of the journey.

They entered the missionary's house to find, first of all, that there were very few chairs. This gave the Sisters an opportunity to practice the Japanese custom of sitting on one's heels on the floor. Meanwhile, the good Father had a fire going and was making soup, the principal dish of the meal he was able to offer them that evening. The ingredients were not quite in proportion to the amount of water necessary to provide a portion for each of the guests; but, at any rate, they were all able to have a bowl of hot water that tasted faintly of bouillon and vegetables, and had some bread floating in it. Since there were only a very few dishes, the Sisters had to eat in relays. When the time came for bed, there were, of course, no beds; but the Sisters agreed with pleasure to sleep on the floor of the chapel. However, it was very cold that night, and there were no more blankets than there were beds. Père Faurie sent his catechist out into the highways and byways to borrow blankets from the neighbors, and when he returned, there were not only enough to provide them with a warm covering, but also to give them something fairly soft to lie on.

At ten the following morning they steamed out of Aomori for the six-hour journey to Hakodate. Although they landed at four o'clock, and the convent was only a few miles out of the city, they stopped overnight with the Sisters of Saint Paul of Chartres.

CHAPTER VII

ANOTHER ORPHANAGE

Excited curiosity had been accumulating in the hearts of all the exiled Sisters as the journey had drawn to its close, as well as relief and thankfulness that it was over, and joy at being able to return to the regular, peaceful, silent life to which they had been called by God. For this their souls had been crying out, obscurely but insistently, all through the long weeks of movement, excitement, and change, vicissitudes and dangers even, that had accompanied their voyage half around the world.

Now, at eight o'clock in the morning of February 28, 1902, in the drab streets of this small Japanese city, under a cold, steel-grey sky, heavy with the threat of snow, Mother Berchmans looked at the dark green hills and jagged mountains inland, where they were going, and her heart sank within her. Soon it would all be over. She would see and know the worst. There would be no more doubt. No chance to imagine things better than they were. She would be imprisoned forever in an inescapable certainty that the rest of her life was to be spent in a poor little wooden hovel at the ends of the earth.

The Trappist monks took their leave, now, and headed for the monastery of Our Lady of the Lighthouse (Notre Dame du Phare), out on its bleak headland, dominating the sea. Probably that was the last Mother Berchmans saw of them, or they of any of the nuns. The Sisters, meanwhile, separated into groups, riding perhaps in rickshaws; we are not told. But they left the city; and in an hour or two of a long climb, they reached their destination. The last group to arrive saw their traveling companions gathered, awaiting them; and in the midst of these, in black scapular and white robe, stood the Trappist priest, their chaplain, their future confessor, spiritual director, and instructor in Japanese, a French monk, Father Robert Lepasquier.

As for the convent, it was almost unnoticeable. A long, low wooden building, standing at the edge of a field. If you looked twice, you could see a belfry, not dominating the building, but clinging to the side of it. Mother Berchmans was to write back to Laval explaining that the belfry was not on top of the house because they feared that the ringing of the two little bells, Marie-des-Anges and Marie-Joseph, would end in the whole place, roof, rafters, belfry, and bells, being pulled down on their heads.

There was an enclosure fence, but it was easy to see that there was not much to enclose. A tiny garden, a couple of pine trees, a chicken house, and that was all.

Suddenly, as the last group of nuns joined the rest, were welcomed by Father Robert, and turned to the little gate of the convent to go in, there was a great rustle of ropes in the little belfry, and the bells began to ring, both of them, one high, and the other, not low, but a little less high. Happy bells! That was the sort of thing reserved for big feasts. Feasts of sermon. The Gloria of Holy Saturday, when Lent, liturgically speaking, comes to an end. Ordinarily, only one bell rings at a time.

With these two poor bells welcoming them in, the nuns entered the enclosure, and the gate closed on them. Did any of them ever leave it again? Mother Berchmans did not. She had seen much of the world, perhaps, in the last month, but she would never see any more of it. Indeed, from now on, she was hardly ever to cast even a glance out of the convent windows at the magnificent view that spread out before them. She would pay but little attention to the long jagged range of mountains, the torrent twisting in the valley below, the plain beyond, cut up into unnumerable neat, rectangular fields and farms and small gardens, and the huddled houses of the city, and the sea. She would not look out at the sea or the headland that pointed out the long road back to Europe and to France. But if her eyes would not turn that way, it was harder to keep her desires from beating against the wooden walls of this enclosure.

Meanwhile, however, she was not thinking of such things. The Father chaplain was leading them into his share of the convent church. The tiny sanctuary and transepts served not only as the chapel of the extern Sisters, but also as the secular church, for the few Japanese Christians living in these hills. With the bells still ringing and the whole building shaking with the work of the ropes, the nuns knelt before the tabernacle, not separated from their Lord by the grille, as they would be from that day on, but right under the hanging sanctuary lamp.

What did He say to them, or they to Him? What mute, half-helpless acts of loving adoration and submission, in the darkness of faith? Perhaps He struck some hearts with deep shafts of consolation, and spoke some word of kindness that brought tears to the eyes. What did He say to Mother Berchmans, or she to Him?

The next thing was to meet Reverend Mother Scholastica, their new superior, from whose lips they were to learn so many of the details of God's will for them. Indeed, it was not many hours before Mother Berchmans was to receive an important employment from her, that of vestiarian. She would have charge of making and repairing all the clothing, of caring for such crude linens and blankets as the convent possessed, and, the biggest problem, of providing something to serve in their place, when there was nothing.

It was clear that the contemplative life at Our Lady of the Angels was not yet possible, in any real sense. Martha had succeeded, after all, in getting Mary to help her with her many duties, and Mother Berchmans was to be sanctified by an immense amount of work and sacrifice. She would have the merit of much prayer, indeed, but not the enjoyment of it. Her prayer would be offered up more as a sacrifice than as a prayer. She would pray by wishing that she had time to pray.

And still they had not entered the convent itself. Noon came, and they remained in the guesthouse for what Father Robert innocently calls "one last meal." During their journey, of course, they had not kept the Trappist fast, or confined themselves to the meager Trappist diet. They had been allowed not only fish and eggs, but even meat, which the regulations permit to those who travel by sea—and that explains the so-called bouillon they accepted from the good missionary at Aomori.

As they dined, the snow began to fall, but that did not prevent Father Robert from showing them around part of the convent. Yet it was not until three o'clock that they all gathered once more in the exterior church, that is, the sanctuary, outside the grille.

The fact that they had been waiting several hours for what now took place, only served to accentuate the great importance of this event in the history of the new convent. For the first time a ceremony was to be held that would become part of the tradition of the house and be repeated often in the years that followed, whenever reinforcements came from Europe. Even as we write these words, we wonder if it will not be held again someday, when the French nuns, expelled by the Japanese government during the second World War, will be able to return to their Japanese sisters. Or will they ever return? We pray that it may not matter whether they do or not, and that the strong and fervent Japanese community may be able to continue without any need of outside help. But we are still considering the days when Our Lady of the Angels was a pioneer foundation, and when to save it from total ruin, the first group of volunteers from France was arriving to join the pioneers.

The nuns who had first come from Ubexy to start the first convent of Trappistines in the Far East had landed only a bare four years before. On April 30, 1898, they had moved into the little wooden building that had first been erected to house a boys' orphanage. But the orphan asylum had failed, and the building was left empty. Empty it was, indeed; so much so that the only furniture of the first colonists had been a few packing cases and some folding stools.

And when they set the "table" for dinner—that is, laid out a couple of tin plates on top of a packing case—and drew up their stools, there was nothing to eat but some two weeks' old bread, brought from Yokahama. This they tried to make palatable by boiling it in water, a process, which, at least, made it soft enough to be swallowed.

We do not have to go back to the great days of the Middle Ages when the courage of the Fathers of the order did not fail on a diet of roots and boiled elm leaves. The spirit that sustained Abbot Richard of Fountains and his companions, when on St. Stephen's day, December 26, 1132, they left the habitations of men to sleep on straw under a tree in the wild, rocky Yorkshire valley of Skelldale had not died. Even in the nineteenth century, at Bricquebec, we read of the monks being so short of food that they mixed in with the "salad," which was the staple of their diet (and to a French peasant, salad generally means dandelion leaves), a generous portion of forest foliage.

The good Sisters, from the mountains of Alsace, had at first faced all this with plenty of strength and courageous joy, gladly rising from their meal of boiled bread and carrying their stools into the empty chapel to serve as seats in choir. But flesh is not iron. With all the hardships and labors of a new foundation, every relief permitted by the rule, in the way of diet, is usually given, if not expected. It is necessary that monks and nuns who must sacrifice everything, even much of their prayer, to extra work, should at least have a little cheese or butter or milk or fruit, in addition to the generous helpings of potatoes and turnips and cabbage and beans that are the usual fare in winter.

These Sisters, with little to eat day after day but a few vegetables and some bread, soon became anemic and, therefore, unable to resist any of the common diseases that afflict men in the winter and early spring. Several of the Sisters became so weak that it was decided to send them back to France. For six months, there were only two choir nuns at Our Lady of the Angels.

When influenza fell upon the little family of Sisters, only one choir nun was left on her feet, and she valiantly carried out the obligation to keep the work of God, the divine office, going in choir at the appointed times. She would ring the bell for office, go to the grille of the choir, and recite the psalms, alternating with Father Robert who stood with his breviary on the other side of the grille.

Thus, from the day the convent was founded, not an hour of the choral service was omitted. But even now the choir of two was eagerly awaiting the four choir religious from France, and the three lay sisters were a welcome addition to the three or four who had first come from Ubexy.

Such was the situation, when seven Sisters filed into the sanctuary at three o'clock that snowy afternoon in February, 1902.

As they knelt in adoration for a moment before the tabernacle, a rustle, a movement of nuns rising from their knees was heard in the hidden choir, and a clear, pure voice intoned that wonderful psalm of hope and joy, *In exitu*: "When Israel went out of Egypt, the house of Jacob from a barbarous people....

The nuns in the sanctuary, with their breviaries open, took up the next verse: "*Facta est Judaea sanctificatio ejus....*"

"Judea was made his sanctuary, Israel his dominion.

"The sea saw, and fled: Jordan was turned back.

"The mountains skipped like rams, and the hills like the lambs of the flock...."

Wonderful psalm! We wonder if they sang it on the special tone reserved for that psalm alone, the ferial vespers for Monday in our Cistercian Psalter. There is no tone more stirring in all our liturgy, in its tremendous and solemn simplicity. It is said that this tone is so ancient that it goes back to the time of the Old Testament; perhaps our Lord Himself, and St. Joseph, and the Apostles, and St. John the Baptist chanted this holy and austere music. At least they chanted the words, and we can guess with what reverence and love they did so!

"What ailed thee, O thou sea, that thou didst flee? And thou, O Jordan, that thou wast turned back?"

During the singing of this psalm, one evening, in the choir of the Abbey of Grandselve, Blessed Bertrand, of that abbey, one of the ancient abbots and holy patriarchs of the Cistercian Order and a man as simple and holy as Abraham, looked up and saw Jesus walking quietly down the middle of the choir.

"At the presence of the Lord the earth was moved, at the presence of the God of Jacob."

What one of the Sisters did not feel the presence of the Lord, in a special way, in their hearts, at that moment? He was working there. This was His doing. He had brought them to this hill among the mountains of Japan. These mountains skipped like rams as the nuns sang, for the Lord was in them. The sea had fled from them, because they were full of God.

"*Domini est terra!*" they sang, after *In exitu*. "The earth is the Lord's, and the fulness thereof: the world and all they that dwell therein."

They had come from France and had found Him in Japan, yet they had neither left Him in France nor had He ceased to hold them in the palm of His hand, He who had been, all the while, with the little nuns in the deserted orphanage outside Hakodate. And He, who was with them, was also with the Sisters they had left at Laval, those for whom they wept and sorrowed in their hearts.

"Lift up your gates, O ye princes, and be ye lifted up, O eternal gates!"

More rustling behind the grille, the turning of a key, and the humble wooden door swung open.

"Lift up your gates, O ye princes, and be ye lifted up, O eternal gates, and the King of Glory shall enter in."

The door swung open, and the Sisters saw the faces of their new sisters, smiling. "And the King of Glory shall enter in." "Who is this King of Glory?"

One by one the French nuns went into their new home, this tiny choir with its white stalls and no *jube* and a bench at the back for the lay sisters.

"Who is this King of Glory? The Lord of Hosts, He is the King of Glory."

Indeed, it was Christ, the Lord of Hosts and the God of armies, passing through the grille into the choir of the nuns, hiding in the heart of Mother Berchmans.

There is no denying her happiness. She was probably filled with joy even at the "Ecce quam bonum," that psalm whose metaphors had so disturbed her in the novitiate at Laval, and which was now sung, for its sentiments were always in her heart, no matter how black her trials.

But above all, her heart was full of happiness and gratitude and fervent love when they ended the ceremony and made all things perfect by consecrating themselves to the Holy Mother of God, whose statue smiled gently upon them from the middle of the choir. No matter what sufferings were to come upon her, and no matter how little she might understand them, she would always find peace and strength at the feet of this statue, all the rest of her religious life. No matter if everything else failed her, our Lady of the Angels would always be a sure refuge, and at her feet she could always find comfort, strength, and light.

This consecration was more than a formula or a ceremony for Mother Berchmans. She had consecrated herself to Jesus through His Mother many times since she had climbed the hill of Fourvières as a child in Lyons, and each new consecration answered to some new spiritual necessity because it corresponded to some new spiritual growth. The immense step that she was taking now was also to be taken hand in hand with this kind Mother who was to guide her safely through much darkness and many storms.

The Sisters would see her kneeling at the feet of Mary's statue, deep in peaceful recollection, oblivious to the winter wind howling through the open windows of the little chapel, or to the flurries of snow that burst from time to time into the empty choir. And when the Sisters, knowing that she was sick and weak and probably running a temperature, urged her to be careful, she replied: "When I am near her, I feel nothing. *Tout près d'elle on ne sent rien.*"

On another occasion, she told someone that she wanted to get very close to the Mother of God so as to catch from her a few germs of that tremendous love of which she had died, in order that she might die of the same sickness—as indeed she was to do, by the great grace and favor of the Lord God, through the intercession of the one from whom she had certainly caught these "germs" of divine charity.

Meanwhile, however, she began, with her companions, to inspect their new home, and in great good humor too. There was something ridiculous about this poor, little, wooden house, built for fourteen people—most of them orphans, at that—and now already overcrowded by the arrival of seven Sisters.

She wrote back to reverend mother, at Laval, describing the convent, beginning with the chapel:

"The part destined for the community is about as big as the novitiate at Laval. On either side of the grille are placed a statue of the Sacred Heart and one of St. Joseph. In the middle of the choir is the statue of our Blessed Mother, and that is my favorite place when my heart is full. I let my tears fall into her motherly heart, and when I am with her, I gain strength to keep going and to be a worthy daughter of Laval. Our stalls are of white wood, and we have no screen. A long bench replaces the seats. At the back of the choir is a third bench for the lay-sisters. The stations of the Cross are along the wall....

"Near the chapel is Reverend Mother's room. It serves at the same time as pharmacy, library, and classroom for the Laysisters' catechism. A little further on, I have the honor, my Reverend Mother, to introduce you to our own new domain: the vestiary, and there, like everywhere else, there is not much room to dance around."

She then goes on to the infirmary, remarking that she is temporarily sleeping there, not because she is ill but because there are only ten cells in the dormitory, and two nuns were relegated to the infirmary which, we may guess, was probably one room with two or three beds in it.

Her letter continues:

"We then go down a few steps and come to the novitiate, which is as big as a pocket handkerchief.... Facing that is the laundry, in which there are no modern conveniences. Now, on the ground floor: first the refectory. It is the largest room, but not the prettiest. It amuses me to look at the pieces of white tin which doubtless conceal some hole, to prevent the snow and rain from coming through. Thence to the Chapter Room. It is a good thing that our Most Reverend Abbot General will never come here: if he did, he would have to bend double to get to his place."

The abbot general referred to was the Most Reverend Dom Sebastian Wyart, a tall man of imposing presence, with a great black beard. He had been in the Papal Zouaves defending Rome under Pius IX, and had afterward entered the Trappists at Mont des Cats, becoming the first general of the Cistercians of the Strict Observance after the reunion of the three congregations, in 1893. He would have made a pretty picture walking along "bent double" through a little room in a Japanese boys' orphanage, between two rows of bowing and awe-struck nuns.

"Then," continues Mother Berchmans in her letter, "we come to the workroom, but I dare not take you inside, since the laundry is drying in front of the fire. Let us, instead, go right away to the garden. It is about twice the size of the refectory. You might go through it from end to end without finding a single pebble in the soil. That is very nice as far as gardening is concerned but in bad weather you sink in as though you were walking around in a lot of ointment."

A little later on, in a letter which, from the fact that it mentions mosquitoes and various other unpleasant insects, must have been written when the warm weather came, she describes some other minor hardships of life at Our Lady of the Angels. "As I write to you, dear Mother, I hear a patter of feet in the ceiling. That reminds me that I have not yet told you about our charming boarders...*messieurs les rats.* They are very numerous in this country, dear Mother, and they have so much nerve that it would knock a man off his horse! At night they dance around above our heads, and indeed we are lucky if they don't do so actually on our heads themselves, for they make no bones about coming and giving us the kiss of peace during our slumbers. During Sister A's first days here, a great big rat, desiring, no doubt, to make her acquaintance, came and sat down in a familiar sort of way on the top of her head: imagine how scared she was, poor little sister! In the evening, and also at night when we are not asleep, we can see these ladies and gentlemen promenading about on the partitions between the cells."

Since she speaks of lying awake in a cell, and also, later, of empty cells, this letter evidently dates from a time when there had been some improvements made in the house. But it will serve our purpose here. She goes on:

"Imagine, dear mother, that a whole family of them decided to take up its residence in an empty cell where we had put the extra blankets. Papa rat made a hole in one of the quilts, and there, in a nice warm little nest, he settled down with his spouse and all his little heirs: but all this was not exactly convenient, as far as we were concerned. One day I am sweeping, and I go to fix the blankets a little, and what do I see? A large rat, scared by my audacity, goes galloping off at top speed. I decide to go into matters a little more deeply, and lift up a few of the blankets. *Quel désastre!* They had eaten through two, three, four blankets, and there, in the quilt at the bottom, *voilà!* two pretty little rats, peacefully asleep!

"Poor little rats! I did not want to disturb their sleep, but the noise woke them up. Not seeing their parents anywhere about, and frightened at being all alone, they huddled up one against the other. They were still unable to walk, and so it was impossible for them to run away.

"I did not quite know what to do with the poor little things. I went to find Rev. Mother and she said flatly: 'They must be killed.' I didn't have the heart: they were crying too piteously! I felt rather like going and getting some milk to console them. How did the gory drama end? I don't know. I did not have the courage to stay to the end, still less to find out what became of the little creatures."

The poverty at Our Lady of the Angels also appealed to her sense of humor, and instead of being one of the heavy crosses of the new foundation, served to make the others somewhat lighter by raising her spirits.

As vestiarian, one of her first duties after arriving was to provide towels for the mandatum on Holy Thursday. Unfortunately she did not realize the lack of them until Holy Thursday morning.

She writes: "I went to acquaint Rev. Mother with my difficulty and she, after having vainly sought for a few somewhat decent rags, ended up by giving me three flour sacks, to cut up according to my needs. At half past five we went to the work room for the washing of the feet"—another defect, apparently, of the low roofed chapter room was that there was no room for the mandatum—"and everything was ready. Some gasoline cans, with the tops cut off, served as foot-baths."

The mandatum was very gay. Mother Berchmans, as might be expected, forgot St. Benedict's warning: "*Risum excussum non amare*," and laughed joyfully several times during the ceremony.

The eucharistic Jesus shared their poverty and, no doubt, Mother Berchmans' joy. The altar of repose was suitably decorated with flowers and greenery; but the vases were not only not elegant, they were not even vases. In the same letter she says, referring to Dom Eugene, Abbot of Port-du-Salut, who had been instrumental in sending the two nuns from Laval to Japan:

"How pleased our good Reverend Father, being such a friend of holy poverty, would have been with the altar of repose. Everything reminded us of the Child Jesus in the manger. All the pots and pans from our kitchen went on exhibition: water jugs, milk pails, the coffee pot, everything was transformed into a flower-vase."

We must not think that the nuns were without the skill, that all nuns seem to have, of disguising all this so as to make it look as if the flowers were placed in receptacles of fine porcelain or ancient jade. But Mother Berchmans admits that the disguise had to be good, for several missionaries visited their chapel that day, and, as she says: "our dear missionaries do not keep their eyes in their pockets, and nobody is quite so frank as a missionary!"

Outwardly, it would have appeared to her sisters that Mother Berchmans bore all her trials with equal good humor. She always had a cheerful face and was always ready with a smile for her sisters, even though they could see that she was tired and preoccupied. If she was inwardly tempted, as we shall see, to movements of rebellion and impatience, even anger and revolt, and if, in her own estimation, she became an intolerable cross to her sisters by her evil disposition, all this was not observed or even dreamed of by any except those who knew the deepest recesses of her conscience. Of course, it is undeniable that they could sometimes see that something was wrong, that poor Mother Berchmans was suffering, that she was feeling the hardships of her position. But the truth is that the physical and outward trials and difficulties of the life at the new foundation were little or nothing to her, except in so far as they contributed to the anguish and darkness and bitterness that seemed to saturate her whole soul within her.

These things did not appear to the casual observer, even to the nuns who were with her day after day, working and praying and suffering with her in the narrow confines of the transformed orphanage. One would have thought that she suffered far less than anyone else, and yet it was she who had the bitterest and most appalling chalice of them all: more bitter and terrible by the very fact of her far greater gifts of nature and of grace, which now made her more acutely sensitive than any of the others to the total lack of all natural and supernatural consolation in this new situation. Jesus seemed to remove, with one sweep of His divine hand, every veil or curtain of sensible joy that concealed from her the thousand imperfections still stubbornly rooted in her soul.

From all eternity and from the creation of the world, her Lord and merciful Creator had formed, in His mighty love, a natural instrument to try and purify her soul. It was almost as if He had planned the whole continent of Asia and the huge Pacific and placed them where they were, and Japan where it was, that their mighty weight might bear down upon this nun and overwhelm and oppress her soul even unto death, that she might know that He alone was God and that she was nothingness. But it was not for her alone, this tremendous, inexorable, and yet gentle scourge, but for the trial of a whole race.

From the south Pacific and the tropics there flows northward a mighty ocean current, called the *Kuro-Sirvo*. Another current sweeps down from the north, from the lonely islands of the Arctic, and these waters bring with them icebergs; they are so cold. These two great currents meet in the straits of Tsaugaru, off Hakodate, and from their meeting and mingling in the silent depths of the sea, there rises into the air a vapor heavy with certain salts in solution. The wind takes these warm, malignant airs and carries them across the land, where they saturate the atmosphere, the clothing, and even, it would seem, the bodies of men: with some, the hot, damp wind seems to burn its way right into their minds. This quiet relentless scourge is called the *Yamasse*. Two or three days before the Yamasse, or east wind, begins to blow, people feel it coming in their flesh and in their bones. And then, woe to those who have weak nerves, or are tired or exhausted, underfed or overworked.

Père Robert, speaking from his experience as a confessor and guide of souls, both European and native, admits that the depressing effect of this wind upon the systems even of those hardened to it gave a special opportunity to the devil to exercise all his evil power to lead souls into sin.

As for Mère Berchmans, who had entered Laval in such weak health that she felt she would be quite satisfied if she could bear the life long enough to receive the habit before collapsing, and who was now under the great emotional and physical stress of the sacrifice she had been called upon to make, it is clear that she was fitted to be a perfect victim of this scourge of God. She had been exquisitely prepared for all the intense and subtle suffering that the Yamasse could draw from the nervous system of a human being. It was as if a perfect violin had been taken and attuned with the most consummate skill, only to be placed in the hands of some lunatic musician drunk with hatred of life, that he might exercise his perverted talents in producing all the discords that could offend the ear and mind of men.

And so she writes, in a letter to Laval:

"Sometimes we are visited by an evil wind called the Yamasse, that is, the wind from the mountain. You can feel it coming three or four days ahead of time, and it exercises a great effect upon various temperaments. Nervous people feel it the most. It is like a cloak of molten lead draped over your shoulders. And on those days, everything is black. To tell the truth, I think it is the devil making his rounds. It is hard work to overcome oneself, with the weariness you feel. Another way to gain souls for the good God! May He be blessed for giving us a chance to suffer a little more for His glory."

And she adds:

"If the Yamasse only affected the body it would not be so bad. What do I care for a little fatigue, more or less! The trouble is that the brunt of the burden is in the mind and will. Character is so closely tied up with the nervous system! And here a person can become very mean-tempered."

Let the reader here be warned not to take too literally what she says about the effects of the climate on her own conduct. Père Robert admits that she exaggerates a great deal. "It may be true," he writes, "that she was tempted to impatience a little more often than she had been in France, and that she even had a few minor outbursts which were very quickly overcome and made good, but that is all that we can reproach her for." So much for her external acts. Nevertheless, we can tell how she *felt* from her own testimony. Father Robert himself adds that the Yamasse alone is enough to drive some people to a nervous breakdown.

To return to Mother Berchmans' letter, then, with all these qualifications in mind:

"A person can become very mean-tempered. Does that come from the devil or from the climate? I don't know. But what I do know is that since I came here I have turned into a little porcupine. To console me, they tell me that I have seen nothing yet. This year is going to be much worse than the one that has just passed. *Ce doit être l'année terrible.* It is going to be the 'terrible year,' that makes you or breaks you. The year in which you really feel the difficulties of getting used to the climate worse than any other time."

For Mother Berchmans, it seems, there was to be not one "crucial" year, but three or four. And, physically speaking, the Yamasse never spared her as long as she lived.

The crux of the psychological suffering caused by the Yamasse was her feeling that she had become a trial and a burden to others. It was almost unbearable to her to think, as the devil and the Yamasse made her think, that everyone was suffering on account of what she supposed was her bad temper and mean disposition. "Considering her habitual considerateness, and kindness, and charity," writes Father Robert, "these few extremely trivial faults appeared to her to be very regrettable and grave. But it is very doubtful whether they were voluntary." However, Mother Berchmans herself tells us sorrowfully:

"I wish I could learn to suffer all things without causing suffering to anyone else. What pains me most is the thought that I myself am a source of suffering to others.... Added to the little difficulties I have with my own character, there is this physical exhaustion which makes everything look blacker than it really is. I really love this bodily suffering, in itself. It is always welcome! It comes from God, and I am happy to see this body of sin taking punishment."

Here, however, we come to one of the major sacrifices demanded of her by the climate. So powerful an effect did the Yamasse have on her nervous system that she could not swallow the Host, and consequently was often deprived of Holy Communion, which was the chief joy and consolation of her life. Indeed, Jesus in the Blessed Sacrament *was* her life. Or so He had been at least at Laval. Even on the boat coming from France, there had been daily Communion except for the few days of storms in the China Sea. But now....

"I am deprived sometimes," she writes, "of Holy Communion. Whether it is because my mouth is too dry, or because of my nerves, I hardly know, but I cannot swallow the Host. As a precaution I have to carry a little bottle of etherized water in my pocket, and that costs me enormously. Lately our good Father has been giving me a half a Host, and Jesus, hiding in this little fragment, still refused Himself to me."

It was not merely a question of her own physical condition, however. Certain reasons, which Father Robert calls "valid" but does not explain, had caused the higher superiors of the order to approve the denial of daily Communion to the nuns of Our Lady of the Angels. They went five times a week, and six if there was a feast. This nearly broke Mother Berchmans' heart as soon as she arrived there. One of her first letters to Laval complained: "There are great sacrifices here.... Even Jesus has cut down the number of His visits. He does not want to be with His little spouse so often, any more, and I am very much afraid that one day He may make me take St. Teresa's fast." (St. Teresa of Avila had to go for long periods without Communion, at a certain time in her life, because for many years she was regularly afflicted with attacks of vomiting every morning.) "However," she continues, with resignation, "if that is His will, I want it too, for only by this union of will and judgment with Him will I be able to give Him glory, and save souls."

The nuns used to arrange it so that one of them would communicate alone on the days when the others did not receive, and Mother Berchmans writes: "How cold is the feeling within me when I see one nun, all alone, approaching the table of the heavenly banquet! And there are even some days when Jesus does not visit a single one of His spouses."

Another trial for the purification of her soul was her difficulty in getting used to her new spiritual director, Father Robert Lepasquier. We must not exaggerate the difficulty, but it was nonetheless real, and caused her pain. Nor was the good Father unaware of this fact—there is a slight trace of sensitiveness left in his own brief account of those first days of their acquaintance. He recalls, somewhat ruefully, the "famous prophecy" of Father Polycarpe—the one where he told her that she would be left in desolation, abandoned and misunderstood by all, even her *confessor*. Father Robert's comment on this is that Père Polycarpe was a holy old man, but he did not have the gift of prophecy. Yet one cannot help feeling that perhaps Mother Berchmans was truly tempted, in the early days at Our Lady of the Angels, to think that the prophecy was being fulfilled.

There was a contrast between the two priests, but, above all, there was a great difference in the circumstances in which they found themselves. Father Polycarpe was an old man, directing the nuns of a big, well-established convent in France. He had known Mother Berchmans from the very beginning of her vocation, and had given her the most careful and gentle formation, evidently considering her to be a chosen soul. He did not conceal from her the fact that he thought she was destined to become a second Margaret Mary—and no matter how much he humiliated her, or how much she suffered from other causes, she always left the confessional with some sense of the magnitude of her special vocation to console the Sacred Heart, by love and sacrifice, for the ingratitude of men.

It would undoubtedly have made the trials of the first years in Japan much easier if she had been able to console herself with the confident certitude that this was indeed her vocation.

But Father Robert Lepasquier was different. He was a young priest. He was energetic, vigorous, zealous, busy with the direction of three convents in a missionary land. He did not have too much time to spare for his penitents, and felt that he could not allow them many "confessions of devotion." One feels that while he was still new to his task, he was being very careful to protect himself against encroachments—he was perhaps a little suspicious of these nuns: if he indulged their fancies, he might find them taking advantage of him, and using the confessional as a resort for gossip.

When Mother Berchmans went to him to confession, he left her with no sense that she had a special vocation. He did not see anything in her difficulties except her own self-love. He told her she lacked generosity, and that her problems would be settled by "one good *fiat*."

That did not mean that he was impatient with her, or that he neglected her needs. Father Robert left behind him, in Japan, at his death, a reputation for the most extraordinary and unselfish devotion to the community of nuns whose director he was. On the testimony of a neighboring Trappist abbot, Dom Benoit, of Our Lady of the Lighthouse, it was largely due to the devoted cooperation between Father Robert and Reverend Mother Scholastica that the little convent was able to survive and eventually came to flourish as it now does.

Indeed, there is not a missionary in that territory, who served in Father Robert's time, who will not testify that he was a model priest and a perfect Cistercian monk. Besides, he had been appointed by Dom Vital Lehodey, who knew how to choose his men.

But not everything went smoothly for Mother Berchmans. She often came from the confessional with hurt feelings. The situation cost her a struggle, but, after all, she realized well enough how God was working, and what he wanted of her. In the last analysis, her summary of the situation was this:

"I have the greatest esteem for Father Robert. In spite of his firmness, or rather because of his firmness, I feel just as free with him as I did with Father Polycarpe. He tells me that if there were not a grate between us, he would have given me the discipline many a time. And yet he can be very good to us, especially he knows that we are having a hard time of it. I am perfectly satisfied with his direction: I could not desire anything better."

As time went on, and Father Robert got to know this little Sister better, he evidently moderated his irony and scolded her a little less sharply: as the years passed, and she began to weather her trials more steadily and to abandon that last, half-deliberate velleity to return "home" to Laval, he too became aware of her unusually fine and ardent soul. Before he was done, he had gone far beyond Father Polycarpe in praising her virtues. In the years after her death, he devoted himself to the long, patient, and painstaking labor of collecting all the material for a biography of his little penitent—a biography which extends to some eight hundred manuscript pages.

All this material is ordered in a way that reflects the temperament of the good priest. It is so orderly, so systematic, as to be almost entirely unappealing to the ordinary reader. He has set forth all Mother Berchmans' virtues, one by one, in their genera and species, divisions, and subdivisions. There is no questioning the fact that he was a painstaking theologian. Perhaps he had in mind some future process of canonization. But he would have been very much surprised if anyone had suggested such a thing to him in 1902.

CHAPTER VIII

AT WORK IN THE HOUSE OF GOD

The physical hardships of the new foundation did not try Mother Berchmans' patience. On the contrary, one of the things that annoyed her was that she was not allowed to fast as much as she had at Laval; for here, owing to the extra work, there was also extra nourishment, and she had to take the "indulgences" offered in the refectory, much against her desire. She might have preferred the very earliest days of the foundation when the Sisters had all nearly died of undernourishment. But another trial was to impose a great and increasing burden upon her in the first few years in Japan; it was the fact that she often had to sacrifice so much of her time of prayer, because of the work demanded by her various employments.

St. Gregory the Great has pointed out in the *Moralia*, that most souls called to a high degree of contemplative life are sooner or later subjected to this trial. God allows them to experience the sweetness of intimacy with Him in prayer and leads them to expect a much closer and more perfect union with Him, a deeper and more excellent peace; then, suddenly, these souls find themselves involved in works of active charity which make the repose of prayer and the sweetness of contemplation almost impossible. Not only is their time for prayer drastically reduced, but when they actually can get a few minutes to fall on their knees before the tabernacle, their minds are as crowded and noisy as a railway station in a big city, and they seem to be completely helpless, overwhelmed by distractions arising from their work, utterly unable to pray.

The anguish this can cause in a soul truly called to a life of union with God is one of the greatest sufferings of the contemplative life. It is a purification that is hard to bear because it is so hard to understand. The soul realizes, or begins to realize in a dim way, that this is necessary for union with a God who unites us to Himself in order that He may work, through us, for the salvation and sanctification of our neighbor; but it can never get rid of the fear and anxiety that arise from the obvious fact that we are distracted because our natures cannot help getting caught in these active occupations in some way or another, in spite of ourselves. It is only after long years that a soul can become so detached as to work for God alone, without danger of becoming too implicated in the work done; and some souls never arrive at this detachment. On the contrary, there is always the chance that we will let our natures run away with us, and come to put our own wills more and more into these activities until they actually do gain the ascendancy and drive out the spirit of prayer.

As vestiarian, Mother Berchmans had been given charge of all the clothing, linens, and bedding of the little convent. It was her duty to make the clothing, mend it, and see that it was washed. She had to supervise the work of one or two other nuns, or lay sisters, who helped her with the sewing. She needed much tact and charity in a position that brought her in intimate contact with such a fundamental need of everyone in the community. If a robe or cowl had been worn thin by age, she had to face the dilemma whether to take a chance on giving it out for another winter, and seeing if the poor nun who wore it would be able to bear the cold, or to try and replace it; but then, with what? and how?

As everyone expected, Mother Berchmans was an excellent choice for this employment, both materially and spiritually. First of all, she was very skillful with a needle and thread; she knew how to make clothes and take care of them. She was exceptionally neat and orderly, and loved cleanliness almost to a fault. Although, interiorly, it cost her considerable sacrifice at first to lose part of her precious "intervals" (time for prayer and spiritual reading) to make up absolutely necessary work, she nevertheless not only never refused such sacrifice, but also never tried to compromise by finishing in a rush, leaving everything badly done or imperfect.

Especially during this first year or so, her repugnance was so great that its effects were much more lasting, and the resulting distractions much worse than when she became able to accept these demands more peacefully. Then, too, each Saturday afternoon, after the distribution of the clean clothing for the coming week, there was likely to be some complaint. These she always received with love and gentleness and a desire to set everything right as quickly as she possibly could; if something had been forgotten she did not delay in making up for the oversight, but went and got what was needed and took it to the Sister's cell before compline. She did not waste her time arguing within herself, that it was somebody else's fault, or that the Sister could very well wait. She did not think her private devotions more important than this small sacrifice for the sake of fraternal charity. And so she proved how truly she loved the Lord, who left us an example by washing the feet of His disciples, and who lived among us on earth as "one who serves."

"It was always a pleasure to ask her for anything," Father Robert says of her, speaking on behalf of the nuns, since he probably had nothing to do with the wardrobe of the convent. And when she had to make some correction of work poorly done, it was always with the greatest simplicity and good humor. She had the gift of telling people they were wrong and showing them what was right without either humiliating them by a kind of breezy superiority, or hurting them by too much criticism.

When the feast of the Purification came, in 1904, bringing with it the annual redistribution of employments our Lord chose to console His little nun with a charge that was by no means a sacrifice. She passed from the vestiary to an employment which was always to remain her favorite. She called the sacristy the "antechamber of heaven," and when she was appointed sacristan her heart was flooded with a joy and gratitude that she could scarcely express.

If, before, her extra work had been a burden to her because it deprived her of the presence of her beloved Lord in the Sacrament of His Love, now all her work-time was an adoration of the Blessed Eucharist, and it was not a sacrifice for her to go to work, but to stop work at the ringing of the bell.

All the nuns lived separated from the sanctuary and altar by the heavy iron grille. She alone had the key. When their Beloved chose to show Himself to them, at Benediction, or during Expositions, it was she who opened the dark curtains. At the *Asperges* on Sunday mornings, and at the processions on feasts like the Purification and Palm Sunday, it was she who unlocked the grille. Best of all, when the Sisters went to Communion, it was she who opened the way for them to go, like wise and peaceful virgins, to meet the Bridegroom in silence and joy, with their souls trimmed like lamps and shining with the pure and steady flame of faith, and fed with the oil of charity, the unction of the Holy Spirit.

Her greatest privilege and responsibility was the key to the tabernacle itself. Christ was her prisoner, or rather, she was His chosen messenger. Almost as much as the priest, she gave Him to souls. Any secular, any visitor, any poor Japanese Christian, whether a neighbor or from more distant settlements, who came asking for Christ from the priest, depended on her. In fact, the priest could not even say Mass without her. The Sacrifice in which the salvation of the world was renewed each day upon this remote and pagan mountain, depended on her. She guarded the chalices and patens, corporals, and purificators; she not only kept the fresh hosts, but also baked and trimmed them and made them ready for the Mass. And she was privileged to handle all the consecrated objects.

It is not hard to realize with what a spirit of faith and reverent love she took care of the vestments and altar linens, the monstrance, the holy oils, the censers, and all the vessels of the sanctuary; with what tender devotion she would prepare a tabernacle lined with silk for the altar of repose in Holy Week. The sacristy was dry and clean and wholesome, heated in winter to keep the damp out of the sacred linens, and fragrant with clean herbs to keep the moths from the vestments. The sanctuary and the altar were always spotless. This house of God, under her care, with all its Cistercian poverty, had also true Cistercian simplicity and dignity and cleanliness. It reflected the purity of that house of God which was the soul of this unstained bride of Christ. And because her soul was a house of prayer (even though to her it sometimes rather seemed a den of thieves), so this house of God built by hand out of boards and beams was also a clean and quiet house of prayer, whose very walls and floor and benches breathed devotion because of the spirit of devotion and love with which Mother Berchmans kept all things in order there.

In her first period of service in the sacristy (she was to return again to her immense joy, several years later) Mother Berchmans found much more work to do than is ordinarily asked of a sacristan. Besides the usual duties we have mentioned, and the baking of altar breads, she was also called upon to do all the cleaning and repairing of the poor vestments and to prepare new corporals and purificators: extremely close and painstaking work, slow work, hard on the eyes, and for which there was all too little time. For it must not be imagined that she had nothing to do except attend to her duties in the church. Not only did she have to perform most of these unaided, but her help was often necessary at the common work in other parts of the convent, especially in the laundry on washdays; and then, if she could, she would hasten to the sacristy when the greater part of the work was done and try to catch up with her duties, or her needlework, or perhaps the decoration of the altar for a feast.

Here it was that the greatest sacrifices were imposed upon her, when the bell for the end of work made it impossible for her to go on and make the decoration as complete and handsome as her devotion and affection would have liked. Perhaps a big feast was coming, and getting rapidly closer and closer; she would find a few minutes to sit down and take her needle and colored silks and work at some badly needed repairs on a chasuble or maniple or chalice veil, for the greater honor and glory of Christ in the Eucharist. And before she had had a chance to accomplish anything at all, the bell ringer would be heard, entering the chapel and pausing to kneel in the middle of the choir before going to the bells. It was the end of work. God, in His signified will, demanded the homage of her own heart and will as something far more pleasing than the homage of needle and thread. And so she would fold her things and put away her sewing in an act of sacrifice so small and insignificant in human terms that to those who do not understand God's ways with souls it would seem ludicrous.

With unconcealed joy she announced the good news of this consoling appointment to those at Laval.

"Oh! What a fine position!" she writes, "How happy I am to get it! To be in constant contact with my Beloved! I think one would have to be as wicked and as hardened as I am, not to become a saint very soon, in this employment. Has not Jesus put me in the very heart of His Mystical Body?[1] And I not only take care of the choir of the nuns, but also of the sanctuary. Every Saturday and on the vigils of the big feasts I go with one of the young Sisters to do the cleaning in the sanctuary and decorate the high altar."

In another letter (dating, it is true, from her second time in this position) she writes: "I am sacristan again. I am always close to the great fire of Love: is it possible that I can go for long without being consumed?" In another letter to a religious (perhaps a Trappist at Bricquebec) we read: "I have become the happy little servant of Jesus in the Blessed Sacrament, and I spend a good part of my time close to that great fire of Love. And so it is my hope that one day a few sparks will fly out into my poor heart."

Perhaps her greatest joy as sacristan was to bake the altar breads and fill the ciborium with hosts for the Communions of the Sisters, and this favor came to her from the hands of the young Jesuit saint who was her patron. She wrote to Reverend Mother Lutgarde, at Laval:

"You will never guess how I spent the morning, yesterday, the feast of my little St. John Berchmans. I must tell you, and spare you a long inquiry: you will envy my happiness. Well, here it is: I made hosts. Now you can understand my joy. But please ask the good God not to take this favor away from me! I am not without fear, in this matter, as it is a bit tiring. But what difference does a little fatigue make? I am glad to sacrifice myself to pay for so great an honor."

We see by this that it was not merely a question of nervousness and strain or the malignant climate; her health was already giving serious concern to her superiors, and she was being carefully watched already in 1903. Another Sister offered to take over the work of baking the hosts, but Mother Berchmans would not hear of it. She jealously guarded her great privilege, and continued her work with all her devotion and zeal. So absorbed was she in this work of love, that merely to see the tender reverence with which she disposed the unconsecrated hosts in the ciborium was as good as many sermons on the Blessed Sacrament.

And then one day she was found lying unconscious on the floor in front of the little oven.

From that time on, she was deprived of the consolation of baking the hosts, and the duty was confided to someone else. But she had already fainted many times and would do so again, before there was any real appearance of danger. Nevertheless, the shadow of death had already made more than one threatening, though brief and transitory, appearance in the neighborhood of the little convent.

In her very first year there, the bell had rung at the convent gate and mother prioress had been called to the parlor where she received official notice of something that she had probably already known for some days. There was a fairly serious epidemic of cholera in the province and many cases had been reported in the immediate neighborhood. The Sisters should take every precaution.

The announcement was duly made in chapter, and counsel given. But Mother Berchmans only smiled. She did not see the shadow of the eerie visitor who lurked below the convent in the mists of the valley. All she knew was that she had seemed to catch a glimpse of the gates of heaven, standing momentarily ajar.

"Cholera," she said afterward, "that is one of those sicknesses that strikes you down without warning. So much the better. We'll be in heaven all the sooner."

The shadow passed. The gate fell shut. Two years later—another glimpse. One of those wild and frightful hurricanes swept in from the strait and lashed the mountain with wind and rain, bombarding the woods and fields around the little convent with almost continual thunderbolts while the whole sky cracked and roared, tumbling and rolling down the weak wooden roof of the convent as if to shake it to pieces and grind them all to powder. But the lightning spared them, and, when the skies were again clear, perhaps one of the nuns, at least, was a little disappointed. Mother Berchmans had been not only calm but full of great joy and peace all through the storm. God did not mean to take her with so much noise and confusion. She was not to die like a heroine in an opera.

And yet her continual fatigue, her headaches, her weakness, her sleeplessness, her occasional fits of feverishness were worrying mother prioress, and letters had been exchanged with Laval, on the subject. Then one day Mother Berchmans was called to mother prioress' room.

"Here is some medicine," said the superioress. "Reverend Mother Lutgarde has sent it for you. You are to take it; it is for anemia."

What was in that bottle that had come all the way from France? We can guess that it was one of those bottles of pink medicine that never does anybody any good. Anyway, it was extremely sweet.

"My Reverend Mother," she wrote in acknowledgment, "I have taken your anemia medicine. I am indeed very grateful for it. At one point I thought I was going to turn into a second Moses, for sweetness,[2] after having had to swallow so much sugar. But I do not think the good God is going to allow it to work, in my case. His divine will is that I continue to suffer: that is the better part."

However, about that time too it was decided to have her examined by a doctor, which was after all a much more sensible move than to give her some medicine sent half around the world on a guess as to what *might* be wrong with her. What preoccupied the doctor most was her lungs. However, when he folded his stethoscope and put it back in his satchel he announced that she was not consumptive, but he added a most significant little word—*yet*.

"The doctor says," writes Mère Berchmans, "that I am not yet consumptive, but that I am just the type to develop consumption. And so,"—she adds, with the intense certitude of one who seems to know by what road she is to leave her land of exile, and is determined to go by that road, too—"And so it cannot be avoided. It is in my constitution. That is the way I am built. That is the mould in which God shaped my being. This is good news I am writing to you, my Reverend Mother: a little fore-taste of home, of heaven. Oh! When will I be able to write you that the first breach has been made in the wall? Whenever Jesus wills: that is the answer...."

And so she went on, with her continual head colds and headaches, and with the pains in her chest and back which, for the time being, were called rheumatism and left at that. Reverend mother prioress tried to make her stay in bed and take a little extra rest, getting up at three o'clock in the morning instead of at two like the others; but Mother Berchmans was inclined to resist this dispensation in her favor, and to do everything she could to have it revoked. Later on she succeeded, even though by that time she was almost bent double with pains and stiffness in the night hours and found it absolutely impossible to give any voice in choir, simply because she had no voice to give. But that was later.

Meanwhile, she was taking the extra hour of sleep (although sleep was probably a euphemism, in her case) and receiving an extra indulgence in the refectory.

Mother Lutgarde was able to do much more for the natural well-being of the poor little exile than could be done by any sweet-tasting medicine. And there was one dispensation which Berchmans did not try to avoid. Mother prioress was allowing her, in view of her intense homesickness to write many more letters to her superioress and sisters at Laval than Cistercian customs would ordinarily countenance. And her dear sisters there were quick to reply, with all their tender affection, to her somewhat plaintive letters. Poor Mother Berchmans! If she wanted sacrifice, it was here that she could offer it to God, and not in being so particular about getting up for the beginning of the night office. But it was to take time, and even a certain amount of coaxing, before she could bring herself to give up these long and frequent letters to the convent at Laval.

From the very beginning, however, mother prioress had been very tolerant. It was during the Lent of 1902, in her first few weeks in Japan, that a handful of letters arrived at the little convent addressed to Mère Berchmans. Since mother prioress could see that the Sister was inclined to be a little dejected by her exile, she permitted her to open them all and read them—even, it seems, to answer them, although the custom of many houses forbids all letter writing in Lent and Advent.

"It was my desire not to read these letters until after Easter," she wrote, in replying to Mother Lutgarde and thanking her for them all, "but I admit, my Reverend Mother, that this was a sacrifice which was, I think, beyond my strength. And the good God, out of pity for my weakness, did not ask me to go through with it. Reverend Mother (prioress) said to me: 'No, read them right away, so that you will be able to answer them as soon as possible.' Before settling down to read them I said a little prayer to Our Blessed Mother, asking for strength to get through with them: I was so full of emotion! I was about half way through reading them when I heard the bell for meditation. Of course I dropped everything at once, but Reverend Mother, you can imagine what kind of a meditation I made! My heart kept repeating: Dear God, thank You: but this is too much happiness all at once! What will it be in heaven, when, there with Jesus, I shall find my religious family, and mother and my little sister and all those whom I love, when now the mere memory of them fills me with such joy?"

What deep and tenacious roots this natural affection for her old convent had in her heart can be read in every line of her many letters to the Sisters there.

"Oh! Laval!" she writes, "how many times in the day I pronounce that name. For me, it has become a kind of ejaculatory prayer: for it is to God that I address it. And He alone knows all that it contains, in my heart, of love, prayers, and petitions. And if, as you tell me, Reverend Mother, my religious family retains an affectionate remembrance of me, I assure you it is mutual; I keep a list of all the names in our breviary, and, even more, in my heart."

We see her, in the summertime, picking a few flowers in the convent garden, drying them, and pressing them carefully between the pages of a book in order to send them to the Sisters in France, accompanied by a letter filled with the sentimental overtones of a nineteenth-century novel:

"Verdure and flowers on every side!" she exclaims. "Here I have plucked a few, and send them to you. Indeed, it pained me just a little to press them in a book, their life is already so short. True, though, far from cutting short that life, I have made it longer, and I have given them a noble end, since they are about to cross the seas to tell you of our gratitude."

The strength of her affection! And the stubbornness with which her heart clung to these memories! Father Robert may well have had his doubts as to the efficacy of "Oh Laval!" as an ejaculatory prayer, for though it may have expressed deep and sincere desires for the welfare of all her sisters, it was true that this affection still had so much of nature in it that it was eating her heart away, instead of feeding and strengthening it as true charity would. He could see this, and it was this, no doubt, that made him most of all impatient with her.

It may have been true that these letters cheered her up, and seemed to give her back some of her spirit and energy. Yet that was, at best, only temporary. She herself realized that, ultimately, it was all a sterile and useless expense of natural emotions that devoured her spiritual energies, and gave her no real strength. But several years were to go by before she would resolutely face that fact, and give up her writing to the Sisters at home.

Meanwhile, however, she wrote:

"To compensate for our many sacrifices, the good God gives us, from time to time, some very sweet consolation: I mean your letters, Reverend Mother, and all the others that come from our poor France. They are like warm rays of sunlight which penetrate the very depths of our hearts. Reverend Mother, I have not the courage to end this letter. If you only knew what joy I feel in being with you and with my dear family!" And then, this sudden cry of conscience: "Oh, why is it that I do not love the good God more? I feel, within myself, such a strong power to love, and yet Jesus allows me to exhaust myself upon creatures, when I so much desire to attach myself to Him alone."

Here we can see clearly enough what was the big cross of these early years; not the climate, not the difficulties of the new foundation, not her health, not even the fact of her exile as such: no, what was tearing her soul apart was this internal contradiction which God would never allow her to forget. She knew, in the depths of her soul, that He wanted everything, every last shred of her heart, every last breath of her love.

Oh, there is no question of sin, hardly of imperfection. In itself, this was a praiseworthy natural affection; Father Robert includes even her devotion to her community at Laval, later on, in his catalogue of virtues, and of course all the letters were written with the blessing of obedience. Besides, she soon enough renounced all fully deliberate thoughts of returning to France, for that was clearly out of the question, and all too evidently against the will of God. No matter how her feelings might rebel, there was never any hesitation in her mind about accepting the signified will of God.

"Yes," she writes, "it is for Jesus that I am here and I do not want to look back. It is necessary for me to suffer in order to be able to tell Jesus that I love Him. For what sort of a love is that which has nothing to suffer? As far as my return to my dear family (at Laval) is concerned, I have no hope that this joy will be granted me. I do not believe that it is the will of God—and as for going to France against that divine will—*never!*"

If we were to judge this situation solely by the standards of moral theology one might ask why there was so much trouble and concern about something so obviously right and proper. What fault could be found with her obedience, here?

Even where her letters were concerned, and her natural affections, once they were approved by her superiors, what more was there to be said about the affair? Why should she be so troubled?

But she knew, and Father Robert knew, and so did mother prioress, that God wanted much more of her. He wanted a total and wholehearted and joyful sacrifice, and that sacrifice was not possible as long as her mind, at every moment of the day or night, was apt to be wandering back across the sea, or calculating the date of the arrival of the next letter from France.

On the fifth of July, 1903, the feast of the Precious Blood, she wrote in her notebook:

"It seemed to me this morning that Jesus was pointing out to me the road I am to follow, after Him. Ah! I too easily forget that all Christian life, and, above all, all religious life is nothing but the way of the Cross. When I entered into life, I made a pact with death, and from that moment, death had looked upon me as his future prey. My first step was to go and sign my death warrant, and the little room where I was born, was my pretorium. But before I reach my Calvary, the room in which I shall die, the road I am to travel is stained with blood!..."

And so she goes on, in her meditation of the feast. Beautiful indeed; but the pith of the whole thing, for her (as for us all), is in that sentence: "I too easily forget...."

Mother Berchmans had to cry out, like St. Paul, to be delivered from the body of this death, even though her pure soul would have found it difficult even to imagine what it was to commit a mortal sin.

"I can no longer recognize myself," she writes: "both physically and morally I am a mass of sufferings. Oh! How hard it is for me to get along without the love of creatures! I am still too natural, too much of this earth. Creatures are necessary to me, to lift me up to God."

After this misapplication of a principle belonging properly to the order of cognition and understanding, Father Robert, in his manuscript, characteristically writes three big question marks. But Mother Berchmans goes on to tell us, in one sentence, the whole truth and *raison d'être* of her suffering of these early years in Japan:

"How much I suffer, *to feel myself continually in opposition with His Divine Will, without feeling that I have any courage to carry it out.*" (She means, of course, in this final and total sacrifice of her legitimate affections.)

The one thing that remained for her to discover was that God wanted her precisely to accept this weakness and incapacity for the final act of heroism, and go on trusting blindly in Him alone. Father Robert had not the words to convince her of this secret. He did not possess the key to let her out of the prison in which she languished, and no one else seemed able to help her. But God, in His own good time, was preparing to send someone to her rescue. It was perhaps well that her confessor and her superiors were not able to give her this help, for in the intensity of her joyful gratitude she would probably have become attached to them; and we shall see with what affection she rewarded the one who finally extricated her from her chains.

Later on, looking back without too much regret, upon these years she was able to write with complete understanding of all that had once so perplexed her:

"At the very first, we do not realize that *just by coming here to Japan we have given our Beloved the greatest proof of our poor, feeble love.* All we look at is the sacrifice; we do not turn our eyes to Jesus. The cross seems so heavy. Poor nature suffers: but it is entirely our own fault."

NOTES

1. Literally: Has not Jesus given me the role of the heart (to play). *N'est-ce pas la part du coeur que Jesus m'a donnée?*

2. I.e., *douceur* which means both mildness and sweetness in French.

CHAPTER IX

THE CHICKEN COOP

In one of her letters Mother Berchmans had sent the nuns at Laval a photograph of the little wooden convent of Our Lady of the Angels, and received, in reply, a letter in which Mère Lutgarde informed her that they were all amused at "the picture of the chicken coop."

Father Robert quotes her brave attempt at a witty defense of her new home, but her smiles are all somewhat strained. Clearly, she could not yet summon up any spontaneous natural enthusiasm. Nevertheless, from this time on, she is going to continue with greater and greater determination to try to overcome all her natural repugnances, and to force herself to break through the obstacles which her natural desires threw in her way. It is important to remember these efforts: for they lead up to the solution of her difficulties. And even though that solution is one which can best be expressed in the familiar term of "abandonment," yet that term has certain passive connotations, and because of them we must not be allowed to forget the intensely active labor of the will, and the long and bitter struggle Mother Berchmans had in order to arrive at that solution.

The secret of that childlike faith, or abandonment, to which Mother Berchmans was progressing is that it so divests us of our own wills and human desires and judgments and activities, that it allows God to act in us, in all that we do. But since He acts in our acts, it means that we are really acting too, with Him. The acts are ours, but they are sublimated by grace, so that all our acts are supernatural; even our breathing and walking, our eating and sleeping, our getting up and sitting down, and all that we do, are charged with the glory of God because they are all done for Him in the way that He wills and because He wills them, and for no other reason. But if a soul is to arrive at the point when its activity is all completely directed by the will of God, it cannot sit down and wait, idle and useless, vegetating and dull, for the Holy Spirit to swoop down upon it, and make it act in some new and extraordinary way.

Mother Berchmans was no quietist. Always, and in all things, she was filled with an earnest and most positive desire for the will of God to be done, no matter how she felt about it.

And so she writes: "I feel the weight of the Cross, and the magnitude of the sacrifice which God demands of me; but for all that, I am firmly resolved to carry out, in all things, the holy will of my Divine Master, no matter what happens." And again: "I am ready to make all the sacrifices which the Divine Master may ask of me, and I want to devote myself, as much as lies in my power, to the new religious family which the good God has given me. My own sorrows mean nothing at all, if only God's will gets done.... No matter how much I suffer, I am happy to see the divine will accomplished in me. Provided only God is glorified, what does it matter how much my nature cries out and complains?...Oh, my divine Spouse, He knows well enough that I desire no other will but His!"

Then, in another letter to Laval: "Oh, Reverend Mother! You can hardly conceive how Jesus has been at work in my soul. For some time now I seem to see Him, the divine Gardener, cutting and pruning, not merely dead branches, but branches full of life—but of a life that is, perhaps, too human. My nature feels it, but then, I am glad to suffer."

It is easy to see that on this basis, and on the basis of her obedience and mortification and self-sacrifice, as they shall be revealed to us in these pages, Mother Berchmans was not going to develop a quietistic and inert form of abandonment which gives up all struggle against faults and imperfections and sits down to enjoy a false "peace," resulting only from the renunciation of all struggle, and which our consciences, if there is any life in them at all, will never leave us to enjoy for very long. Indeed, that kind of "abandonment" would soon lead to serious sin!

The source of all her strength at this period, and indeed throughout her religious life, was her devotion to the Sacred Heart; that means devotion to Jesus in the Blessed Sacrament, for the two are inseparable. Her devotion to the Holy Eucharist, says Father Robert, was the sun that filled her life with light.

Practically the last words of Father Polycarpe to her, before she left France, were to tell her that she must become "the dove of the Tabernacle," and indeed her soul was to fly and hide itself in the wounded Heart of Christ like the dove in the cleft of the rock. White and silent and motionless in her cowl, with her big sleeves joined before her breast and her head slightly bowed, she would spend whole intervals in adoration—when they were hers to spend there. Sundays were her best days for prayer and for peaceful converse with her God, dwelling in the secrecy of the tabernacle. Apart from the time set aside for spiritual reading and that demanded by the constitutions of the nuns for a little walk in the garden to get some fresh air, she spent practically the whole of Sunday on her knees, in the silent chapel, deep in prayer. Sunday was her day of rest and that was what "rest" meant to her—resting in the sweet experience of her Beloved's presence.

In these hours of prayer and silence, rare as they may have been, she began to learn new things, imperceptibly, about Japan, and about the reason for her being there. Her Lord was teaching her, as He teaches souls that love Him, not in signs and wonders, not in astounding manifestations of His power and glory, but feeding her with a secret manna, teaching her with grace that appeared without her knowing how in the depths of her soul.

Kneeling before the tabernacle, she gradually began to realize the connection between her presence there and His presence there. Why was she here on this mountain in Japan? Because He was there. And why was He there? The answer was to be found out in the hills, in the cabins of the farmers among the terraced fields. The answer was to be found in the gongs that sounded from the darkness of the pagan temples, out under the twisted pines. The answer was in the strange, hot incense that went up to the blind, dead, wayside gods of bronze.

All around them, in this land, were souls locked and helpless in little prisons of everlasting darkness, going about their daily life with a strange futile intensity that was robbed of all real purpose because, ultimately, there was nowhere for them to go. Now they were on earth. They breathed the air from the sea, they bowed their backs in labor under the hot sun; heat and cold and hunger and thirst made them forget the helplessness of their imprisoned souls; they could not realize what it meant to be, as they were, without God's grace. Where were they going? What were their lives for? Their souls would one day leave their bodies, and then their own prisons would close upon them and they would fall like plummets into the deeps of hell.

All around them, in these gardens and fields, but above all in the city by the sea, and in all the other cities, in China and Manchukuo beyond the grey-green water, were souls crippled by appalling pagan hatreds and lusts and envies and dark superstitions and despairs from which they had no way of freeing themselves. All their movements, all their attempts, only seemed to entangle them more in the great web of sins woven by centuries of paganism and idolatry.

Yet every one of these hopeless souls was fashioned by the immense love of God to receive into its pure depths the light of His infinite goodness and joy. How were those depths to be purified of their darkness? Only by the light of grace, freely given by God. No work of theirs, no effort, no good will, no good desire, no striving was sufficient to win them this light that would give them faith, this faith that would begin to work in them, with the work of Christ's love, and purify them and set them free.

And Christ had been born on earth for each one of these souls. Souls of poor, thin, brown, bent, despairing, half-starved fishermen and rice growers whom she would never see; Christ had seen them all as He lay in the manger at Bethlehem. Christ had seen them all as He worked at the bench in Joseph's shop. He had seen them all when the disciples slept by a boulder under the clouded moon, and His blood ran down His anguished body and moistened the roots of the olive trees. Their frightened, almond eyes had looked at Him out of the chalice that His Father wanted Him to drink. And so He had died for them on the Cross. If He was here, now, in the tabernacle, it was because He had come to get them. He had bought them, now He wanted them. They were His.

In the tabernacle, hidden from the eyes of men, His mute and glorious wounds pleaded to the Father for these souls. And that was why she was here, too. Not to go out among these people and try to preach to them, or teach them her religion; no, but simply to stay here, with the hidden, glorious humanity of Christ, and share the patience, helplessness, and abjection which love constantly drove Him to assume, hiding in the thin white Host in order that men might learn from Him the meaning of prayer and love.

It was her part to kneel with Him, and share His immensely powerful silence, and lose herself in the incomprehensible strength of His secret adoration of the Father. And now she was beginning to see more and more that it was not for herself alone that she was here; not only that her soul might be filled with His mighty, purifying grace, but that her will be so filled with the power and charity of the Holy Spirit that it would overflow in a love that would pour out grace upon the whole of Japan.

She was there in order that the special souls whom Christ would choose, through her prayers, from among the scattered Christians of these northern mountains, might come and see and desire to be there also with her. She was there in order that the souls who would soon begin to feel the love of Christ and know the power of His great and gentle spirit, might know what to do in order that they also might overflow with this same charity, and fill other souls of their own race, until there were many of them, in different places, adoring God.

And then, because of this adoration, and because of God living, now, in so many hearts, hundreds of other souls would be drawn gradually from perilous darkness into safety. Because of this pure prayer in so many hearts, the spirit of God would spread like fire from the lips of the missionaries and the teaching Sisters, still so ineffective and helpless in this unreceptive land.

What did she have to do? Only suffer what she was already suffering, pray as she was praying, but, if possible, more joyfully, with more generosity, greater trust in Him, closer union with His own sufferings, and a more complete annihilation of herself to belong more and more entirely to Him.

She wrote to Father Polycarpe: "When I reflect on the great grace Jesus has deigned to grant me, choosing me in preference to so many others to come and work, through suffering and annihilation, for the salvation of these poor infidels, I begin to realize how happy I ought to be at so much kindness! Jesus has conceived designs of great mercy for my soul. He has confidence in me, and He expects a return of confidence from me, in Himself. Oh! Dear Father, beg Him not to let me deceive the expectations of His Divine Heart, but to make me win many souls for Him. That is the end for which He brought me to Our Lady of the Angels, after having broken the chains that attached me to creatures, and torn me away from the cradle of my religious life."

In another letter we read: "Oh! How beautiful is our vocation as cloistered missionaries! It is the vocation Jesus has, in the Eucharist. I hope I may never keep merely for myself alone the rays of heavenly light that are in my daily Host, but pour them out upon all the poor souls around about us, still immersed in the shadows of paganism." Again she returns to the theme that so impresses her: that her vocation is a sign of the confidence Christ has in her, an augury and a promise of the great work He can and will do, in and through her, if she will submit herself entirely to His will. "In calling me to Japan," she continues, "did not my beloved Spouse give me a sure sign of His confidence in me? Yes, Jesus is counting on me. May I never fail His Divine Heart in its expectations.... By my prayers and sacrifices I must come to the help of our poor missionaries, who have so little consolation in this country."

She adds significantly: "There is no harder mission-field in the world than Japan."

Are there still Christians in the world so ignorant of the ways of God, and of the power of prayer, that they would assume, from this statement, that what was needed in Japan was not contemplative, cloistered nuns but missionaries? If any still think so, they have not read Pius XI's constitution, *Umbratilem*, where the Holy Father wrote: "Those who devote themselves to the practice of prayer and penance exercise a more potent influence upon the life of the Church and in regard to salvation, than others who labor assiduously in the Lord's vineyard: for if the former did not call down from heaven an abundance of the celestial fertilizing waters, the latter would not gather in so large a harvest."

Yet if the essence of her vocation was prayer and reparation by sacrifice in obscurity, nevertheless she could not remain completely unaffected, in the natural order, by the fact that she had been transplanted into a totally unfamiliar culture. On the contrary, there were problems of material adaptation to her new environment that were going to provide her with matter for her most bitter sacrifices in these early years.

She was praying for conversions, for vocations to her own convent. She was praying for the grace of God to bring good Japanese Christian girls to join them and learn their life, and eventually replace them altogether. After all, this was to be a convent for Japanese Cistercians in future years. But at the moment, the only one in the whole house who could speak any Japanese was Mother Scholastica, the prioress. The older one grows, the harder it is to learn a new language. Mother Berchmans was among the youngest of the choir nuns, and also one of the most intelligent. Not that she had any aptitude for languages, especially for a language of such extraordinary difficulty as this one. But when all things were considered, the other nuns had even less aptitude than she.

A most important consideration was her holiness of life. We must not forget that this was something that had already impressed her mother prioress and all the Sisters in the little community.

A soul endowed so richly with gifts of nature and of grace, as intelligent as she was holy, as cheerful as she was prayerful, as sensible as she was recollected, free from any of the harshness or eccentricity or coldness or oddity which tend to make some fervent souls so unpleasant to other people, was evidently sent by God to fill the most important offices in the little community, in future years. She would, for example, make an excellent mistress of novices.

When it was first proposed that she take up the study of Japanese, Mother Berchmans was frightened. Who would not be? The average nun is liable to be filled with a more or less excusable panic merely at the prospect of studying Latin. But Latin at least is written in familiar letters and syllables, and in the same way as our own modern languages in the Occident. But here, before she even got to the complexities of grammar and syntax, she would have to master a whole system of terrifying hieroglyphics, and try to frame her mouth and throat to the formation of sounds utterly alien to anything her ear had ever heard before.

Then, another complication was the fact that her teacher was good Father Robert, whose caustic tongue and intolerance of her timidity only served to confuse and frighten her more, and make the difficulties seem even more impossible to overcome. There is not the slightest doubt that it was when these two met in the parlor, over their Japanese grammars, that they found the greatest difficulty in getting along together. Nowhere is Father Robert more caustic in his discussion of her imperfections than in his account of her backwardness at Japanese, and we may assume that in the classroom he was scarcely as restrained as he is on paper.

It is no wonder that, at first, Mother Berchmans failed to see any connection between this new trial and her fervent prayers for vocations. This did not fit in with her conception of her vocation as a cloistered missionary as she had envisaged it before the tabernacle: but that did not make it any the less an essential part of God's plan for her and for the convent.

The difficulties of the study oppressed her mind, distracted her at prayer. She was harassed by the sense of her inability to make progress in it, and by the pain of feeling herself a burden to her teacher. Day by day, it became more and more difficult for her to concentrate on this extremely distasteful work.

And so, day by day, confronted ever more clearly with her

weakness and incapacity, she began to make frequent representations to her teacher and mother prioress, pointing out that she was not fit for this sort of thing, she was destined for a life of obscurity, for the most menial and humble place in the monastery. She was a more or less useless thing, fit only to be left in a corner where she would not get in the way of the others. And since the fact of her helplessness was so clear to her, we need not raise any difficulties about her sincerity.

Father Robert, however, was able to see the connection between this overanxious humility and the natural desire to avoid the labor of study and the responsibilities that would obviously follow from her having learned Japanese. Of course such a desire was not at all deliberate in her; indeed, there have been scores of holy men and women in whom such a retiring disposition, in the face of material responsibilities, has been counted as virtue.

One day the bell rang at the gate and the portress looked out into the anxious face of a young Japanese girl, accompanied by someone who was evidently her mother and carrying a small bundle of belongings. The first postulant had arrived.

Mother Scholastica did not show great haste in accepting postulants. She had to be very careful. Even girls with the most thorough Christian training were still very far from having a clear idea of what it meant to be a contemplative nun. It was rare enough when one of them had any but the vaguest notions of the Christian life, and what it really involved. Yet girls began to come in, not only from the city, but even from distant settlements in the mountains or by the sea.

What were they looking for? Peace, happiness: that was certain enough. They were devoured, all of them, with a deep and burning sincerity, a real longing for something undefinable, some vague good, some happiness which they could not identify. Someone had told them that they would find it here, in the convent.

Unfortunately, the longing for some vague undefined happiness is a thing so universal that it is not even the beginning of a vocation to such a strict religious order. The postulant should have some conception of the means by which he thinks this happiness is to be attained, because, after all, *everybody* wants happiness.

In all the cases Mother Scholastica had to accept or reject, she found very little to go on except this obvious sincerity and the rudiments of faith and charity and the Christian virtues. She made her choices as best she could, and soon there were three or four little Japanese Sisters in the house, wearing the habit of oblates.

A good Swiss nun, Mother Léonie, who was struggling with Japanese like Mother Berchmans, was appointed mistress of novices to take care of these poor strangers. Mother Scholastica would not have them begin their canonical novitiate for some time. And as it was, there was all the more reason why they should remain as oblates, since the only one who could really talk to them was the first superior of the house. Mother Scholastica was constantly occupied with more important duties, and even then she had to sacrifice everything whenever some workman came to do anything that was required in the house, in order to accompany the outsiders, according to the rule. Of course, it always had to be Mother Scholastica since she alone knew Japanese.

However, there were three times in the week when the prioress turned over her room to the lay sisters, who used it for their catechism class; and consequently, on those occasions, the Japanese oblates received instruction in the rule and usages of the life they thought they wanted to embrace.

When Mother Scholastica received the poor, bewildered recruits in individual direction, she soon discovered that the life was far from what they had been expecting. And this soon became evident to everyone else in the community. Left so much to themselves, and being so helpless and so lost, the oblates tended more and more to form a forlorn and separate group, within the community but not of it, huddling together, as it were, for sympathy in the face of the austerities which no one had time or was able to make them understand.

The nuns and lay sisters were brokenhearted at the evident dejection of the little Japanese oblates, but even more so at their own helplessness in making matters better. It was all very well to try and express sympathy by a smile or a sign, but what good were signs to someone who could not read the book that explained what the signs meant? And experience shows that mistaken signs can cause confusion and pain enough even in monasteries where all the religious are of one country and culture and have, more or less, the same attitude toward life.

Some of the oblates had applied for admission, more or less, under the impression that the Trappistine convent was a kind of school, and they were soon very surprised indeed at the cold and poverty and hard work and manifest lack of educational facilities. Now, bewildered, they stood in choir in an attitude of mute dejection. At work their movements became slower and slower, their eyes wandered more and more to the windows and over the enclosure fence. When someone tried to explain something to them they stared with an incomprehension made all the more blank by hopelessness. They would receive no comfort, or, if they did, it was with a smile so wan and pitiful that it made the Sisters want to cry. And then, one by one, they left.

There were, however, new arrivals to replace them. Not many, of course, but enough to keep three or four or half a dozen always in the house. And soon, in spite of their difficulties, there were one or two who remained not only a month or two, but a year, then two and more. Eventually they became novices, and were professed and stayed for good. One of them is now the abbess of the monastery.

But in those days that time could not be foreseen, and of all the Sisters in the house, none was more depressed by the new oblates than Mother Berchmans. There were several reasons why.

In the first place, it is easy to see that this was all part of the purification especially designed by Providence for her. The Sacred Heart, whom she so loved, and whose love she so desired to bring to these poor people, was again teaching her that the love which is His very Being has to burn, here below, in darkness and desolation, and will not tolerate the movement of mere natural affection or desire, until these become transubstantiated into Himself by trial and suffering. If she really loved the Japanese, let her prove it, not alone by words and holy aspirations and desires before the tabernacle, but by concrete and actual charity for real, individual souls of the race she wanted to save. There is no question that she had this charity, and did give her whole heart to trying to help the unhappy strangers. That was why their ever growing dejection and lack of response was all the more painful to her.

In the cold little novitiate of Our Lady of the Angels there was very little of the joy which Mother Berchmans had seen all around her in the first days at Laval. The Japanese postulants were bewildered by the unfamiliar life, often crushed by burdens which they were not quite able to understand because no one knew enough Japanese to explain them. They had come to the convent not quite knowing what to expect, except that they wanted to find happiness, and someone had told them they could find it here. But it was hard for them to understand that happiness consisted in sacrifice and doing God's will when hardly anyone could explain the meaning of such thoughts to them. Mother Berchmans, for her part, was distressed and discouraged. She too, at first, was a little bewildered. She did not see why the postulants were so slow and halting in choir, at work, at their books.

But there was another thing about this situation that caused her a special unhappiness. It became increasingly clear that she would someday, perhaps soon, receive the full weight of this immense responsibility on her own shoulders. And the harder life became for the postulants, the weaker and more helpless did she find herself. How could she ever face the task of mistress of novices? Impossible! It was far beyond her! She was the last person in the world to put in such a position! It would be insanity!

So she began to renew her representations of her weakness and incapacity to her prioress and Father Robert. Beyond question, she should be left where she belonged, in obscurity, *dans son petit coin*, in a little corner, out of the way!

Of course, that meant that her efforts to study Japanese became less and less enthusiastic as time went on. Finally she wrote:

"My Reverend Mother (Lutgarde), next time you write you must give me a good Chapter of Faults. The trouble is this: I have not yet applied myself seriously to the study of Japanese, and you must know the reason why. You will see that there is something, if not a great deal, to be said for my side of the argument. At the moment we have four Japanese postulants. They are all the time with the community, since there is no novitiate. Not that we haven't a room for that purpose: what is lacking is a Mother Mistress.... Our little sisters suffer from all this. They are left pretty much to themselves. It is absolutely necessary that some nun get a thorough knowledge of Japanese. Reverend Mother is counting on me, a little: and it would be a chance to give myself up for these dear little souls that I love with all the strength of my heart. But such a responsibility terrifies me: it literally paralyzes my mind! To be Mistress of Novices out here means a much greater responsibility than it would in France. These souls are so new to everything in the religious life. First impressions will be too deep ever to be removed, and their perfection will depend upon the direction they receive in the novitiate. To really fill this office well, one would have to be another Margaret Mary; one would need to read what was going on in those young souls, and be led by the true Spirit of God." And she adds, to the horror of Father Robert, "Reverend Mother, pray for your little daughter, that her shoulders may never have to bear so terrible a burden."

Perhaps her good confessor is right when he says that this last somewhat unheroic sentence does not show anything but an illusory humility, which masks a real, but unconscious, lack of trust in God. But Mother Berchmans was certainly not wrong when she looked into her own soul and found neither the natural aptitude nor the supernatural grace and strength to even begin the task. Later on, however, that same Spirit of God, in His own good time, was to give her all the light and strength she needed, just when and in the measure she needed them, and she, in a much more perfect spirit of faith and abandonment which she was even now learning by this trial, was not only to accept the responsibility but to form some ten or fifteen Japanese Christians into holy and perfect Trappistines: nuns who would form the foundation of a strong and lasting edifice—a community that would be able to dispense with all European aid within a single generation, and which would become the largest convent of nuns in the Order.

As time went on, Mother Berchmans' health grew imperceptibly worse, and yet she was able to persuade Mother Scholastica to let her get up, with the community, at two o'clock. She persisted, and was to persist for several years to come, in ignoring her pains, her upset stomach, her headaches, and even the peculiar attacks which always seemed to arrive on First Fridays, when she would frequently be overcome by weakness and drop unconscious to the floor.

The choir at Our Lady of the Angels had few voices and poor. Even ordinarily speaking Mother Berchmans was the poorest of them all, but now she was frequently unable to sing a note during the night office, being completely robbed of her voice. All she could do was stand in her stall, moving her lips and offering up to God, in the tabernacle, the sacrifice of the pains in her chest and head. Perhaps it was the chantress, Mother Angelica, who suggested that Mother Berchmans pray to get her voice back, seeing that there were so few in the choir. At any rate, one of the nuns did so, but Mother Berchmans preferred to leave that to the good God. "He has given me this Cross," she said, and left it at that. It was to be her way in all her troubles, especially of the body. Let others pray for her to recover if they wished, she would only do so under obedience.

Perhaps, indeed, she was already suffering from tuberculosis without the doctors being able to discover any real proof of its presence. In her last years, analysis of her sputum was to give the impression that her lungs had been attacked by consumption once or even more times before, and she had partially recovered.

In 1904, the year of the great storm that has been mentioned, the little convent was threatened by yet another danger. This time it was the war between Russia and Japan. Any day, now, they might expect a Russian cruiser to steam into the strait and train her guns upon the city and the surrounding hills. And Our Lady of the Angels was less than two miles from the sea. It was Mother Berchmans who was appointed to prepare a French flag of blue, white, and red, to fly above the undefended convent. Probably one shell would have been enough to wipe out the whole community and send all the nuns to heaven. However, that never came to pass.

Working on the flag, Mother Berchmans reflected peacefully on these things. And there was a kind of joy and happy pride in her heart to be doing so. She loved France so much. These colors meant so much to her.

There were some new recruits from France. Some of them apparently felt the bitterness of the sacrifice far more than Mother Berchmans ever had. With one of them, her action was characteristic. The poor Sister was walking alone in the garden in a flood of tears, sniffing and sobbing and brandishing her handkerchief like St. Arsenius in the martyrology—but for a far less worthy cause than that holy ascetic. Mother Berchmans finally went up to her with a gentle and humorous impatience, took the handkerchief away, and threw it into a puddle. After all, that was the most effective way of getting it wet. The Sister understood, and the tears dried of themselves and gave place to a smile.

Mother Berchmans wrote: "I do not like to see people cry, especially in a Trappistine convent, where nobody can talk. I always feel very sorry for saints who lived in communities and who received the gift of tears. That is a gift which I can only appreciate in a hermit."

Now that charity was gaining ever greater freedom of action in Mother Berchmans' soul, she began to run more swiftly in the way of God's commandments and to perform with ever greater facility those countless little acts of renunciation and mortification which obscurely sanctified her day as a Trappistine.

But, first of all, what was her day? Father Robert had the good fortune to find and piece together her private daily "schedule" which, like all good religious, she had made and submitted to her director for approval, and followed faithfully. For this is not a way of enslaving our wills to routine, but of liberating them from the tyranny of caprice and self-indulgence. This submission of our desires and judgments to the approval of our legitimate superiors is the one sure defense against boredom in the religious life, because boredom cannot exist except where there is self-will.

From the time when the clangor of the dormitory bell rang the knell of self-love at two o'clock every morning, until the time it rang again at seven and she stretched her aching body on the straw mattress and couch of planks, Mother Berchmans' day was a constant elevation of the heart to God. It was a constant act of love. Later on, when she was mistress of novices, and the tattered schedule could no longer help her much, as none of her intervals belonged to her any more, a novice asked her: "What is your private schedule?" and she answered: "My schedule is: Love." She made acts of love all day. Every step she took was an act of love. Every breath was an act of love. Every action was an act of love of God. Not all these acts were formal or explicit or conscious, but her whole day was a virtual loving union with God, renewed from time to time by a few vocal prayers or simple elevations of the heart and mind to God in the midst of whatever she might be doing.

One day, after much prayer, no doubt, and plenty of meditation, she took up her pen and wrote:

"For the greater glory of God and the spiritual profit of my soul, I resolve to keep the following schedule as closely as circumstances may permit, in the desire, above all, of submitting myself to holy obedience." A truly Benedictine beginning. Without obedience there is no charity, says St. Thomas, because charity is a union of wills: *idem velle et nolle* between man and God. If her day was to be an act of love (and she did not make *that* her resolution) it would first have to be a day of constant and total obedience.

"I will get up at the first sound of the bell...." And she did. We have the testimony of the whole community that she was one of those religious who have the happy gift of a constitution which enables them to be invariably one of the first to arrive in choir and kneel in adoration of God a bare minute or two after the bell has rung. But the important thing was that from the very first waking moment she took care to direct her heart to heaven. She made the sign of the cross, knelt a moment by the couch, and sent her first petition of the day to Mary, Mother of God and Queen of heaven, "for her maternal blessing." Simple and easy; no complications!

And then, with the same directness: "On my way to the chapel I shall give my heart to God."

Mother Berchmans had a little book of vocal prayers and aspirations copied from various sources—to read them all one might get the impression that she always had them on her lips. They served her, no doubt, on special occasions when she happened to have some leisure. But the essence of her prayer was this constant swift flight of the mind and will directly to the Heart of Christ: ever repeated, simple offerings of her whole self, not so much in words as in the *will*. There were still words; she liked words, but they were not the chief thing.

She took care to realize what she was doing when she took holy water at the entrance to the chapel, and then, on her knees, putting herself into the presence of God, she made a more profound act of adoration and consecration of herself to the Sacred Heart, offering the office and all her day; and so the day began. Mother Scholastica would give the signal, and bowing almost to the floor, in the darkness, on their knees and knuckles, the Sisters would hear the *Ave Maria gratia plena*—the first cry that rises from every Cistercian soul in the solitude and silence of all the cold mornings of the world.

"The Lord is with Thee!" And the Lord was with Mother Berchmans, especially in her meditation. Here she was free to let her heart go, and even on days when her heart seemed to refuse to go anywhere, to do or say anything, she was still able to offer all her helplessness with great peace to God, supplying for it with the love and merits of Mary. She always prepared her mental prayer. Sometimes she sought assistance from a book, but not always, not even as a rule. Her prayer was mostly affective: acts, as one might expect, of love. But she believed in variety, choosing, always something simple. Of this we shall see more in another place.

During the canonical office (though she does not mention this in her schedule), she generally occupied her mind with the passion of Christ. She often had to fight, like every other religious, with distractions and all the usual trials by which the weakness of the flesh tends to destroy the value of our praise of God. From the very first days at Laval she had attacked the problem at its root by guarding first her exterior senses and then her imagination. She did both by the same simple means of keeping her heart occupied with Christ in His passion. When she was acquiring the habit of keeping her eyes down, in order not to see anything that might take her mind away from the office, she did so by reminding herself of Jesus blindfolded by Pilate's guard, in the Pretorium, and mocked by them. Was He not even now almost at her side, in the actual physical Body which had suffered all those outrages and torments and insults? And when distractions came nevertheless, she turned her heart, rather than her mind, once more to Christ in His passion.

Was any great effort necessary? Did she have to force her way to the unscalable heights of some empyrean heaven to bring Him down to her? No, He was in her heart. The uncreated and eternal Word of God was present in her soul: and to that Word was united the soul and flesh of Christ, not only as it is now, glorious in eternity, but as it was at each successive moment of His earthly life. The face of the thorn-crowned Christ, the outcast of His people and of the world, bleeding to death under the terrifying burden of the sins of a thousand generations of murderers and adulterers and thieves, was looking at her out of the very depths of her own soul. His eyes were scrutinizing her from the recesses of her own interior darkness, and compelling her compassion for Himself and for His murderers—for thousands of souls that she had never known. She was not only singing in the presence of Christ, or rather trying to whisper the words inspired by His Spirit, in her voiceless throat, but it was He uttering those words, singing and suffering in her. Her cracked lips, her dry throat, gave forth the words of the psalms half audibly, like the "*sitio*" of the thirsting Christ. And in her, He thirsted still, not that he might have anything for Himself, but that souls might drink of the living waters of grace and live forever.

Was this hard? No. Yet her mind could not always conceive it, nor her memory call it back. Even when she was robbed of all power to think of anything that was not an absurd confusion of distractions, her will in anguished resignation relived the struggle of the soul of Christ fighting its way out of His dying flesh on Calvary.

After the Angelus, at four o'clock, she was on her knees before Our Lady of the Angels. Every day she was there, summer and winter. In winter, at that time, when the choir was empty but for Mother Berchmans, all the windows had to be opened to let in a little fresh air. The snow would blow in and fly about her frail shoulders, and flakes would fall and melt upon her perhaps feverish cheeks. But every day she was there.

Then Mass and Communion except when there was no Communion. But there was always the Mass, and she would try to warm her empty heart with at least a spiritual Communion. After Communion, peace: a long thanksgiving in the dark, silent chapel. It would seem as though she had escaped from time into a quiet and deep and wonderful eternity. Then she would open her eyes and, most of the year, she would see the windows growing pale with the faint new light of dawn.

At her Communion Mass, she always united her offering of herself to God as victim with the offering of the eternal and only perfect Victim on the altar at the Consecration, when she renewed her baptismal and religious vows. It was her intention, certainly often actual rather than virtual, to renew this offering at each *Gloria Patri* of the various offices during the day.

Most of her morning intervals were devoted to prayer. That meant that in the season of the fasts of the order she probably had between an hour and a half and two hours free for prayer and reading between chapter and dinnertime. This time was divided between a visit to the Blessed Sacrament, the rosary, the study of Japanese, and a few minutes for general private devotions.

After sext in winter, or after chapter in summer, came the morning work, which Mother Berchmans, according to her good resolutions, sanctified by uniting it with the work of Jesus and Joseph in the little carpenter's shop at Nazareth, and of Mary in their house. If the work was quiet and reflective, like sewing, then she could easily pray as she worked. If, on the other hand, she dug in the garden or pitched hay in the field, or if she had to bend over a washboard and sink her arms deep into the thick suds and scrub and rinse the week's laundry, then she could offer the work, not so much as a conscious prayer, but as a penance. For such work grew to be more and more of an effort and strain on her frail body as the years went on. Nevertheless, Father Robert says, if she had any preferences in the matter of work, they were for what was hard and penitential; wearying to the flesh and even to the spirit.

Mother Berchmans was remarkable in the refectory only for the fact that, after several years of observation, no one was able to tell what she liked and what she disliked on the Sisters' simple bill of fare. She took a little of everything that was given her. She never refused to eat anything that was displeasing to her, and even when she felt ill, and her stomach resisted the very smell of food, she would eat anyway. There were things that never agreed with her, but she always ate them.

An important item on the Cistercian menu is cheese, for the nuns, like the monks of the order, are always dairy farmers. Unfortunately, Mother Berchmans was one of those people who cannot eat cheese without getting slightly sick. It was a long time before anyone found this out. Even in summertime, when the cheese was dry and moldy, she would eat it without even bothering to remove the rind. God had given it to her with the rind on it, she explained, so why should she cut it off? Some of the Sisters developed the wise habit of carefully paring any fruit that came to the convent from the itinerant Japanese peddlars; Mother Berchmans did not go to the trouble of doing so. Father Robert asserts that if a fly happened to drown in her soup, or a worm turned up in an apple she was eating, she would swallow it down along with the rest.

As the Japanese postulants began to arrive in greater numbers, and some found their way into the kitchen, Japanese dishes sometimes appeared on the table, and these were not always to the taste of the French nuns. But Mother Berchmans made a point of always eating them.

Even during the summer, she would not drink anything between meals unless she was forced to do so.

The constitutions of the Sisters prescribe a little walk in the open air after dinner, all the year round, for the sake of health, since the Trappistines do not have as much outdoor work as the monks.

This walk is of course in no sense a recreation as that word is understood in other contemplative orders. The nuns continue to keep silence, and do not indulge in any amusements or games together. They walk peacefully together, with their rosaries, or go apart to pray at various shrines in their garden, or else take a book with them. In summer, this walk was very pleasant at Our Lady of the Angels, although it was sometimes hot. The Sisters would go outside their little garden and pick flowers in the shady glen and bring them in for the decoration of the altars. Out on the flowering hillside, Mother Berchmans would let the wonderful view of the deep green valley and the wall of mountains over against them raise up her soul to God in adoration, but she did not make the mistake of allowing herself to get attached even to this harmless natural pleasure. For the rest, she kept herself from enjoying the flowers and the lovely countryside for their own sakes, and when the Sisters presented their bouquets for her to smell, she would smile and turn her head aside.

In the winter time the walk was another matter. Snow lay thick on the ground and the biting icy breath of Siberia and the Arctic swept along the ridge, and most of the nuns were glad to stay in the chapter room with their books. But since it was the rule that the nuns must take a walk, Mother Berchmans always went out for a walk.

Yet in summer, when the time prescribed for the walk was over, she was sitting at her usual place in the chapter room, composed, quiet, erect, her feet together and tucked under her robe, and, unless she was holding a book, her hands were always in the thick woolen sleeves of her cowl. To look at her, no one would have thought it was hot. She would not even move over to the open window.

This was her time for spiritual reading. She was not a great reader, and certainly not a curious one, but any curious avidity for books and information makes true spiritual reading impossible. She was devoted to her reading more as a form of prayer than as reading in the sense in which it is understood by a devourer of all the latest novels. She carefully studied the lives of holy and contemplative Sisters in different orders, mystics mostly, of a generation close to her own, like Elizabeth of the Trinity, Marie of the Agnus Dei, Marie of the Divine Heart, and Sister Gertrude Mary. From these lives she lovingly copied out thoughts and reflections and prayers, and especially things that had been revealed to these holy women by our Lord: and all this material went to make up a collection which she called the "Mirror of my Soul."

From the very first, however, her greatest devotion and her most lively interest had been in the lives and revelations of St. Gertrude and St. Margaret Mary—the latter not yet canonized in Mother Berchmans' time. Indeed, so deeply and prayerfully had she studied the lives and doctrine of these two great apostles of the Sacred Heart that by now she no longer read them; she knew most of the revelations of the Sacred Heart to Margaret Mary by heart.

Every day she recited the Little Office of the Sacred Heart, which is made up of the words of our Lord to St. Margaret Mary, and these were always in her mind. They had shaped her whole life. They had given her devotion, her prayer, and her vocation the strong character of love and reparation which they possessed; they had given her the intense and consuming desire of her whole life: to be a victim for God's love—a victim of reparation for the outrages and insults offered to the infinitely loving Heart of Christ. But as long as this desire to be a victim went no further than the traditional lines laid down by St. Margaret Mary, Mother Berchmans' spirituality was incomplete. There was one thing yet lacking to set free all her energies to love God in the way He had created her in particular to love Him. This she was to discover, in a very short time, in the pages of the autobiography of a Carmelite nun, a little Sister who had died some years before in the obscurity of a convent in Northern France, not very far from Laval. That was the *Story of a Soul* by Sister Thérèse of the Child Jesus, and from the moment she read that book, Mother Berchmans had no doubt at all that its writer would soon be called not "Sister" but Saint Thérèse.

So her day went on. The interval she devoted to spiritual reading would be followed by the afternoon work, and then, as always during the day, she would keep lifting up her heart to God. She always remembered to do this when she heard a clock strike, and at three in the afternoon she still said her little prayer to Jesus dying on the cross. Every day, too, after work, she made the stations of the cross with great recollection and love. As the sun sank behind the hills and the lengthening shadows gradually enveloped the little wooden convent, Mother Berchmans would be on her knees again before Mary's statue, and there she would prepare her mind and heart for the next morning's mental prayer.

Now her period of trial was drawing to its close. Not that her sufferings were to cease; far from it—they were only just about to begin, but her faith had been tested now. And in this darkness she had been made stronger than she realized, for she had been confirmed in a strength that was not and never could be her own, or from herself. While she had been fighting with all these repugnances, God had been secretly tightening the grip and deepening the power of grace upon her soul. Now the repugnances were to wither away before the intensity of a new charity that she was to find within her. And with this greater strength of faith, all the hesitation about accepting her exile was to cease. Her feelings would still fill her with yearning for France, but the yearning would be easy to disregard, and would be ignored until it gradually died away altogether.

Not long after her arrival at Our Lady of the Angels, she had contrived to get rid of everything that she had brought with her from Laval. She acquired a different breviary and exchanged all the other little things (few enough they were!) that might remind her too much of her first home in religion. But now she was to shake off at last the anxiety of will that kept drawing her back there all the day long.

An indication of the end of this preliminary struggle was given her when the Father Immediate, that is the higher superior responsible for the little convent, came at last from France to make his regular visitation. This was the abbot of the Cistercians at Bricquebec, Dom Vital Lehodey. This man was one of the pillars of the vigorous new Order of Cistercians of the Strict Observance. He was an abbot of singular prudence and wisdom, a true contemplative, and a director of souls who had wide and deep knowledge of the trials of those whom God has chosen for a particularly intimate union with Himself.

When Dom Vital met Mother Berchmans again and spoke with her, he realized at once that she was a person of great purity of life, called to high sanctity, and generously doing her best to respond to that call. And he also recognized, after a more intimate acquaintance with her interior life, that she was undergoing a siege of purgative trials. We do not know how deeply he entered into the problems of her spiritual life, but surely, no prolonged analysis of her situation was necessary. Nor was there need of long discourses to give comfort to her mind and restore her to peace and resignation, which her own efforts could not procure, and which Father Robert seems to have had so little success, at first, in bringing to her soul.

No, all was well with her. There was no cause for surprise in her trials, her weaknesses, her homesickness, her inner movements of rebellion. God was working in her soul. He was pleased with her. She should let Him work, and not be too disconcerted at the feelings she found arising within herself. Let her trust in Him, love Him, and look ahead, not back.

And then he asked her: "Will you be willing, then, to make your new stability here in Japan?"

The time had come. Her whole sacrifice would finally be consummated. The last ties that bound her to Laval, the technical bond of obedience that still made her the subject of Reverend Mother Lutgarde and her successors, would be severed. She would solemnly renew her vows and bind herself, even unto death, to this little plot of land on a mountain in Hokkaido. She would never go back home again. This was the end. Irrevocable. Final.

But there was no hesitation in her answer: "Of course, Reverend Father. When will I be able to do so?"

CHAPTER X

NEW STABILITY

Mother Berchmans had arrived at Laval on the feast of the Sacred Heart, and had thus begun her religious life on this day consecrated in so special a manner to the love and the sufferings of the Man-God dying a Victim for sin, living always among us in the obscurity and abjection of the silent, helpless Host on our altars. On the feast of the then uncanonized saint who had been chosen by Christ as the apostle of His Sacred Heart, she had offered herself as a volunteer to go to the new foundation in Japan. On the feast of one of the first of the great mystics who initiated this devotion, St. Gertrude the Great, Mother Berchmans had made her perpetual vows, giving herself entirely to God forever. And now, on the feast of the Sacred Heart, in the year 1906, after four years in exile, she was to consummate this sacrifice, giving it a final and complete totality by renouncing all freedom to return to the cradle of her religious life, to her country and her own people, and bind herself irrevocably to all the uncertainty and difficulties and trials and hazards of this remote foundation in a strange land.

She had always known that her vocation was to a life of suffering and reparation for sin. She had always realized that without sacrifice there is no love on this earth, and that she, being called in a special manner to a life of love, was therefore called to a life of suffering and of sacrifice.

"To love," she wrote, "is to suffer; to suffer, and suffer well, is to love. True love lives only on sacrifices."

In a letter to one of the nuns at Laval, she said: "Remember, my dear Mother, that it is in the mould of the Cross that the Divine Master shapes the souls that He deigns to call to greater love. Oh, if only we were really docile under the hand of the heavenly Sculptor, what masterpieces He would make of His little spouses! Let us then allow ourselves to be carved by love and abandonment. The consolations of this earth are not worthy of us. Jesus wants a complete immolation. Let Him then do as He pleases, and take as long as He likes."

One afternoon in the chapter room she had read in the life of some mystic these words of our Lord to that soul; she had copied them out into her "Mirror" and made them her own: "My child, forget, if you can, Heaven and its delights...forget all my promises and rewards and think only of the joy of pleasing Me and of suffering for My glory...."

It was as if Jesus had appeared and said the same to her. And she wrote in another letter: "I have to suffer, in order to be able to tell Jesus that I love Him: for what is love that has never suffered?"

She had written of the same things in her notes in the novitiate at Laval; she had prayed to be left without consolations. Her prayer had been answered, and in a way that had surprised her; she had begun, indeed, to suffer, and to realize her inability to suffer heroically by herself. For a long time she had been confused by the unexpected form her trials took.

Yet now, once again, she was writing about suffering, praying to suffer, offering herself for more and more suffering. And this time, there is a new sureness in her voice. She seems to know what she is talking about. She seems to realize what she is asking for. There is a greater peace in her words. Her voice is more tranquil and more strong. It is no longer the voice of a romantic adolescent.

Her prayers were going to be heard this time, too. Not right away, it is true, but soon enough, the answer would come. And this time they would be real sufferings. Not that all her trials, up to now, had been nothing, but they had not all the full, stern impact of the hardships that were to test her in her last years. All these, even the worst, we must remember, were never extraordinary or spectacular. She was to suffer the ordinary, obscure, purifying trials of work and desolation and sickness which are the common lot of all religious, more or less; but she was to suffer them with an extraordinary degree of trust and love and abandonment.

Yet, the fact that one of the chief elements of her sacrifice would always be her exile, far from making her forget her country, could only contribute to giving France, as a nation, a place in the forefront of all her intentions in making this sacrifice. She was convinced that if Christ had torn her up by the roots from her native soil, against every instinct of her nature, so strongly attached to her land and her people, it was in order that her sacrifice might make reparation for the sins of that land and win grace to save it from further disasters.

Mother Berchmans was a Catholic, but she was a French Catholic. And although the word Catholic contains the notion of a universal love and faith, there is no contradiction in speaking of a French, or English, or Irish, or American Catholic. Mother Berchmans was destined to nurture in her French soul this universal love which is the love of God for all men. But she was always French, and she loved her own people in a way someone who was not of her blood and country could not do: with an understanding that such a one could never fully share.

Her soul had deep roots in her nation's Catholic past. It was not hard for her to conceive her sacrifice as an atonement for the awful disorders into which her land had fallen; she had been torn out of her native hills to atone for the sin of those who had uprooted their country from the fertile field of Christ's faith. Her heart loved God with the clean and ardent love that had burned in Joan of Arc. She belonged to the land that St. Bernard had filled with abbeys dedicated to the Mother of God; the France that was, and is, the finest jewel in the Queen of heaven's dowry, the France of Lourdes and La Salette—is there a wood or hill or mountain of France where Mary has not appeared to someone?

But where was this heritage? Whose was the sin, the immense sin of its loss? What man shall be judge of this crime, or assess the reasons of this great disaster? When Christ appeared to St. Margaret Mary at Paray-le-Monial, did He not show her the wounds He was receiving from His chosen people? from those, not only of favored France, but of the whole world, who had received the special, invaluable, immense grace of vocations to the cloister or to the priesthood?

In century after century of growing cruelty, injustice, and greed perhaps some, and perhaps many, of God's human ministers had betrayed Him and His Gospel, some by weakness, some by malice. And in punishment (or rather, out of mercy, lest the evil spread), Christ had allowed men without faith to make this their excuse to attack and crucify Him again in His Mystical Body in France.

The blood of the harmless and the innocent had been cruelly spilled in every city and town of this elect nation, and the doors of convents and empty monasteries had been closed as if forever. The body of the Son of God had been torn from His tabernacles and scattered in the mud of the streets, devoured by dogs, to atone for the cold hearts and stony wills of those who, abusing His grace, had for centuries received Him without gratitude or love, or who, professing to love Him, had despised and forsaken Him in the needy and the poor, in the prisoner, in the man dying of fever, in the cripple and leper, in the starving peasant.

And now this lovely and chosen country belonged to a tribe of mean and crafty bureaucrats, little fat atheists with false teeth and carefully curled mustaches, stingy men who sat for hours in the cafés reading the socialist newspapers through their weak spectacles: the men who played interminable games of cards in the *gendarmerie*, or who betrayed their civil marriages with cynical and regular openness. Christ had made His life in the souls of this people depend upon the whims and undependable tolerance of dishonest deputies and subprefects. The first Communions of the children were contingent upon the moods of freemasonry; their education in the faith upon the good pleasure of communists; their perseverance might at any moment be poisoned and die at the hands of incipient fascism, or be stifled by the thousand appeals to sensuality and materialism that made themselves heard in every café and theater, at the corner of every street, on the pages of the papers and magazines that fluttered like flags from the sides of the *kiosques*.

In 1903, Mother Berchmans had written: "Poor France! No, the good God cannot go on leaving her to her own devices. Is she not Mary's kingdom? It is His Mother's honor, then, that is at stake! If you but knew it, Reverend Mother, sometimes I get angry with Jesus. It seems to me that just now He is being more severe than Assuerus! Am I not His little Esther? Have I not forsaken my country, and left my people for Him? Instead of hearing my request, He seems, by His actions, to give me the answer He once gave His Blessed Mother: 'Woman, what is that to me and to thee?' But what care I for this severe tone? I will continue my importunities until He stretches forth His scepter and has mercy on poor France!"

And indeed she had continued to beg Him in the name of His apparitions and promises at Paray, and of His Blessed Mother's love for France, and of the ancient alliance of France with the Church, and of the thousands of French saints, to have pity, to send down His grace, to spare His people.

But now, as the day for her final gift of herself approached, she found the thought of France's tragedy more and more insistent in the forefront of her mind. What could she do to emphasize the sincerity of the desire with which she was ever renewing the consecration of her country to the Sacred Heart? Was there anything she had to offer? If there was anything left at all, that was her, it was only her life. Let Jesus, if He would, deprive her of it with whatever sufferings He pleased, under whatever circumstances; she would be a willing victim, and go joyfully to whatever cross He chose.

It was on the sixth of June, 1906, only a few days before her new stability, that she wrote out this offering of herself which was folded away in a locket and rested there, for the rest of her life, next to her heart.

"Oh my dearly beloved Jesus," it began, "led by my Immaculate Mother I come to Thee to renew all the consecrations and offerings I have been able to make up to now to Thy Sacred Heart, and to offer myself anew to Thy Divine Mercy as a victim of love. I pray and conjure Thee to purify, sanctify, and immolate me entirely in the flames of Thy holy Love, in reparation for the outrages and bitterness which Thou dost taste in our unhappy nation. Oh my good Jesus, it is necessary that Thou be loved by this whole nation, that Thou be recognized and acclaimed by every true French heart. It is necessary, O Jesus, that the very government of France, humbled and abject, fall at Thy knees to implore Thy forgiveness and consecrate the entire nation to Thy Sacred Heart. And if, for that, oh my good Jesus, a victim is necessary to Thy outraged and despised love, I conjure Thee, take me. Take all that I have, all that yet remains to me; here are my body, every drop of my blood, my heart, my soul, my whole self. I unite my sacrifice to that which Thou didst consummate upon the Cross for the salvation of the whole human race. And if there be, in this offering, anything that is in opposition with the designs of Thy love upon my soul, I renounce it altogether. I desire but one thing only: that Thy divine will be done, in its entirety. And from now on, I take the resolution to accept generously all the sufferings and crosses which it shall please Thee to send me.

"I also implore Thy infinite mercy, oh my Jesus, for my land of adoption. Let fall upon her a ray of light from Thy divine Heart and so dissipate the shadows of error that engulf her, and give Thy Church the consolation of seeing all these lost sheep gathered in Thy fold.

"Oh Mary, my good and tender Mother, place me upon the Heart of Jesus as though upon a burning fire, that I may consume all that is natural in me, and that I may become less unworthy to be offered to Him. Offer me thyself to thy divine Son, and beg Him, in return, to deign to grant graces too powerful to resist to all the souls I desire to save for Him.

"Sr. Marie Berchmans, Spouse of the Sacred Heart
of Jesus and loving child of Mary Immaculate."

Such dispositions were growing stronger and stronger in her now. Nor could she be content with desires alone. The spirit of Christ, her Lord, who had been stripped of everything and nailed to a Cross, kept stirring in her, demanding of her something more concrete, more tangible, as a pledge of her sincerity.

In the little private box allotted to her in the chapter room, where she kept her notebook and a handful of papers and little odds and ends she needed, there was also a sizable packet of letters. They were all that had come to her from the Sisters and her former superiors at Laval. Often she used to take them out and leaf through them and read them over tenderly with, now and again, a prayer. She liked especially to do this in the *meridienne*, or afternoon rest, prescribed in St. Benedict's rule for his monks after the midday meal, in summertime, when the work is heaviest and the heat hard to bear. The patriarch specifically mentions that no one is obliged to sleep, but all must be on their beds in the dormitory, quiet, reading, or sleeping according to their pleasure or ability, as long as they do not disturb others.

But now she began to feel that this innocent pleasure was no longer for her. If she really meant to give up everything that was hers, everything that attached her to this earth; what about all those letters? And so, one day, she took them all, and threw them into the fire. And then she had a little peace.

That did not, of course, mean that she altogether ceased writing to Laval. Far from it. It was still to be a long, slow struggle for her to persuade herself that she really could reduce all her correspondence to the minimum of a letter or two each year to Mother Lutgarde, in other words, to the bare minimum required by gratitude and filial charity. However, here is what she said of the sacrifice to the mother abbess of Laval:

"Jesus is taking everything I have. In order to satisfy the desires of His Divine Heart I had to burn up all our letters: yours, my Reverend Mother, and those from Reverend Mother Antoinette, and even those of good Father Polycarpe. And you know what a little package of them I had accumulated since my departure. It was a real treasure for me. From time to time, especially during the *meridienne*, I enjoyed myself reading them over again. And now that is all over. Sometimes Jesus is very exacting!"

Father Robert gives few details about her vow of stability. She left no notes about it. We may assume there was a fervent retreat of a week or so for the several nuns and lay sisters who were making this final promise together. The ceremony itself was extremely simple, if not austere.

And yet it was a joyful day for the little convent of Our Lady of the Angels. No matter how many fervent novices or unstabilitated Sisters there might be in a house, the heart and soul of the community is in the nucleus of solemnly professed religious, bound by all their vows and firmly rooted there by stability. Only death can make a break in the solid ranks of these determined souls, and they have special graces proportionate to the magnitude of their sacrifice. No matter how many good religious may be there under temporary vows, they are only *in* the community. But those bound by perpetual stability, they *are* the community.

So, on the morning of the feast of the Sacred Heart, 1906 (we do not know if it was sunny or rainy, or what kind of a day it was), the seven Sisters, with Mother Berchmans in the midst of them, filed into the tiny chapter room and prostrated at full length, on their faces, on the floor before Mother Scholastica, begging the mercy of God and of that community.

The words of the mother prioress in her allocution to them are easy enough to guess. There was no need for many words. They knew what they would have to face. They had known it for a long time now. They also knew how much depended on them, on the generosity of their sacrifice. That was evident enough when they looked around the half-empty benches of the little room. No, the significance of their sacrifice was not hard for them to grasp, under such circumstances!

The main ceremony, in the church, was scarcely less perfunctory. After the Gospel of the Mass they filed up to the grille and arranged themselves before it as best they could, in the middle of the narrow little choir.

Mother Berchmans' hand probably did not tremble, or her weak voice quaver much, when she took the schedule of her new stability in her hand. There was not the emotion of the day of her perpetual vows.

"Ego, Soror Maria Joannes Berchmans....

"I Sr. Mary Berchmans, nun of the Order of Reformed Cistercians, promise my stability under perpetual enclosure and obedience according to the Rule of St. Benedict, before God and His saints...."

She read it a second time in French, and placed the paper in Father Robert's hands, with a profound bow, and all was over. *Consummatum est!*

Now she knew that this was to be her body's home and resting place until the day of doom. She would never see France again. It was all irrevocably over and done with. As far as her human nature and affections were concerned, she might as well be dead. Yet her life was only really to begin on this day. Only now would she begin to know a purer and rarer peace than she had ever experienced before.

"It is in the Heart of Jesus that I have made my stability," she wrote shortly afterward. "He will answer for me Himself.... I made it with my whole heart, and since that day I have never had a single regret for the vow I have pronounced.... " And she added, with a note of gratitude that has a new depth and a much more profound humility than she had ever shown before, in spite of all her sincerity: "Jesus, knowing how weak is the heart of His unworthy spouse, has, in His divine jealousy, hidden her away from the eyes of all those who were dear to her." With this new light in her soul, her life began to change rapidly and completely, says Father Robert. And from now on, he tells us, there were no more regrets: not the slightest thought of looking back. She had such a horror of pretense and artificiality and duplicity that the slightest movement of the heart toward France would have seemed to her, after her vow, a rapine in the holocaust.

But the effect of her vow was a final and complete severing of all her attachment to Laval. Now that the vow had been made with her whole heart, there was no more real temptation to regret, no more real homesickness, except of course a transitory feeling, now and then, on the surface of the emotions, the sort of thing that no one can either forestall or prevent and which does not strike deep into the will, or affect it at all for that matter.

Her new detachment was soon enough put to the test. One day she heard—perhaps Mother Scholastica told her privately, or perhaps the news was announced in chapter—that several more nuns were going to be sent to Japan, to Our Lady of the Angels from her dear Laval—Sisters she had known and loved there. Naturally, she was glad. Her heart was filled with pleasure and anticipation. Who would they be? Perhaps even someone who had been with her in the novitiate!

All these surmises, whatever they may have been, were vain. They came to nothing. The news proved to be false, and her expectations without foundation.

She felt a little disappointment, but it did not affect her peace, or disturb her in any way. She was perfectly satisfied. It really made no difference to her at all. In a day or two the whole thing was forgotten forever.

And this was a manifest sign of her progress. In her first year in Japan, and even after that, this would have been a real calamity, and would have caused her great pain.

She wrote to Mother Lutgarde: "Perhaps you were worried, to think of the rude awakening I would get, on discovering that it was all a nice dream with no substance to it. Oh! Set your mind at rest! Since the good God does not will it, I do not want it either, and it does not cause me any pain. I admit that at the time I felt it keenly—all the more keenly because my joy had been so great: but it only lasted as long as it takes to say: 'Anything You want, Jesus!' and now, as a matter of fact, I am happy that He has refused me this consolation, and that He leaves me my sacrifice in all its fulness. I acted like such a coward all the time, until I made my stability here, that now it is about time for me to make a little reparation on that score. Since leaving my dear Laval I can say in all truth: 'Lord I have given up everything, yes, everything.' There is nothing left, now, but the total sacrifice of myself. Oh, if I can only arrive at that, some day!"

But as time went on, her peace grew deeper and deeper, more and more pure each day. She was soon to write:

"Oh, yes, exile is a beautiful thing! For in it, we love Jesus with a far purer love. I believe that in heaven, our true home, there will be *particularly intimate delights reserved for those who have suffered voluntary exile*; Jesus will do everything to make up for all their privations here below....

"Here in Japan, we find the same Jesus, or rather I should say *a Jesus who is still more loving and more tender, a Jesus who thirsts to give Himself ever more and more to souls who have left all, but left all for love of Him!*"

This peace was the true peace, the peace that only Christ can bring to the soul and which the world cannot give, because it consisted not in the absence of suffering, but was the very joy of suffering for love of God and counting all sufferings as nothing for that love. She adds, in another letter:

"My Reverend Mother, you know the tender and affectionate heart of your child, always so ready to give herself to others. And so, Jesus, jealous of the heart of His little spouse, is bit by bit cutting off all supplies for my poor nature: but far from complaining of this, I rejoice at it."

If there was anything that troubled her in these days, and during the rest of Her life, it was the growing sense of what she considered her cowardice and infidelity before her stability. The more she looked back upon those days of hesitation and homesickness and regret, the more clearly she saw, with the growing light of grace within her soul, how much she had been deceived by her own nature. The more she realized how much unconscious weakness and sentimentality and self-pity had influenced her acts and judgments during that time. She began to accuse herself of having been a great cross to her superiors by her "disobedience," "lack of docility," and "rebelliousness."

So greatly did this thought grow upon her that in the last days of her life, when she was on her deathbed in the infirmary, she wrote a note to Mother Scholastica, expressing her deep sense of sorrow at all her imperfections.

"My Reverend Mother," it reads in all its perfection of simple sincerity, "it really gives me great sorrow to think how much I made you suffer during my first years here, and I beg you to forgive me. Jesus has taken account of all your sufferings, and guilty though I may be, I have contributed to your crown in paradise. It looks as though I am going to have a bad night. I offer it all up for your intentions. May I, by that means, make up to you for all the pain I have caused you."

Of course, Mother Scholastica did not agree with this at all. We have seen how she held up Mother Berchmans as a model of obedience and docility, saying that she had *never* seen her disobedient either to the rule or to her superiors. And Father Robert reminds us that many religious would be very satisfied if they could live up to her standard, even as it was in the time of her greatest difficulties and "imperfection."

The keen sense of her weaknesses and miseries grew upon her as the days went on, but it did not rob her of her peace or disturb her soul with that nervous, melancholy brooding shame which is nothing but self-preoccupation and pride.

In the same letter where she had acknowledged herself as having been "such a coward" up to the time of her stability, and declared that it was time for reparation, she went on to say: "Ah, if I could only start over again!" But at once she realizes that this regret is useless, not merely because of the impossibility of turning back the clock, but above all because of the mercy of God, who wills that we make use of our past faults and present helplessness to draw closer and closer to Him in humble and loving confidence that He alone can deliver us from our miseries. And so she exclaims: "But no, I would much rather offer to Jesus my weakness and cowardice: that is what His infinite mercy requires of me."

This sentence alone would be enough to explain all her peace, all her tranquil courage, her new sense of purposefulness and determination in the face of all obstacles. She no longer trusted in herself, relied on her own virtues or generosity; she trusted in God. She had discovered the secret of perfect confidence and abandonment to His merciful love, the secret which the proud can never learn, because it is *hidden* from the wise and prudent and revealed only to the little ones.

It is a wonderful thing that the Gospel should go to great pains to tell us that Jesus (who, being the Son of God and united to His Word, always enjoyed the beatific vision) was transported out of Himself as it were in ecstasy; what a light, what a glorious intuition it must have been, to fire the mind and heart of the Man-God with such a transport of spiritual delight and joy in His Father's mercy! And yet that is what happened when Jesus was seemingly forced, by the vehemence of the Spirit, to cry out as if in spite of Himself, "Thou hast hidden these things from the wise and prudent and revealed them to the little ones: yes, Father, for so it hath been pleasing in Thy sight!"

This truth, that helplessness, humility, and trust in Him are things that God cannot resist, had now begun to shed its sweet and penetrating light upon the soul of Mother Berchmans. This discovery was, indeed, one of the greatest graces of her life, if not the greatest of them all. Perhaps her Lord and Spouse had been reserving it for her, to reward her for her sacrifice in making her stability, and to comfort her after all her sufferings, as well as to prepare her for the greater sufferings that were to come.

What was the occasion of this discovery? How was this truth brought home to her? Under what circumstances was this great grace bestowed upon her soul? Now is the time to see how marvelously God works through His saints.

CHAPTER XI

A VOCATION WITHIN A VOCATION

The autobiography of St. Thérèse of the Child Jesus tarried a long time in finding its way to the poor isolated convent of French Trappistines on their hill in northern Japan. It was not until the spring of 1907, nearly a year after Mother Berchmans had made her stability, that a friend of the Sisters presented them with a copy of that remarkable book. But at once all the nuns were conquered by its doctrine. Father Robert tells us of the enthusiasm that swept the little convent, and which he himself shared. The single copy of the *Story of a Soul* was apparently far from being a complete edition, and it was soon worn out in passing from hand to hand, and from penitent to confessor and back again. However, it was not long before other and more complete editions found their way into the Sisters' "Common Box." Within a few years Mother Berchmans was to have access to every edition, and to know them all, practically by heart. If she had so desired, she could have written a detailed textual criticism of the separate printings and their variations. More than that, she could have written a deep and moving spiritual commentary on the doctrine of the Little Flower.

Of all the Sisters at Our Lady of the Angels, none needed the help and consolation of the "Little Way" of spiritual childhood as much as Mother Berchmans and none profited by it more than she. And we may also say that no one there was better prepared to receive and understand this doctrine than she was. It was not merely that she had been conditioned and attuned to this simple and fundamental spirituality by the failure of the conventional methods to solve her greatest problems; long since she had received a sound intellectual preparation.

The spirituality of Thérèse of Lisieux is influenced by that of St. Margaret Mary, on many points; it is in some sense a development of Margaret Mary's notion of the vocation to be a victim to the love of God. And St. Margaret Mary had, up to now, shaped the whole of Mother Berchmans' life.

The young Trappistine had also been well prepared to understand such teachings by her study of St. Gertrude the Great. That Cistercian mystic had learned confidence from the lips of the Lord Himself, and in the same way as St. Paul. For St. Gertrude, in spite of her visions (or perhaps, like Paul, because of them), was permitted by God to suffer temptations that keenly brought home to her, her own weakness and infirmity.

If Mother Berchmans had read St. Bernard, especially his final sermons on the Canticle of Canticles, which she probably had not, she would have realized how important a place is held by confidence (*fiducia*), in the mystical doctrine of that great Master of the spiritual life. But in any case, she was a true follower of the abbot of Clairvaux and his true child without knowing it, having absorbed his teachings on love and the whole Cistercian mystical tradition, through St. Gertrude and St. Mechtilde, and her own spiritual directors.

No better preparation was needed to enable her to draw the greatest fruit from her reading of St. Thérèse. However, as if this were not enough, our Lord saw to it that the ground of her soul was still further softened for the reception of the good seed He intended to sow there. About the time of Mother Berchmans' new stability, the life of a Poor Clare who had sanctified herself and won untold graces for souls in an obscure and hidden life in our own day, Celine of the Presentation, fell into her hands.

Father Robert points out that the similarity between these two souls made this book one which was bound to have a deep and lasting effect on Mother Berchmans. Both of them, he says, were chosen souls, endowed by God with a sensitive, tender, affectionate nature, full of candor, innocence, and fervor. Both burned with a holy desire to live for God alone, and to suffer and die for His glory. They were both called to a hidden life of contemplation and penance, and they were equally generous in accepting every suffering that came to them from the hand of God, since they were both alike consumed with thirst for His infinite love.

But in reading the life of this saintly nun, Mother Berchmans realized something about her own vocation that had never been made clear to her before. In her preoccupation with the visions and extraordinary interior and exterior trials and sufferings of St. Margaret Mary, and the other saints she so revered, Mother Berchmans had come to take it unconsciously for granted that sanctity was hardly compatible with a completely ordinary life. She had never consciously worked all this out into a well-formulated belief, but the prejudice was there in her soul, and neither of her confessors, apparently, had done anything to disillusion her. On the contrary, Father Polycarpe had perhaps unintentionally favored its growth by encouraging her to look forward to an extraordinary future as a second Margaret Mary.

In the life of Celine of the Presentation, Mother Berchmans first discovered a wholly new standard of values, which was nevertheless the pure teaching of the Gospel. This Poor Clare had never done anything extraordinary. She had sanctified herself by doing all the things that the other nuns did: but *how?* The difference lay in the intense and perfect purity of intention in which she did all these ordinary acts for the love of God, and saw Him in all things, and made use of all her obscure and common duties, the events of her daily life, as means of increasing and deepening and perfecting her union with God in faith and hope and love. Hers was the heroism of complete simplicity, or pure faith. She was what is known as a "little soul." That means, she was a soul who did not trouble to try to achieve a heroism understandable to men. She was content to let God Himself be her heroism and her sanctity, holy will, which found her always totally abandoned to His dwelling within her, working in and through her with His all-desires and His good pleasure, an instrument perfectly attuned to the inspirations of His spirit.

The impact of this truth struck Mother Berchmans with all the force of a revelation. Father Robert tells us that the book proved to be, in her case, the occasion of a great grace and infusion of light from the Holy Spirit. She went to Mother Scholastica with her eyes bright and her cheeks aflame and told what she had found.

"How did it happen," she asked, "that this little novice who did practically nothing remarkable could reach such high perfection? The only possible reason for her rapid progress was the *intensity* of her acts."

This concept of intensity contained the solution of all her problems. It was not a question of a multitude of acts, of their external greatness, or their difficulty. All that mattered was intensity of love. One act of pure love of God, silent, wordless, deep in the faithful soul, could do more for the Church, merit more graces, give God greater glory than great works and sufferings without love, or with *less love* of God. To a soul that knew the power of love, and knew that God is Love, and realized His mercy, could there be any further sadness or dejection or perplexity over little faults and imperfections? Was it not certain that the smallest act of true and trusting love, sincere love that contains and implies all contrition and sorrow and purpose of amendment and much more, would wipe them instantly away? Was not this love, and repeated acts of such love, the surest way to conquer our failings?

Indeed, imperfections and failings were necessary to make this love grow in us. Celine of the Presentation had written: "How would our confidence and love be put to the test if we never fell? Little souls are always falling: that is to be expected. Children continually fall down. As for us, let us not seek to grow up. It is better to get a few scratches: the good God will heal them all on the Last Day. It won't take Him long to wash up His little child and make her fresh as a rose."

Good, innocent Mother Berchmans, so tormented with her inner movements to rebellion and impatience, her human attachments and affections, and her own strong judgment so hard to repress, gratefully copied this down in her "Mirror."

From now on, she was well prepared to discover, as the Little Flower had discovered, that there are *some faults which do not offend the good God at all*—they are mere weaknesses, faults of character, and not formal sins. From then on, her progress was assured, because from then on she would advance by the path of faith and hope and love, with her eyes fixed on God alone and His perfection and His strength, freed from all trivial preoccupations with her own helplessness and her tiny, but stubborn, imperfections.

The first thing that Mother Berchmans realized, in reading the *Story of a Soul*, was the inescapable fact of the sanctity of this humble little Carmelite.

But at the same time she realized something far more important still. This Thérèse of Lisieux was a saint, indeed. But also, even in the natural order, her life and even her character closely resembled Mother Berchmans' own. She never did anything extraordinary. She simply lived the normal, everyday life of her convent. She kept her rule, she performed all her duties as well as she could—not always to the perfect satisfaction of everybody else, either. She was sanctified, not by the temptations of a St. Anthony or a St. Catherine of Siena, not by visible attacks from the devil, but by the usual, humble purifications and trials with which all fervent religious, and many not so fervent, are constantly visited. Undoubtedly St. Thérèse was a mystic, with a high degree of union with God, enjoying certain graces of infused prayer, suffering the trials of passive purification, but she seems to have enjoyed these things and suffered these trials just like countless other religious who have enjoyed and suffered them without really knowing what they were, and without being able to dignify them by any technical title. Mother Berchmans did not possess the technical knowledge to analyze and describe such things, nor did she need to do so.

Thérèse had also had to serve her community in the very position which threatened to rob Mother Berchmans of all her peace of mind: mistress of novices. Of course, the young Carmelite had only been submistress, officially, but it is well known that, in actual fact, she exercised all the influence of one completely in charge of the souls entrusted to her, and she had shouldered the full responsibility for them.

Finally, what was most important of all, Thérèse of the Child Jesus also shared most of Mother Berchmans' weaknesses and little faults—and had one or two, besides, that Mother Berchmans had never had to worry about. For example, there is no denying—and Thérèse makes no attempt to hide the fact—that the Little Flower, as a child, was a trifle spoiled and very much a crybaby. Mother Berchmans had had fits of bad temper, but she had not been quite so lachrymose. Then also, the Little Flower seems to have had a lot more natural vanity, in her early years, than Mother Berchmans ever had. But in both of them, their faults and imperfections were simply the products of a sensitive and affectionate and lively temperament. Both of them had hearts made for love, full of tenderness, delighting in the presence and affection of their relatives and Sisters in religion. If Mother Berchmans had to struggle against her overpowering natural attachment to the community at Laval, Thérèse had had to fight against temptations to spend too much time in the company of her own natural sisters, born of the same flesh and raised under the same roof, whom she had joined in the convent. Indeed, Thérèse had never had to consummate such a sacrifice as Mother Berchmans had made. What must have been the latter's feelings, what joy and consolation, when she read a page like that in which Thérèse describes her own thoughts of a vocation to a Carmel in Indo-China.

"My heart is not insensible," wrote the Little Flower, "and it is precisely because it is capable of so much suffering, that I desire to offer to Jesus every possible kind of suffering that heart can bear. Here I have your love, Mother, and the love of all my sisters, and this affection is sweet to me indeed! And that is why I dream of a monastery where I should be unknown, where I should have to suffer *exile of the heart....*"

At the same time, Mother Berchmans read in these pages the truth which she had long felt in her own heart, concerning this natural affection. After all, it was a natural good. It was implanted in our souls by God for a purpose, and God, always, has only one purpose: to bring us to Himself. Thérèse was never able to understand saints who did not love their own families, for she knew that this natural love is given us, not to be crushed or torn out by the roots, but sublimated in the service of divine charity. It must be turned to a higher purpose than the gratification of our own hearts; it must be offered to Christ, that He may use it as the instrument and means of *His* love for the ones we love.

"When the heart gives itself to God," Thérèse wrote, "it does not lose its natural tenderness: on the contrary, this tenderness increases, becoming more and more pure, more and more divine."

But for this, the sacrifice of our own natural desires and satisfactions is absolutely necessary if they stand between us and God. Perhaps that was why Thérèse had never been asked to leave France and go to Indo-China; her love was selfless enough already. Instead of hindering her union to God, the presence of her own sisters only helped it to increase in purity and perfection.

There was another thing, another most important consequence of the tender, sensitive, and affectionate temperament shared by these two souls. Perhaps Mother Berchmans had never realized the fact until now, but she could well say, with St. Thérèse:

"My nature is such that fear only *drives me back*; but with love, I not only advance, I fly."

If we examine this sentence of the Little Flower, we will find in it the psychological basis of her little way—the natural reason for its necessity, in certain souls. The Little Way of abandonment and trust may be regarded, from the psychological point of view, as a supernatural device for facilitating action, for setting souls free to do the work that God desires of them. For God does not want pure passivity in souls. Love must act. "*Probatio amoris*," said St. Gregory, "*exhibitio est operis*—Prove your love by showing forth your works." And our Lord Himself said: "My meat is to *do the will* of Him that sent me that I may *perfect His work*" (John 4:34). And also: "I must *work the works* of Him that sent me, whilst it is day: the night cometh, when no man can work" (John 9:4).

The very words of St. Thérèse, "...fear drives me back...love makes me *advance*, makes *me fly*...," show that the saint's only concern is with hastening toward divine union, the possession of her Beloved, and with avoiding all that impedes her progress toward that goal. But, with the penetrating eye of spiritual genius which comes to God's saints in the Holy Spirit's gift of Counsel, St. Thérèse had seen that the most dangerous, the most universal, and often the most hidden obstacle to our progress in sanctity is the fact that we rely upon our own powers and place our trust in our own miserable efforts which, without the assistance of grace, are absolutely incapable of any good in the supernatural order. She had seen, as St. Bernard saw before her, that those who live too much on the natural plane are inevitably doomed to fear, because their lives are so largely taken up with changing and transient and unsubstantial things which must betray them at last. The only way to be delivered from this fear, which paralyzes action and cripples love and makes perfect charity impossible, is to remove our trust from creatures, and from our own feeble powers, and place it entirely in God who alone can never fail us, because He alone is infinitely powerful and loves us with an infinite love.

But, on the other hand, God resists the pride which trusts only in the feeble judgment and efforts of men, for the simple reason that this pride, by its very nature, resists Him, and implies a categorical refusal of His grace. "He that is good shall draw grace from the Lord: but *he that trusteth in his own devices doth wickedly*" (Prov. 12:2). Christ said to the pious Pharisees, who trusted so much in their own fasts and observance of the law, their own wisdom, and their own great sanctity: "You are they *who justify yourselves* before men, but God knoweth your hearts, for *that which is high to men is an abomination before God*" (Luke 16:15).

St. Thérèse's reply to pharisaism and pelagianism is the perfect humility which Christ came on earth to teach. Writing to her sister, Celine (Letter 4 to Celine), she says: "If you are willing to bear peacefully the trial of not being pleased with yourself, you will give a sweet refuge to our Divine Master. *Si tu veux supporter en paix l'épreuve de ne pas te plaire à toi même, tu donneras au divin Maître un doux asile.*"

At one glance, the Little Flower had seen through all the worries, all the miseries, all the anxieties, all the restlessness, all the anguish that turn the life of some religious people into a hell on earth. It all comes from the futile struggle of their pride which refuses to accept the fact of their own helplessness, their own incapacity for supernatural good without the grace of God. They want to do things their own way. They will not accept situations as God plans them. Consequently they do not get the graces God planned to give them, if they had cooperated with Him. Consequently they fall into faults and sins, and then they are plunged into utter dejection. And if their pride persists, they will fall further and further until finally they become hardened in some utterly stubborn incorrigibility which makes them a penance to all their neighbors and a still greater penance to themselves. If the process is allowed to go to its ultimate limit, they will become perfect pharisees.

Thérèse of Lisieux, with the wisdom that is granted only to the little ones, refused the greatness and self-sufficiency which are an abomination in the sight of God, and exclaimed: "*Quel bonheur de porter nos croix faiblement!*—What joy to carry our Crosses in weakness!" And she continues: "We would like to suffer with generosity, in the grand manner; we would like to go without ever a fall! What an illusion!...But I, little grain of sand that I am, I want to go to work [note that, she wants to *work*] without courage, without strength, and this very powerlessness will make the task easier for me, because I want to work for love." This very powerlessness will make the task easier, the burden lighter! What kind of a strange paradox have we here? How can weakness make our burdens easier to carry? How can helplessness make our work less difficult, or utter incapacity bring us more swiftly to our desired end?

The solution of this paradox is that there is no paradox at all. The realization of our weakness, helplessness, misery, incapacity, delivers us from the illusion of our own wisdom and sanctity; and if this realization is born of grace, as is supposed by the saint, then at the same moment that we learn the truth about ourselves, we will also see the truth of God's almighty love, presented to us in the obscure light of faith. Then trust and absolute, uncompromising love will teach us to turn spontaneously to Him, expecting everything from His mercy, and He will do the work. Then we will be able to say, with St. Paul: "I have learned in whatsoever state I am, to be content therewith. I know both how to be brought low, and I know how to abound...both to be full and to be hungry, both to abound and suffer need, *I can do all things in Him who strengtheneth me*" (Phil. 4:11–13).

Echoing the Mother of God, Thérèse of Lisieux could exclaim: "He that is mighty hath done great things in me, and the greatest of them is to have shown me my littleness, my powerlessness for all good." Her whole joy, she said, was to see herself as she was in the eyes of God, "*un pauvre petit néant et rien de plus!*" Nothing but a little nonentity.

For those who cannot understand such things, it must be explained that the tremendous reality of this joy springs from a sense of liberation. The soul that discovers the way of spiritual childhood is happy in a way that it had never before imagined possible, because, by discovering its own nothingness, it is at last liberated from the prison of futile introversion and fruitless self-consideration, and can devote itself altogether to the one thing necessary: the knowledge and love of the great, immensely good God. And how happy an occupation that becomes, when the very contrast between our insignificance and His immensity tells us, better than anything else could tell us, the infinite marvel of His love for us.

Father Robert Lepasquier speaks of the Little Way of Spiritual Childhood as a "second vocation" and as a "vocation within a vocation." That was certainly what it proved to be for Mother Berchmans. Entering upon the Little Way was, for her, the beginning of a new and more perfect life within the religious state. Now at last she had found out how to give herself entirely to God, and thus fulfill the object of all her vows. Now at last she had entered upon the way of simplicity which must necessarily be the way of every true contemplative, and which is most characteristic of the Order of Citeaux. Her life had finally reduced itself to one single-minded preoccupation: the love of God. And it was St. Thérèse of Lisieux who had shown her how this could be done.

And Mother Berchmans really followed the Little Way. She really understood it and practiced it—which is more than can be said for some of the people who imagine that they are disciples of the Little Flower. For her, Spiritual Childhood meant something more than mere spiritual baby talk. It was not just a matter of acting cute, and developing a lot of coy and sugary expressions and mannerisms to decorate the outer surface of the same old sham—the egocentric piety of the pharisee.

The one true test is the love of one's own nothingness; and that love is proved by interior peace in times of stress and failure and trial.

Now at last Mother Berchmans had discovered that her weaknesses, her stubborn imperfections, the faults that seemed so great in her own eyes, and which had caused her pain for so long—all these things now appeared to her for what they were: fuel to cast upon the fire of God's merciful love that the flames might altogether consume them.

"The more rotten the wood is," she used to say, "the quicker it will burn!"

What did it matter if she was still so attached to creatures, still proud or distracted in choir, still tempted to impatience, or still feeling movements of rebellion against the unforeseen inconveniences of the poor little foundation in Japan? God's mercy was infinite; He needed only to be asked, and He would do away with all these failings in His own good time and in His own wise way. Far from causing her discouragement, they would in the future be nothing but motives for hope and for greater trust in the mercy of God. Should her failures, her little falls, her movements of imperfection cause her to draw back from God, and renounce her aspirations to high sanctity? Not in the least. Sanctity was a gift of God, and all she needed was to ask for it patiently, pick herself up with confident and patient contrition after every one of her falls, and trust lovingly in the good God to raise her to Himself by the power of His love. She did not have to give up the fight just because she happened to be weak; on the contrary, her very weakness was now her guarantee that God would not fail to help her every time she asked Him. To believe otherwise would be a blasphemy against His infinite love.

So she could write: "I, too, would like to die of love (like St. Thérèse), but is that not too high for me? I am so proud, so full of miseries! And yet it seems to me, the more rotten the wood is, the quicker it will burn. No doubt in my case the path of love will be steeper. I am far from being an angel—but what do I care? I must die of love anyway....

"In contact with the Little Flower, my soul regains strength and courage. Yes, her little way is just what she said it was: a way all of confidence and love. She draws one on without harshness, and we soon leap over all our miseries and pass on, seeing nothing but the infinite love of the Heart of the tenderest of Fathers."

Yes, she could continue with full confidence to ask for sanctity, and high sanctity at that. In another letter we read:

"So I too, little Sister Misery, I can have confidence. Jesus will work that miracle (of sanctity) for me too, but only when my exile is drawing to its end.... What a consoling thought. Do not be surprised, then, if I am in a hurry to die, in order to belong all to Jesus, sooner, and forever."

To Mother Lutgarde she wrote: "If you could walk into my soul and take a look around you would draw back in horror. But no matter. I pass over all my miseries and ask Jesus to let me love Him anyway. Oh, would that I could lay open my soul to you! You would find an abyss of miseries;[1] and yet it is this very abyss which I ask our dearest Jesus to fill up with His Love."

Far from feeling any restraint, Mother Berchmans removed all limits from her desire to love God. Henceforth, with St. Bernard, she would know that the measure of our love of God is to love Him without measure, and she could cry out with the same great Cistercian: "*Quanta in spiritu libertatis fiducia! Quid manifestius quam quod perfecta charitas foras mittit timorem!* What confidence is given to us in the spirit of liberty! And what is then more obvious than that perfect charity casteth out fear?" For here, the saint is speaking of that degree of love in which the soul "is so intoxicated with its love that it no longer stops to consider the majesty of God" (Serm. vii. *In Cant.* n. 3).

Mother Berchmans reminded her former abbess that Father Polycarpe had told her she was "called to love much." But she adds: "That is not enough for me. I want to answer that call, and throw myself into the furnace of love which is the Heart of Jesus.... Oh, I want to love Jesus so much here below; ask Him to let me participate in His immensity, in order that I may love Him all the more...." Only the immensity of God's own love, which is His own divine Nature, could satisfy her desire to love and adore this Jesus who had overwhelmed her poor heart with the secret of simplicity and joy!

"Pray for me," she continues, "pray for your little girl. Beg that she may love her Beloved Jesus, and love Him until she dies of love. I thirst, I thirst for love. Ask Jesus to give me a little of that divine fire which He so desired to cast upon the earth."

In proportion as her confident desire for sanctity and perfect love increased, there also grew in her heart a tremendous sense of solidarity with all the other "Little Souls" who were, she knew, giving themselves to God in obscure lives of sacrifice and love in all parts of the world. Who were these souls? They belonged to every walk of life. Some of them were poor people in the world, working girls, mothers of families, perhaps little children who had barely learned to lisp the name of Christ but who could already love Him. Many of them were priests; she felt more and more closely united, now, to priests. That is something that St. Thérèse seems to inspire in the hearts of her disciples—and perhaps that explains why she has been named patron saint of all the missions. Many of them were souls, like herself, living in convents, in orders of active, teaching, and nursing nuns, or orders of cloistered contemplatives. Most of all, she was conscious of an increased solidarity with the contemplative souls who were adoring Christ with their hidden sacrifice of prayer and penance in her own former convent of Laval. That community was now becoming one of the most fervent in the Cistercian Order. It was continuing to attract more and more chosen souls to its novitiate, and many of them had already consummated their sacrifice, being called early to heaven as the Little Flower herself had been. If anything was evident in all this, it was, once again, the all-pervading influence of Thérèse of Lisieux.

Only a few months before, a disciple of the Little Flower, a young religious whom Mother Berchmans had never even known, had died at Laval in the odor of sanctity. Born of one of the noblest families in France, Marie-Antoinette de la Tour d'Auvergne, after struggling to decide her vocation, gave up her desire to enter the Carmel of Lisieux when God's manifest will brought her to Laval. There, as Sister Mary of the Incarnation,[2] she became a novice who edified the whole house by her simplicity, humility, and obedience—in a word, by the perfection with which she followed the "Little Way." Now she had been called home to heaven, to the joys of perfect and untroubled and everlasting contemplation in the light of glory, in a way that filled poor Mother Berchmans with holy envy. But she consoled herself by a renewal of confidence and the thought that her own turn would come. Meanwhile, she rejoiced all the more in this fulfillment of Thérèse's prophecy that every victim of love would be a saint at the hour of death.

The conception of her own place in the Legion of Little Souls, that had risen up all over the earth at the bidding of the Carmelite saint of Lisieux, added a particular note to Mother Berchman's own vocation. She began to be filled with an intense desire to sacrifice herself, not only for the world at large, but in a special way for the other souls called to share the grace which had now transformed her own life. She wanted to offer up her whole self, her littleness, to God's merciful love, precisely in order to obtain for others the new-found confidence and love that she herself now enjoyed. It was her role, she believed, to deliver other people from temptations to discouragement with their faults, and bring them sweetly and gently into the Little Way.

Therefore she began to consider herself as the "standard-bearer" of the Legion of Little Souls. This concept had a very definite meaning in her mind, and she took it so seriously that she did not rest until it was more or less approved by a letter from one of

Thérèse's own living sisters, at the Carmel of Lisieux. Her notion was simple enough.

"The standard-bearer," she said, "although he does not fight, runs more of a risk than anybody else, because he is carrying the flag, and cannot defend himself. On the contrary he must let himself be cut to pieces rather than let it go."

In other words, of all the Legion of Little Souls, she was to be the littlest and the most helpless, the one most obliged to rely on Jesus in the most perfect and entire trust and abandonment; and in return for such faith on her part, her Beloved would pour out His grace upon souls in convents and monasteries everywhere to deliver them from discouragement, and from vain preoccupation with their own miseries, that they might swell the number of His great saints.

"Yes," she said, "I would raise up aloft the standard of love, in order to lift up downcast hearts and fire them with new courage."

Her desire did not go unheard. She was to suffer many an hour of darkness and spiritual aridity to win grace for these souls, as her subsequent letters testified.

A soul as enthusiastic as that of Mother Berchmans could not be content with the interior and essential devotion of her heart to the Little Flower. She had to express herself in many other ways. Indeed, her zeal and energy in propagating the doctrine of the Little Way and devotion to Thérèse went so far that her mother prioress finally said: "I think you are out of your head over this Little Thérèse of yours!"

Mother Berchmans did not consider this to be an insult. Perhaps, in a way, it was quite true. She paid little heed to the decrees of Urban VIII, and had no intention of waiting upon the pronouncements of Rome before she started putting the title "Saint" in front of Thérèse. And she had a nice new reliquary all dusted and ready in the sacristy to receive the first relic of the Little Flower. Indeed, she was greatly surprised and disappointed at not yet being able to obtain, on demand, a first-class relic of her beloved patroness.

In addition to the liturgical cycle of the Church, Mother Berchmans kept the whole cycle of Thérèse's personal feasts, from her birthday to her entrance into Carmel, her reception of the habit, profession, and so on, until her saintly death. We have already said that she knew the *Story of a Soul* practically by heart. When she became cellarer, she took advantage of her contact with the outside world to beg quantities of pictures and souvenirs of the Little Flower for her convent and for distribution among the missionaries and their flocks. Indeed, when it came to the Little Flower, Mother Berchmans almost found herself entering upon the active apostolate, and it would not be wrong to say that she had a real part to play in introducing devotion to St. Thérèse to the Catholics in Japan, though only indirectly, through the missionaries who came in contact with the nuns at Our Lady of the Angels.

Most important of all, however, when she became mistress of novices, she would be able to turn to great advantage all that she had learned from the Little Way. Now she not only had a solid and coherent doctrine, which she was able to teach others because she lived it herself: but she had a model to imitate. She need no longer be terrified by the task, by the tremendous responsibility of forming souls. She could say, as St. Thérèse had said when she was placed in charge of the Carmelite novices at Lisieux: "Now that I understand that it is impossible for me to do anything by myself, my task seems to be simplified. I occupy myself inwardly and exclusively with uniting myself more and more to God, knowing that all the rest will be added unto me."

Far from dispensing us from all activity, far from killing all our efforts at their very source, the Little Way is the supreme preparation for supernatural activity and the most efficacious way of making our efforts fruitful. Those who pretend to follow the Little Way without really putting it into practice do, indeed, turn it into a false gospel of inactivity and quietism. But in those who really grasp its meaning and give themselves to it with generosity, a change soon becomes evident. Stubborn imperfections begin gradually to yield under the mysterious and secret influence of grace, and they find themselves gifted with courage and strength to overcome themselves just when they seem to need it. Where all their multiple, pious practices, all their self-conscious and agitated strivings for perfection failed them before, they now need only to keep their eyes on their beloved Jesus, and they find themselves advancing in a way that even they themselves are at a loss to understand.

So it was that Mother Berchmans at last completely overcame that most stubborn of all her failings, her attachment to her old convent and to those beloved Sisters she had left behind, nearly eight years before.

In 1908, when she had so much to do and so many responsibilities, her very activity began to argue against her spending her precious time in writing letters that were not strictly in accordance with the Cistercian life, when she needed every moment she could get for prayer before the tabernacle.

Indeed, although perhaps she was reluctant to admit it to herself, all this letter writing was becoming a burden to her. It interfered with the one, deep, vital necessity of her life: the need for prayer, for intimate contact with the Source of all life and joy, with Christ, the Word of God, the uncreated Joy and Glory of the Father, and the Saviour of all souls, the Giver of life to all.

But then Jesus Himself began to speak, loud and clear, unmistakably within her soul. When she was making the stations of the cross, looking with the wide open eyes of faith and love at the sacrifice of God Himself, ever present in His eternity, for her: when she followed the bloody footsteps of Christ, step by step, up Calvary, knowing clearly that she, standing there at each station, was present to Him in the midst of His very sufferings, so many hundreds of years before, could she remain deaf to the voice that spoke within her own soul, urging her to unite her sacrifice with His, and, to console Him, to make her own sacrifice more perfect, more complete, more undivided?

Now, at last, Mother Berchmans realized clearly what was expected of her, and made that final sacrifice. A letter came from Mother Angela. She read it with joy. She commended Mother Angela to God in her prayers. But she did not answer the letter.

Presently another letter came from Mother Angela. Mother Berchmans read it with joy. She prayed for her dear Mother Angela.

But the letter went unanswered. It was the same with her other sisters at Laval.

In writing to Mother Lutgarde, however, she could not refrain from offering some explanation of her silence, and from including a little message of affection for Mother Angela and her other sisters; and this indeed was demanded by charity. Let us see what she said.

"How is my little Mother Mary Angela? Is she not, perhaps, angry with me? Here are two letters from her: they are unanswered, and must remain so. My Reverend Mother, I will tell you the reason, in confidence. For a long time I have desired to make the sacrifice of writing to no one except yourself. Every time I make the Stations of the Cross, I see Simon the Cyrenean helping Our dear Saviour to carry His cross of wood, and I cannot help thinking: What about the Cross of His Heart? Who will help Him to carry that? In the Garden of Olives, He was alone. And then I offer myself to my beloved Jesus to be His companion in His agony by accepting all the interior sufferings He may be pleased to send me.

"But it seems to me that what wounds His divine Heart most bitterly of all is the fact that He sees Himself so little loved. And I, knowing this, am I going to seek after the affection of creatures? Oh, I know well that the affection of my dear Mothers and Sisters is quite permissible and legitimate: but it is for that very reason that I want to be all the more generous in sacrificing it."

By way of a message, apologizing for not having written to another of her mothers at Laval, she wrote: "The closer I get to Jesus, the stronger does my affection for her become also. All that is human in it disappears, so that nothing is left but the soul, that divine breath, uttered from the very depths of the Heart of God."

NOTES

1. For those who do not know it, the term miseries (*misères*) has a certain accepted meaning which has become familiar in French ascetical writings of modern times. It is a kind of a generic term for all imperfections and semi-deliberate venial sins, all the faults which are more or less

unavoidable, and which constantly recur even in the lives of those devoted to the pursuit of perfection, to remind them that they, like everybody else, are still saddled with the defects of a fallen nature. We ought to be sorry for these faults, but we can never hope to be absolutely free of every one of them.

2. Since that time, the usages of the order have forbidden double names. Each religious takes the name of a saint and prefixes the name of "Mary" to it, in honor of our Lady.

CHAPTER XII

THE CHILD OF MARY

If we have seemed to imply that, since her new stability, Mother Berchmans' interior trials had all ceased, it is now time to correct that impression. Ever since that first fall day at Laval when Father Polycarpe had told her to volunteer to go and help the little new foundation in Japan, her life had been one constant trial of faith. True, the trial had varied in intensity, but it never ceased. Nor was it to cease until her beautiful soul, purified by still greater physical and moral sufferings, at last flew from her body into the vision of God's perfection face to face.

Indeed, we shall see that every moment she spent in exhausting and distracting labors for the material maintenance of her community demanded a more perfect exercise of faith. And when she was most occupied with her various responsibilities and employments, she scarcely had leisure for those deeper, more intimate, and more terrifying trials that scour out the depth of the spirit with what St. John of the Cross compares to "strong lye." After all, a soul weighed down with many material occupations can but rarely enter into the depths in which such purifications are felt in all their terrifying force, and though the trials may be going on in the depths, and be felt with great severity by the soul, nevertheless its responsibilities would seem to absorb some of the shock. At least, we offer this as a possible explanation for the fact that Mother Berchmans, although the passive purifications of her soul continued and increased during these years, nevertheless very seldom expressed herself in terms like those of the passage which we shall presently quote.

In other words, the purification of her soul, by which she advanced step by step more deeply into the darkness of perfect faith, took a firmer and firmer hold on her as days went by, but that hold increased not in great and sudden crises of suffering, but rather in a subtle and habitual growth.

She was able to say: "I have never had any consolations in Japan. I have lived purely on naked faith." By consolations, she meant any extraordinary sensible consolations, as Father Robert points out. For it is very evident from the study of her life and of the growth of her spirituality in Japan that her soul acquired a deeper and more joyful peace that grew in proportion to the completeness of her sacrifice. But that is what she is referring to as "naked faith." Later, as we shall see, there were one or two rare occasions when she did receive favors strong and notable enough to be called "consolations" in the sense in which she here uses the word. But they were very rare.

However, once at least the loving Providence of God drew the veil of a more complete and terrifying darkness over her soul, leaving her in such desolation that she sought some relief by trying to express it on paper. Was this the only time? Oh no, surely not! For in these years she scarcely had leisure to keep a complete spiritual journal or any other record of her inner life. We can be grateful that the Holy Spirit prompted her to write down this one account of what she felt in such times, and assume that this was not the only occasion when she saw the abyss yawning before her feet. Father Robert, however, authorizes us to say that such intensity of tribulation was relatively rare with her.

At any rate, she writes: "In the agony which holds me in its crushing grip, I try to lift my eyes to heaven, to get courage, and the sky is made of brass, for me. And then I question hell, which seems to be destined for me as my portion, and hell answers: 'Do I really exist? Heaven and hell, these are only words. After this life, comes nothingness....' On the verge of despair, I utter the sweet Name of

Jesus, from which flows balm for the consolation of every wounded heart. I try to grasp His Cross, but alas, I fall back into the void! It is night, the frightful night of Golgotha, and the shadows of death close in on me from every side."

These words were written, in 1907, when she still had more opportunity to enter into herself than would be allowed her at any other time for the rest of her life. And perhaps because she would stand so much in need of pure faith, in the busy years that were to come, her wise Lord took advantage of this occasion to withdraw every ray of light from her soul and leave her to taste, for a very little while, the intense anguish of this most complete darkness. Indeed, it seems from this and other evidence concerning this year, the one following her new stability, and the one in which she discovered St. Thérèse's Little Way, that God chose 1907 to lay a strong and deep foundation for the final soaring edifice of her sanctification.

The weightiest reason for such a surmise is the fact that in this year she made a special and more solemn consecration of herself to our Lady than she ever had before. And we know that the influence of Mary was all important in the spiritual life of Mother Berchmans, an influence surpassed only by that of the Sacred Heart. The fact that the Spirit of God drew her by His inspirations closer to the Queen of Heaven than she had ever been before is of great significance. It was as if this consecration were to bring her in closer union with that living and powerful Mother and Mediatrix of every grace, in order that Mary might win for her all faith and fortitude.

This new consecration to the Mother of God had already been adumbrated by another during her first years at Our Lady of the Angels, during the years of trial. The document from her hand that records and preserves her first offering of herself to our Lady as her slave is simply a sketch of the later and more complete dedication that was to crown the years of her spiritual maturity.

The earlier gift of herself was made without the full light and comprehension that marks the later consecration. She seems as yet unable to express what she wants to say, or to formulate her offering. It is not that she does not understand how much it is that she means to give; she knows well that she desires to give everything, without reserve. But as yet she does not seem to grasp the deepest possible motives that such a gift might have.

In making this offering of herself as a slave of Mary, in 1903 (it was the feast of the Annunciation, just twenty-three years after she had been confided to the Sisters of St. Vincent de Paul at the Convent of the Redemption), she wrote: "Good Mother, bless your daughter who now becomes your slave, and who is never, henceforth, to *act except by you*"—and this expresses an exalted and perfect ideal of union with Mary and abandonment to her powerful and loving mediation. But her offering seems to lose itself in a more or less external sign or pledge of her fidelity, which, for all its beautiful simplicity and its sincere and childlike faith, still expresses her comparative helplessness, in 1903, to see her way clear to the direct and straight path of sanctity that she was later to travel. She wrote: "As a sign of my slavery, I desire, O my gentle Mother, to wear about my neck (in so far as obedience may allow me to do so) a cord with seven knots in honor of your seven sorrows, and to do so until my death." And she adds, later on in the same formula of donation: "If, at any time, I make any further attempt to do my own will, good Mother, please give a good hard pull on this cord to remind me of my promise; and especially at the hour of my death, pull me so strongly to yourself that nothing may keep me afar from Jesus and from you." Thus the donation spends itself in this lovely, simple piece of faithful fancy.

Came the year 1907. She had traveled far. She had emerged from the confusion of her many trials. She had learned not to fear her human weakness or be disconcerted by temptation. She had become strong in faith and hope and love. She had become spiritually mature by becoming a spiritual child. She was much more closely united to Jesus, in the power of His Holy Spirit and of His gifts. In 1907, she found herself, as we have seen, under the fire of trial and tribulation as she had been in 1903—and indeed in all her years in Japan.

Perhaps this new consecration of herself took place about the same time as the temptation against faith we have just recorded. There is every reason to believe that it sprang forth from a soul that was being crushed in the wine press of strong trials. We do not know the date of the note in her journal about the temptation against faith: except that it was some time in 1907. The consecration of herself to the Mother of God was made on the feast of our Lady's Assumption in that year, and there is every reason to believe that the two events came close to coinciding. The strongest motive for this belief is that the formula is written out in Mother Berchmans' own blood.

Now, no normal person writes out documents and oblations in his own blood, unless he is impelled by some very strong force of conviction or emotion; and generally such a move is resorted to by a soul violently beset with trials, particularly temptations against faith or purity. We recall how St. Benedict killed the temptations of the flesh within him at Subiaco by hurling himself, naked, into a thicket of thorns, brambles, and nettles; and in our own day Dom Chautard, while still a university student, wrote the word "Credo" in his own blood to overcome a temptation against faith.

However, as a warning to those who might be inclined to place too much trust in such pledges of fidelity as these, which are all, in the end, more or less external, we might add that Dom Chautard, after becoming a Trappist novice at Aiguebelle, had another temptation against faith. It was a strong temptation, too. So he resorted to the same means. He made a wound in his flesh and wrote "Credo," once again in his own blood. Unfortunately, when he had finished doing so, the temptation against faith was just as violent as it had been before he started, and it not only continued so, but increased. So then he went and made everything known to his abbot, which is what he should have done in the first place.

In any case, it requires no little courage to do such a thing, and what astonishes us the most about Mother Berchmans' intense desire to prove her love for Mary is the length of the consecration written in her blood. It is not just the word "Credo." The document is nearly six hundred words long and takes up two pages of Father Robert's manuscript.

It is not merely the fact that it is written in her blood that stirs us. Of all the writings left us by Mother Berchmans, there are few pages comparable to this. Nowhere does she display a more complete sincerity and simplicity, a greater perfection of faith, a more burning intensity of love, a more profound depth of true humility. And if we were to select any one from among her papers, and present it to the reader as most characteristic of Mother Berchmans, and as the best and truest expression of her saintly soul, surely this is the one.

Here, more than ever, we see what a strong, clean flame of love it was that burned in the pure heart of this Trappistine nun, this humble, heroic, devoted little Sister who had ceased to take any account of her own generosity, and counted even the purest flights of fervor and consolation as nothing, relying entirely on the love of her heavenly Mother, trusting in her as the guide and protectress and teacher whom Jesus had given her to be her very life itself. Indeed, we see here her conception of abandonment soaring beyond all human limits into the sheer perfection of a supernatural faith that desires to live in and by Mary the way Christ lived in her when He was being formed of her pure flesh within her immaculate womb. And, once again, remember it is written in her blood.

"Oh Mary" it begins, "Oh my dearest Mother, on this glorious day of your Assumption into heaven, where I would so like to follow you, I feel the need to consecrate myself to you in a still more intimate, still more irrevocable manner, if I possibly can, than I have ever done before.

"And for that purpose, O my dearly beloved Mother, I renew all the consecrations and offerings I have been able to make to you until this day.

"I give myself over totally to you, in order that I may no longer live except by your life, just like a little child living within its mother's womb. I abandon to you my heart, my body, my senses, my mind, my reason, my memory, my understanding, my will, that poor will, always so rebellious! with my whole being, and all my past, present, future, and eternity in order that you may use them all as you see fit for the greater glory of the Sacred Heart of your divine Son.

"I consecrate also, and above all else, yes, above all, to you, my dearest Mother, that little spark of divine love which Jesus placed in my heart on the day of my Baptism, and which lies buried under the ashes of my pride. Take care of it, sweet Mother. Make it grow. Stir up this fire into a mighty blaze that will quickly burn me up and cause me to die, as you died, of love, for I desire no other death but yours, dearest Mother! Grant me, then, that I may love Jesus utterly, completely. Make me hungry for love. Make me never think of anything except love. Let me live only for love. Make all my works bear the stamp of divine love, and make my whole life be nothing but a prolonged act of love. Oh yes, sweet Mother, I want to be a victim of my Jesus' love because I am the child of the love of His Immaculate Mother.

"I want to be a victim of love because I am too weak to be a victim of reparation, and because suffering, although I desire it with all my heart, fills me with fear. I am so bereft of virtues! Let heroic souls take the Cross: my portion is to love.

"And now, oh my dearly beloved Mother, let me tell you once again all my love for you. Oh, yes, Mary, I love you because on the day of my Baptism you became my Mother and my Patroness and because your sweet name protected me in the cradle, rejoiced my childhood years, and drew my heart to God.

"Yes I love you, Mary, because you have protected and sustained me in dangers and temptations, consoled me in trials, strengthened me in weakness, and everywhere, and in all things, you have proved yourself to be my Mother. Oh yes, gentle Mother, I love you because you are and always will be the tenderest, sweetest, most loving, most devoted, and most motherly of all mothers, and through You and with You I want to love my Jesus. I want to love Him with the love with which You yourself love Him, I want to love Him with your Heart during my exile here below and in Heaven for all eternity.

"Sr. Mary Berchmans, Spouse of the Sacred Heart,
and Child of love of Mary Immaculate."

There are few more moving and more inspired prayers in the annals of our modern saints than this fervent outpouring of love from the heart of this exiled Trappistine, and there are many who have been raised to the honors of the altar, who have not been able to express so total and uncompromising a humility as that of this little Sister, who wanted to be "a victim of love because I am too weak to be a victim of reparation!" "Suffering," she said, at about the thirty-fifth line of a document written in her own blood, "fills me with fear." She did not see the holy irony of the situation precisely because what she wrote was so true, and because she knew that her very fear and weakness guaranteed her all the strength of Christ Himself, merited for her at Gethsemani and on the cross, if she would only ask Him for them.

When she said, "Let heroic souls take the Cross, my portion is to love," she was not trying to renounce the inescapable obligation of all who want to enter heaven: to suffer. On the contrary, she was offering herself as a victim of any suffering Christ cared to send her, but in the way most pleasing to Him. Knowing she had no strength to offer Him, she was offering Him her weakness and helplessness that He might transfigure them with His grace and suffer, Himself, in her, for His Father's glory. And in this way she fulfilled the fundamental prerequisite of all striving after sanctity: that humility which, as St. Bernard says, is the only thing that can ever make us able to die as martyrs for Christ.[1]

But Mother Berchmans knew well that the shortest way to Christ is through Mary.[2] If Christ was to suffer in her, by His grace, and Mary was Mediatrix of all graces, and the Co- Redeemer of the human race with her divine Son, doing all that she saw Him doing just as He did all that He saw the Father doing, then if she was to suffer and die as a martyr of love, Mary would have to suffer and die in her.

Father Robert's manuscript gives us ample material, from Mother Berchmans' own hand, concerning her distinctive and characteristic doctrine of a life of union with Mary, which gave the keynote to her whole interior life. In all her actions, everything she did during the day, she strove faithfully to preserve in her mind the habitual intention of asking Mary to do what was to be done in and for her. To pray in her, to work in her, to suffer in her, to speak in her when she had to speak, and, within her, to love Jesus all the day long. Her life of prayer was to be a life of recollection in which all her faculties were handed over to Mary to be kept immaculate by her, and preserved from everything that was not Jesus, or His will.

Everything that came to her, in the course of her day, whether bitter or sweet, easy or difficult, came to her as a means of grace, from the loving maternal heart of the Mediatrix of all grace. There was no consolation and no temptation, nothing great or small, important or seemingly trivial, in her day that was not a means of union with Jesus in His loving will, a means presented to her, together with the necessary grace to use it, by the hand of her loving and watchful Mother who was always at her side. She copied the following words and kept them for constant meditation:

"I shall receive nothing that comes to me from heaven or from earth, without realizing that it comes to me from the hands of Mary. I shall offer nothing, either to God or to creatures, without first placing it in the hands of my loving Mother."

As the planets revolve around the sun, so her life was one of constant gravitation about the Queen of heaven, *Maris Stella*, the star that was the center of her love and of her life.

"Oh Marie! Vous etes l'astre bien aimé autour duquel je décris le cercle de ma vie!"

In the little locket next to her heart which we have already mentioned as containing another small document, she also kept a paper on which she had written and underlined the actual triumphant words in which Pope Pius IX had defined and proclaimed the glorious dogma of the Immaculate Conception of the Mother of God. It is said that when the holy pontiff pronounced these words, he received a supernatural intuition of Mary's purity that was so clear and powerful and intense that it almost separated his soul from his body, and if he had not been sustained by a special grace from God, it would have cost him his life. These words rested day and night over the pure and humble heart of this silent nun.

NOTES

1. Sermon xlvii on the *Canticle of Canticles*.
2. Fr. Faber.

CHAPTER XIII

AT THE GATE

It was a good thing that Mother Berchmans had received so full and complete a preparation in the spiritual life, for now she was really going to need it. Ever since she had come to Japan, she had been a busy and useful member of the little community, but the time had come for her to occupy positions in it that were vitally important—what is more, she would have to occupy several of them at the same time.

For the past four years or so she had been sacristan, and had also sometimes helped Mother Leonie with her novices in the quality of submistress, but there had not been much work for her to do. There was still no organized novitiate, as we have seen. The postulants followed the rest of the nuns around and did what they could in the community. It had been just enough to thoroughly frighten poor Mother Berchmans at the difficulty of the task that would so evidently one day be hers.

Sometime before she made her new stability, Mother Berchmans had acquired another employment, in addition to that of sacristan and submistress. It was not one for which she was especially well fitted by nature, it was appropriate to her state of health and allowed one of the stronger nuns to devote herself to harder work around the house. This office was that of treasurer and secretary for the dairy.

Cistercian monasteries and convents are rather well known for the cheese they make, and what monks refer to rather disdainfully as "white cheese" is mentioned by gourmets with a certain amount of reverence as "Port-du-Salut." Trappist cheese goes, in the world, by the name of the monastery whose abbot had been Father Immediate of Laval, and had also been indirectly responsible for Mother Berchmans' exile to Japan.

The nuns at Our Lady of the Angels had imported this simple skill with them, when they came to Japan, and as usual had built up a small reputation for their cheese in circles both European and Japanese. Indeed, when the first World War broke out, at the time when Japan was still neutral, some officers from a German warship that was lying off Hakodate came ashore and visited the convent just to get some of the famous cheese. Mother Berchmans had the pleasure of waiting on them—which gave her a chance to choke her patriotism under a rather chilly display of politeness.

From 1905 or 1906 on, Mother Berchmans was in charge of the shipping of cheese from the convent. This meant a certain amount of manual labor, carrying the cheeses up from the cellar to the "turn" that communicated with the shop of the Brother carpenter outside the enclosure. Brother carpenter then boxed the cheeses for shipping. Mother Berchmans also kept all the accounts of sales and gifts of cheese, and carried on the necessary correspondence with customers and friends of the house in connection with these sales. She was not exactly a business woman. From the rather supercilious attitude taken by her spiritual director toward her lack of practicality, we may judge that she had a poor head for accounts. But anyway, she would write a nice letter on occasion, and she generally managed to alleviate the commercial jargon with a word or two to move souls to the love of something higher than mere cheese.

This work was not altogether easy on her health. Going back and forth from the cellar to Brother carpenter's turn she was exposed to icy draughts, but that did not worry her in the least, any more than the strain of carrying armfuls of large cheeses. In fact, one day she was proclaimed in the chapter of faults for carrying "too many" cheeses in the course of her official duties as sales manager of the dairy department. One wonders if the charitable nun who proclaimed her was worrying more about possible damage to the cheeses than to Mother Berchmans: the answer is that she was probably about equally concerned for both.

Remember that at the same time she had to do all the washing and ironing of altar linens in the sacristy. She had to make candles and vigil lights. She had to bake all the altar breads. She had to mend the vestments, sweep and dust the church, decorate the altar, and attend to countless other little duties besides.

As if all this were not enough, when the feast of the Purification came around, in the year 1908, bringing with it the annual changes of employments, Mother Berchmans was not only not relieved of these offices, but she received two more of the heaviest burdens in the convent upon her poor weak shoulders. We say two, as a matter of fact they amounted to three. She became portress, which meant that she was also guest mistress, and at the same time she became interior cellarer.

Feast of the Purification indeed! The Cistercian nuns seem to be practicing a form of mild liturgical irony when they make all their annual changes in the community on that day.

So in February, 1908, Mother Berchmans found herself holding the positions of sacristan, sales manager of the cheese department, portress, guest mistress, and cellarer: all this on top of a constitution that was clearly pretubercular and the temperament of a pure contemplative who had entered the convent just to be all alone with God and to forget all about the noise and distractions of the world and of base material things.

Her new position at the gate promised to be a very lively one. In the old days she had lamented the occasional loss of a free interval, but now she could not even settle down to the work of God itself—the divine office—without having to beat a hasty retreat from the choir to answer the bell at the front gate. If the work of God was interrupted, much more so the work of man. She would settle down to her ironing in the sacristy, or to her cheese accounts, or to the much more complicated business of cellarer, and then the bell would start ringing again. Things were even more amusing when at precisely the same moment bells would be heard from two opposite directions, one at the front gate and the other at the "turn" in the sacristy. She would pause in a moment of anguish, make a hasty decision and start off toward the one that appeared, under the circumstances, to be the more urgent.

Perhaps no office she ever held at Our Lady of the Angels cost Mother Berchmans more sacrifices than this one of portress. She did not by any means fall into it just naturally. Let us hear what she has to say on the subject:

"The first day, when I had to leave the choir to answer the bell at the gate, I could feel my temper getting hotter and hotter. I was almost ready to tear down that bell. But today I had to run out of choir again, and it didn't cost me so much. As soon as I hear the bell I lift up my heart to Jesus, and for His sake I keep cool and even manage to smile. I hope I won't leave this job until I have arrived at holy indifference and real detachment from self. I dare say it will take time."

Of course we must remember that all this running back and forth was not easy for her in her condition of bodily weakness which sometimes amounted to exhaustion.

Then there was an added difficulty, the obvious one: when she actually did get to the gate and opened up the wicket, her troubles had only just begun. Nine times out of ten she found herself peering through the bars at some polite Japanese countenance from whose lips there instantly began to proceed a succession of strange and unfamiliar sounds which she had to try and interpret.

"Your position at the gate will be an excellent one," Father Robert had said complacently. "It will enable you to practice your Japanese."

If anything, it enabled her to discover just how much Japanese she still needed to know.

She had entered the convent to become a silent Trappistine. Now for six years she had had offices which involved the necessity of speaking more or less, either with those who came to help her, or with those who communicated with her through the sacristy "turn." But if it was bad enough to have to talk French, it was even worse to flounder around in the difficulties of this language which she was sometimes tempted to regard as beyond her capacity to learn.

However, she had gained such control over her feelings, and was able to do all that her office required of her with such simplicity and love of God that she literally charmed everyone who came to the gate. Mother Berchmans was always so pleasant, so polite, so obliging! She never realized what an effect the mere contact with her often had upon visitors to the monastery.

Some of the Japanese peddlers who came to the gate soon learned to appreciate her simplicity in a far different kind of way. In other words, they were not long in detecting her complete innocence in commercial affairs. Since she was at the same time portress and cellarer, she often had occasion to act in both capacities at once, and buy things that were needed in the convent—or rather things that she thought were needed. She gives an account of one of these business deals of hers.

"One day," she writes, " I thought I was getting a wonderful bargain. I bought some fish. They were dead, all right: and yet, if you know what I mean, they were alive. They were almost ready to get up and walk away of their own accord. The smell ought to have given me some idea, but I put all my trust in the sales-talk. I took them in to Reverend Mother and just told her what he had told me. 'It's salted fish,' I said.

"Before the salesman left I had invited him to call back again every week, but he wasn't as big a fool as I was. He took good care not to show up again...."

Her star performance as guest mistress was on the day that Mother Scholastica was entertaining a visiting religious superior at dinner with Father Robert in the secular quarters. They had asked for some white wine to be served, and she hastened down to the cellar to find some. She discovered a bottle that looked like white wine and returned to pass it unopened to the Brother who was waiting on table. She waited, expectantly, inside the "turn" to hear how everything went off, and the first sound that reached her ears after the popping of the cork was the voice of Father Robert.

"Vinegar!" cried the indignant priest, "she's served up a bottle of vinegar!

During the interval in the afternoon when all the Sisters went out to take their walk in the garden, Mother Berchmans could no longer go out along the ridge, under the pine and cedar trees, and pick flowers or say her rosary gazing at the bright sea or the blue-green mountains or the city spread out below them in the distance. She had to take the air within reach of the gate. And not only that, but she used to take advantage of this time to carry on some of the extra work required in the sacristy. She walked up and down along the front of the wooden convent, or around and around the long two-story building, making wicks for candles. To do this she had to braid three threads together. So she would be seen walking up and down, holding the ends of the threads between her teeth, and stretching her arms out in front of her to keep the strands taut, while she braided them together with her fingers. It was not the most comfortable or pleasant way of taking a walk, and it must have given her many a stiff neck or an ache in the shoulders — not to mention the strain of looking cross eyed at three threads in front of her nose.

Yet not all her duties as gatekeeper cost her a sacrifice. Indeed, it was her joy and privilege, in 1908, to throw open the gate of Our Lady of the Angels to welcome another contingent of volunteers from convents in France, mostly from Ubexy. Perhaps she still felt much of the old weakness and helplessness within herself, but the progress she had made since her own arrival, six years before, was evident from the effect she had on the newcomers.

One of them, Mother Gertrude, who was later to become prioress of the convent and who wrote Mother Berchmans' biography in Japanese, recalls her first impressions of her saintly sister.

"I have heard tell that our good Mother Berchmans was not always as perfect as she was in the last years of her life, but that she made great progress after her stability, and climbed gradually to the heights which she reached at the end. I cannot vouch for this, for, since I arrived in 1908, I saw our dear little mother just as she was in the last years of her life: the same extraordinary piety, the same charity toward all her sisters, the same energy in the service of the house, the same obedience, the same spirit of sacrifice and mortification and all the rest. It is this continuity, this habit of doing everything so perfectly and fervently, without ever taking anything back and without letting up for a moment, that makes me certain that Mother Berchmans was a saint, that she was heroic from the very beginning and all along the line. Never did she let the fire of divine love in her go out or even die down—that fire that devoured her far more than her sickness did: she kept feeding it with continual sacrifices and by all her ordinary actions, enhanced as they were by such a supernatural spirit and such holy intentions.

"When I first came to Japan I felt such a veneration for her that I considered myself very happy and did not know how to thank the good God for the favor He had bestowed upon me in calling me to live side by side with a saint. Sometimes I used to make the following little prayer, in that connection: 'My God, I congratulate You on having a Berchmans like her, but I am sorry that You have to have a Gertrude like me.'"

Going on to speak of Mother Berchmans' services to the community, the same good Mother Gertrude writes:

"She was a first class worker. Her superior intelligence, her talents, and above all her admirable devotion to her community fitted her for every kind of a position...and I was stupefied to see that one in such poor health could turn out such a tremendous quota of hard work, doing everything perfectly, without ever neglecting in any detail her spiritual duties and the demands of the Rule."

Perhaps Mother Berchmans' biggest responsibility and her most complicated office at this time was that of cellarer. It was fortunate indeed for her that she was only interior cellarer, and not in charge of all the work on the farm as well. She certainly had enough to do as it was.

As interior cellarer it was her business to feed and clothe the whole community, and to see to it that all the other employments around the house were provided with the necessary materials and implements. In other words she was general housekeeper and *econome* of Our Lady of the Angels. And that was a big enough job, all by itself, for any one individual.

It demanded even more tact than the office of portress. After all, it is relatively easy to dismiss a stranger with a few non-committal words through the grating of the wicket; but when you have to deal with the most intimate necessities of your own companions in religion you need plenty of charity and tact and an indefatigable patience. Mere urbanity, worldly politeness, and diplomacy will not suffice. When people live together at such close quarters as do religious in a Cistercian monastery, only a real patience and a genuinely charitable desire to understand the needs of others and to make every possible concession for their shortsightedness can enable a cellarer to handle everybody with the unfailing kindness and gentleness that his position requires.

Even though Mother Berchmans did not possess a doctorate in economics and scarcely knew the first thing about purchasing supplies for a community of nuns, she made an excellent cellarer because she was obedient and had a heart that was humble and filled with a patient understanding of the needs of others. In the first place, she saw nothing in this uncongenial employment but the will of God. Since perfection consisted in perfect union with the will of God, and since that was why she had come to the convent, it was obvious that all she had to do was to try her best to be a good cellarer. That was her way to sanctity.

"All these employments," she wrote to Mother Lutgarde, "frighten me a little. With all the distractions they bring, the interior life looks very hard to me. And so I recommend myself to your good prayers, so that if I do happen to lose anything along that line, I may make up for it with an increase of devotion to my job and a greater renunciation of myself and all my own tastes."

As cellarer she had much to do with the lay-sisters. One of her most important tasks was to preside at the distribution of the following day's work, just before compline in the evening. Relying on the subcellarer in all that regarded the work on the farm, she assigned the tasks in the light of charity rather than material expediency, always taking care to lay burdens only upon shoulders that could or would bear them. All the people who live in monasteries are not perfect, and some of them preserve very definite likes and dislikes in the matter of manual labor. It may not be to their credit, but the cellarer is bound in charity to consider this weakness as much as any other. Here, as everywhere, Mother Berchmans' charity and tact made her a great success. In any case, she did not take long in giving out the work, but allowed the Sisters to get to church for compline as soon as was humanly possible.

She did everything she could to lighten the task of those Sisters who had to do extra work, as well as those who worked at odd hours, or during the night. Some were apparently a little inclined to criticize her for being too easy on them, but her answer to that was: "I had rather go to purgatory for having been too kind than for having been too hard on the Sisters."

With all these offices, she was not spared her modicum of physical hardship. Although her work kept her in the house, she felt the cold of winter as much and indeed more than those who were out in the barns or fields moving about and exerting their bodies.

She put off her cowl after sext, and went to the cell where she worked on the dairy accounts. She would sit down in the little room without heat and start to write. It is not warm in Hokkaido. She would frequently have to stop writing and rub her hands together, to thaw the cold out of her fingers. Meanwhile an icy breeze seeped under the cracks of the windows, and the cold of the little bare cell penetrated her thin robe and scapular and entered her flesh and even her very bones, until she felt as if she were being transformed into a block of ice. And yet she would not leave that cell until she was forced to when the ink actually froze and it was no longer possible to write.

Then she would pick up her books and her table, and move into the workroom, where there was a fire. And as she did so, she took along the little picture of Jesus in agony in the Garden of Olives which she always kept before her at her work.

Surely the Sacred Heart was not without His consolations from this most fervent and devoted child in those hours of labor and sacrifice. Perhaps He received more love from her, then, than she had ever given Him in her most ardent moments before the tabernacle, in the old days of sensible fervor at Laval.

CHAPTER XIV

A CANTICLE OF GRATITUDE

The years began to pass by more rapidly. Her days were ever more and more crowded with work and responsibilities. Her health was gradually weakening, but she paid no attention to it, since her pains and weariness could not prevent her from working and from going to choir and praying as she had always prayed. In the course of time her work was lightened by an assistant in the sacristy.

Meanwhile, in her seven years in Japan, the little convent had been steadily growing. The first uncertain Japanese postulants had finally yielded fruit in a handful of permanent oblates who remained faithfully at their place in choir and in all the community exercises, day after day, and week after week, and year after year, until they became happy and cheerful and saintly members of the little family. Indeed, some of them were beginning to exhibit a most perfect and edifying simplicity and a spirit of holy joy that was an immense consolation to Mother Scholastica and all the community. Smiling, peaceful, patient, loving, and docile, these little oblates began to show promise of a day when, after proper guidance, with the grace of the Holy Spirit, and a thorough formation to the Cistercian life, they would be able to show the older European Sisters, the veterans of the foundation long accustomed to sacrifice, the way to heights of sanctity that they, perhaps, had not yet dreamed of.

Now more than ever, Mother Berchmans' lessons in Japanese had a direct reference to eight or ten oblates who so badly needed to begin their canonical novitiate. Before, she had found herself well occupied in trying to master the simplest rudiments of the strange tongue. Now there was the problem of learning how to express all the essentials of the spiritual life in an oriental language. For she was not only going to face the responsibility of becoming a spiritual director, charged with the formation of souls to the religious life in one of the strictest contemplative orders in the Church, which is, in itself, no small task, but she would have to do this in a language not only unfamiliar but extraordinarily difficult to master, even in order to express the simplest and most ordinary everyday matters, let alone abstract truths and all the subtleties of the life of prayer.

So while workmen came and began to dig the foundations of a new convent building, just outside the enclosure fence of the temporary house, which was now uncomfortably crowded, Mother Berchmans was given still another important office in the little community, one more difficult, in some respects, than any she had hitherto held. The new post was manifestly chosen to give her practical experience in the guidance of souls. She was relieved of the sacristy but became mistress of the lay sisters, while retaining her post as cellarer and keeping the cheese accounts as usual.

Consequently, during the coming year, in which the foundations would be laid for the permanent building of Our Lady of the Angels, that would one day house a community entirely Japanese, Mother Berchmans was also to lay down a firm foundation of practical experience, cemented in the grace and light of the Holy Spirit, upon which she would build a spiritual edifice of true Cistercian simplicity and solidity in the souls of these chosen oblates, whom Christ had called to Himself from so many millions of their race.

The first "repetition," or conference on the rule, that she had to give was extremely hard for her. It was the first time she had ever had to do anything of the kind, and it gave her many opportunities to offer up her helplessness to God, with urgent prayers for light and strength.

She wrote to Mother Lutgarde: "Today I had my first repetition. If you only knew how much it cost me and how impatient I was to get it over with. I just don't know what kind of a mould the good God is trying to cast me in! I long for the life of silence and solitude, I have an immense need of it, and here I am talking from morning to night, for I still wear my old stripes as cellarer, manager of the dairy and gate-keeper."

Stripes! The word shocks Father Robert beyond measure. The little standard-bearer's implicit comparison of herself to a top sergeant is not to his liking. She had always had military tastes, he reflects, but that does nothing to make such an expression more appropriate for a nun. Stripes, indeed! If she wanted to borrow metaphorical allusions from some army, he feels she would do better to look upward to the heavenly army of the Seraphim and Cherubim.

However, he soon returns to the thread of his narrative. This new office was by no means easy for one without experience in directing souls. It is not child's play for a young nun, thirty- three years old, suddenly to assume the position of spiritual mother over a group of lay sisters all older than herself, all seasoned by longer years in religion, even though they were less blessed with gifts of nature and grace than she had been. Finally, some of them were even of a different nationality, being Germans from across the Rhine in Württemberg or from the Saar, or thoroughly germanized Alsatians.

Would she be able to command a hearing from these Sisters? Could she gain their respect and trust?

She had, as a matter of fact, surprisingly little difficulty in doing so, and the reason for this was her beautiful simplicity and humility, her true charity. These Sisters realized at once that Mother Berchmans was not their mistress but their sister, she was one of them, she loved them, and because they saw at once that she loved and trusted them, and did not think of approaching them with suspicion or reserve, they instantly responded with their love and trust also.

She was all patience and sympathy for their needs; she would hear them to the end, no matter how garrulous they might become; and when she promised to help them, they knew that promise could be relied on, and that she was not merely trying to get rid of them so as to have a little free time for herself.

Mother Berchmans, as a matter of fact, soon had an opportunity to practice humility and self-denial which, though it may seem like nothing on the surface, really demands a heroic, if obscure, abnegation. Her first repetition had been a trial to her, it is true, but we can easily understand that with her warm temperament, her enthusiastic heart, her lively intelligence and imagination, and her fervent love of God and zeal for souls, she soon threw herself with great generosity into these little spiritual talks. Mother Gertrude tells us that she spoke in a tone of voice that made it impossible for her audience to fall asleep.

Mother Berchmans laid special emphasis, in her little talks, on the importance of trust in God and of always rising again after our falls. She preached the love of our own helplessness, of our own weakness. She preached spiritual childhood. The name of Sister Thérèse of Lisieux soon became familiar to the phalanx of seasoned veterans in brown habits who faced her, sitting around reverend mother's room, which was their chapter room on these occasions. Yes, these stolid, matter-of-fact Alsatians, who had grown up in the pine forests of the Vosges and served, some of them, on the battlefields as nurses, began to hear of the Little Legion, of the Little Victims, of Little Souls.

Whether it was the doctrine itself that seemed a little far-fetched to some of them, or whether it was simply that one or two were blessed with the kind of temperament which becomes extremely perplexed at anything sounding new, Mother Berchmans' "message" was not received by all with unmixed enthusiasm.

It is a matter of experience that, in matters of devotion and of means to arrive at union with God, one man's meat is often another man's poison. And so, one of the first lessons the Lord had in store for this future directress of souls altogether new to the Cistercian (and even, sometimes, to the Christian) life was to show her how necessary it was to moderate her own natural ardor and enthusiasms, even in the holiest of things.

She was going to find out, and very quickly, that the thoughts and words and phrases and concepts which filled her with so much joy and peace of soul, and drew forth from her heart so many acts of love and faith and hope, often merely irritated other people, or confused them, or made them nervous. One or two of these good, solid lay sisters were not only left cold by the thought of being Little Victims in the Little Legion, but even grew weary of hearing so much about Sister Thérèse.

Surely, this must have been, in its own subtle way, one of the greatest sacrifices Mother Berchmans had to face; and it was certainly a true test of her virtue and disinterestedness.

It is indeed greatly to the credit of her good sense, and above all of her supernatural spirit, that she did not get melancholy over his initial failure, and begin to try and force her doctrine down the throats of the rebels, with many dark innuendos of heresy, and hints that the rejection of the Little Way might point to a very different lot in eternity from what they had been expecting. She did not lapse into an unwilling public silence on her favorite topic in order to unburden herself in private to those who were sympathetic, and to relate at great length what she thought of the retrograde spirituality of those who could not bear her doctrine.

Precisely because her acceptance and understanding of the teaching of Thérèse of Lisieux were truly supernatural, she was able in perfect tranquility to recognize that perhaps she had been carried away by her own human weakness into as exaggerated emphasis on what appealed especially to herself, without due consideration for the different needs of different souls. And indeed, she must have seen at once that a little more objectivity on her part, a little less freedom in the use of the adjective "little" and of anecdotes about "sweet little Thérèse," would help her to preach the essentials of the Little Way only the more effectively. After all, what was important was not so much the language of a Little Victim but the solid, objective truths about the virtues of hope and trust in God's power, and of divine and fraternal charity, which are not only essential to the teaching of Thérèse, but also to the contemplative life, and *a fortiori* to the Gospels on which both are founded.

With the most perfect supernatural humility and resignation, without any bitterness or rancor, and without putting on the air of a martyr about it, Mother Berchmans ceased almost entirely to mention Sister Thérèse by name in the conferences she gave to the lay sisters in public, out of consideration for the one or two who were irritated by it.

Another subtle temptation arose out of these same "repetitions." Since Mother Berchmans had to instruct the Sisters in the rule and the usages—which all of them, incidentally, had been studying for more years than she had—there were many occasions where she could have put forward and insisted upon some views of her own, or interpretations which had a special appeal to her because they were those observed at Laval. There are countless places in the usages of the order where differences of opinion must inevitably arise, especially when the rules have to be applied to all sorts of different localities and communities and buildings.

However, she rejected this golden opportunity to excel in casuistry, and demonstrate, by subtle hairsplitting, some new way of keeping the rule better than anyone else was keeping it at present. Once again, her sure and faultless intuition, bred of faith and true charity, told her at once that the only thing that mattered about the usages, and the one principle underlying the very conception of such a collection of rules, was unity in charity. But since some discussion and some variety of interpretation cannot be avoided, there is another principle which covers that eventuality also, and preserves unity even then. And that was Mother Berchmans' solution to all problems.

She simply followed the ideas and interpretations of the first superioress of the house, Mother Scholastica. And that was the end of it.

She tirelessly warned the Sisters against all those surreptitious prayers and acts of external piety stolen from the time appointed for other duties, as well as the stealthy labors accomplished against obedience during the time appointed for prayer and reading, under the guise of "sacrifice." Self-will can persuade us of a thousand better things to do than are prescribed for us, but all these things are temptations. There is only one good, and that is God's will. Outside of that, all is evil for us, no matter how good it may be in itself.

In a little manuscript of reminiscences of her saintly companion in religion, Mother Gertrude confesses with charming simplicity to an incident in which she overheard some of Mother Berchmans' doctrine as it was dispensed to the lay sisters.

Mother Gertrude had taken over the sacristy, to relieve her sister in religion, and she found the work and the circumstances under which it had to be performed rather trying. As a result, she found herself making mistakes and committing faults for all of which she began to reproach herself rather bitterly. She tells us that she was "tormented for fear," that she had been doing her own will too much, and that her work was not pleasing to God.

One afternoon, feeling a little depressed with these thoughts, she went and sat down on the steps outside the door and listened to the voice of the mistress of lay sisters coming out through the window. "She was," she says, "talking about conformity with the will of God. No doubt it was an inspiration from on high that made her do so."

And Mother Gertrude proceeds to quote her words:

"What is the use," Mother Berchmans was saying, "what is the use of performing the most pious acts and with the best of intentions, if we do them outside of the will of God? Under such circumstances they only feed our vanity and self-love. Let us do things at the time willed by the good God, without doing more than He wants us to do. On the day of judgement, He won't ask us if we did a great deal: but only if we accomplished His holy will."

As time went on, and her health grew visibly worse, Mother Berchmans' conferences and repetitions would frequently be interrupted by fits of coughing that nearly shook her to pieces, but she laughed at any suggestion that she spare herself.

On the other hand, she always showed a special tender concern for the needs of those Sisters who seemed to be overburdened, not merely for the sake of their health or contentment in the natural order, but with the interests of their souls in view. While giving them, herself, an example of perfect and totally simple generosity that was as pure and humble as it was total and complete, she leaned rather toward indulgence in her dealings with the Sisters who were ill or indisposed or hard pressed with work. She could afford to do so, not only because of the spirit of generosity of the whole community, but also because the force of her own example was powerful in deterring anyone who might have been tempted to be excessively concerned with her own health. If she showed any preference at all for certain Sisters, it was for those who were suffering either physically or spiritually.

It did not seem too much to her for a mistress of lay sisters to mend the clothes of a Sister who was hard pressed for time to spare in her intervals, because of the demands of work. Mother Berchmans was often seen sitting apart, busy with a needle and thread over a stocking that was brown instead of white.

Writing down, after her death, what was evidently the consensus of opinion among the lay sisters concerning Mère Berchmans, Father Robert tells us: "Never, it seems, did they notice any act of their Mother Mistress that was not charitable. Everything about her raised hearts up to the good God; everything was edifying, and produced sentiments of happiness and courage in the hearts of those who came in contact with her. Everything she did seemed to flow from a love that was completely forgetful of self, and which sought after nothing but the good of others and the perfect reign among them of fraternal charity."

As we go on through the years of her life, we find this one characteristic standing out more and more clearly: her life is a life of love. Not a life of sentiment, of emotion, of fervent feelings, but of true love, the charity which burns in the heart of those who are possessed by the spirit of God.

In the spring of 1909, after a hard and busy Lent, in which the long fasts and long hours in choir did not prevent her from working harder than ever in all her employments, Mother Berchmans had the consolation of one of the best spiritual retreats of her whole life. The preacher could not have been a better one for the occasion since it was their own Father Immediate, Dom Vital Lehodey. On this his second visit to Japan since her arrival there, the good Father Abbot of Bricquebec first made the regular visitation of the little community and then preached the retreat.

During these weeks, Mother Berchmans had several interviews

with him, and a better opportunity than before to receive the full benefit of his wisdom and advice in spiritual matters. He, in turn, was impressed by the great development which had been taking place in her pure soul. Until the end of Mother Berchmans' life, Dom Vital Lehodey was to take an ever increasing interest in this saintly nun, so rapidly progressing toward divine union.

But on the occasion of this retreat, the wise abbot and father of souls was able to give Mother Berchmans complete assurance that she was traveling the right road, that God was pleased with her, and was, indeed, drawing her closer and closer to Himself, in spite of all her responsibilities and distractions and trials...or rather, indeed, using those very things as His means.

She told him, above all, of her discovery of the Little Way, and of her new and total abandonment into the hands of God's merciful love; she received his full approbation of her oblation as a victim to that divine mercy.

Her heart full of grace and light and strength, she brought this retreat to a climax by an act which was not only a renewal of this oblation, but a new offering, which, made as it was with the evident approval of Dom Vital Lehodey, amounted practically to a vow, although it did not have the particular force and definiteness of a vow, to do always the most perfect thing possible under whatever circumstances. She did not, it is clear, explicitly bind herself to do always what she considered most perfect under pain of sin or imperfection. Mother Berchmans did not have the type of soul that seeks to bind itself by contracts with every loophole stopped by a water-tight legal sanction. The reason for this is that she did not even consider any loophole. She knew she was weak, and might fail; but she would pick herself up again and go on, trusting in Jesus' grace and mercy to carry her forward over all obstacles. What she did on this occasion was to make a new and more total oblation of herself to God's love in a particular way, which shows what a positive interpretation she had given to the previous act of oblation.

God did not keep her waiting long for signs that He was greatly pleased with her offering, and that He accepted it. At the High Mass which closed the retreat and at which there was a general

Communion of all the Sisters, Mother Berchmans' oblation was received by her merciful Lord with a special sign of favor.

Her heart, dilated with divine love and confidence and overflowing with the powerful desires inspired by the spirit of God, received a sudden and especially strong influx of supernatural light, in which she clearly understood in what manner her offering was presented to Jesus by Mary; she was privileged to enjoy a brief and inexpressible sense of a special contact and close union with Him as a result.

She herself scarcely knew how to express this experience, to convey it to others. It was not an imaginary vision, but rather a realization implanted suddenly, she knew not how, in the midst of her soul, and which she afterward attempted to express in her journal. Her few words, halting as they are, allow us to judge well enough of the intensity and reality of the experience. And though her terms rather tend to diminish that reality than convey it to us, nevertheless we can see at once that the important thing was a vivid, intense awareness of *vital contact* with Jesus Himself, not with an idea or a notion or a symbol or a vision, but with the Man-God, a vital contact with His Soul, His Sacred Heart. Her heart, her own soul, had actually touched the Soul of the Source of life, not after the manner of the five senses, but in the sudden quickening of faith and love within her inmost being.

The scene is, briefly, this. During the High Mass she had made her offering of herself, her resolution and promise to act always out of pure love of Jesus. Then came the *Agnus Dei*. The Sisters began slowly to file out of their stalls. In the hushed chapel, nothing was heard but the quiet movement of their feet, the gentle rustling of the veils as the Sisters gravely and silently bowed, meekly embracing one another with the kiss of peace, and then fell on their knees.

The abbot at the altar turned to give them absolution, and once again, the last traces of natural imperfection and the human dust that all our souls inevitably gather on themselves upon the road of our exile were all washed from her. Then she rose again, and with her soul full of ardent desire and expectation, gently moving her affections with simple almost wordless aspirations of love, she advanced toward the grille.

One last time she cast herself gravely down in adoration. Then, with the long sleeves of her cowl falling down almost to her feet, and crossed in front of her, she fell on her knees to receive the body of the Son of God.

What happened then? She was scarcely aware of what was around her any more; but in the depths of her great joy and peace, she followed, as in a dream, the one in line before her back to her place. The world had become a shadow, and there was, as always, after her Communions, only one reality: the God who was with her and within her, and in whom she was, who lived in her and in whom she lived. But now her heart, in all its earnest simplicity would entertain Him with its one big preoccupation of that day and of her life: her gift of herself to Him. As ever, she would talk to Him with Mary, who was there, too, always with Him. And now it occurred to her what she should say; she should ask the Mother of God to seal this gift, and enter it, for her, for all eternity, in the book of her Son's Heart. Suddenly, when she asked this, came the vivid realization of contact with that divine Heart, the strong, inescapable sense of brief, momentary union, the awareness that with this gift, her life, her very soul, was brushed by the vitalizing presence of infinite Goodness and Mercy.

But let us read her own description of what happened:

"April 28th, 1909. Oh my beloved Jesus! What tender love You display toward Your poor little creature! I desire to reserve the memory of all Your kindness, in order that, on darker days, my soul may still hope in You. When I had the ineffable happiness to possess You intimately within my soul, this morning, at Holy Communion, I felt the desire to tell You again how much I loved You and to renew the offering of my whole being to the merciful love of Your Sacred Heart. Turning to my dearest Mother, I said to her: 'Sweet Mother, a good businessman keeps account of all goods that have been delivered to him; therefore, write down in the Book of Life, which is the Heart of your Divine Son (as He Himself told Bl. Margaret Mary one day), write down that today your little girl delivers herself over *in a very special manner to His divine Love, that she desires only to live for His love alone, and that, whatever she may do, it will never be for any reason but for love of Him*. My worthlessness will exalt His love by contrast, and my weaknesses and lack of generosity will implore that love to heed them.'

"Right away, Your divine Mother wrote down this total donation of myself in Your Sacred Heart in characters of fire. *Then, taking my hand, she made me place it upon this sacred record to show that I ratified all that had just been said there. And then You did the same, Oh my beloved Jesus*. And then, by a happy coincidence, my Reverend Father who was still at the altar, turned toward the choir to give us his blessing. And in this manner, the adorable Trinity Itself sanctioned all that had just passed between the Son of God and His tiny little creature."

Her faith, stirred up to great strength by the impact of this experience, could not help seeing in everything confirmations of it from God Himself, but He too, in His mercy, gave her a stronger proof of His approval than this "happy coincidence." Knowing Mother Berchmans' deep faith in the truth that Christ lived and dwelt in her superiors, and her special reverence for His word and His will as revealed in all their wishes and desires in her regard, it is easy to understand the significance that she attached to the words which Dom Vital Lehodey had to say to her when she met him right after his Mass and thanksgiving in the guesthouse where she hastened to serve his dinner.

Her journal continues: "The assurance that You wished to give me, Oh my adored Jesus, of the acceptance of my offering did not stop there. I had just left the choir and gone to the gate-house to serve my Reverend Father's lunch, and the first words he addressed to me as I came in were: 'I give you my blessing, in order that you may become a seraphin of love.' Oh Jesus! How good these words were to me, placed as they were, by You, in the mouth of Your minister! Oh, my Beloved! Yes, I promise You never to take a moment's rest until I have arrived at the summit of love. I am thirsty, yes, burning with thirst for love!"

In addition to these two "signs," however, Father Robert, who was never an enthusiast in such matters, brings in a third and more convincing one still, which is the fact that she lived up to her offering perfectly, as long as she lived. The only sure way to judge these extraordinary movements in the soul is to observe their fruits, and in this case the test is perfectly satisfactory. Indeed, Father Robert points out, her exceptional fidelity to this promise was something that was, itself, to be ascribed only to a very special grace of God. He concludes that if God had not accepted her offering, and given her the grace to keep it as a sign of His acceptance, she would never have been able to live up to her promise.

This is perhaps the most opportune time to introduce a short account of Mother Berchmans' prayer, and to ask what part was played in her life by graces of infused prayer or phenomena of a mystical order.

To those who conceive the life of mystical prayer as rigidly separated from what is commonly called "ordinary," or "active," prayer by a definite and easily ascertainable boundary line, the answer to the second question will be easy. Since Mother Berchmans had no imaginary visions and no ecstasies or raptures, no spectacular or easily ascertainable phenomena of the kind we read of in the lives of great mystics, we cannot class her among them, except for one or two cases of what the cautious and extremely reserved Father Robert accepts as "interior locutions," and which occurred later on in her life.

In actual fact, however, it is almost impossible to identify at what point a soul passes from "active" to "passive" prayer. There are many fervent souls, in religion and out of it, who lead lives of prayer and union with God and earnestly struggle to overcome themselves for love of Him, to please Him, and to arrive at union with Him, and who, as a result, hover for years just over the border lines of mysticism and scarcely realize it. Therefore, it is hard to give much documentary evidence that Mother Berchmans was a mystic; but at the same time it is impossible to escape the conclusion that her whole religious life, especially after 1907, was marked by close union with God in which, being led habitually by the Holy Spirit, and living under the dominion of His gifts, she was a mystic in the true sense of the word. Her life was hidden with Christ in God. It was the life of the purest faith, of total and generous sacrifice. It was a life of love so supernatural that only the close and constant intervention of the Holy Spirit and her often "passive" obedience to His movements in her soul can suffice to explain it.

Although mystical or infused prayer is very often granted to souls who have by no means reached perfection, and still retain many minor faults and failings of nature, such as impatience, it always bears fruit in an increase of virtue and of peace. Mystical prayer is not always granted in the form of light and consolation. Indeed, severe passive purifications and interior trials are themselves a mystical state and often result from the presence of an infused light in the soul, the very unfamiliarity and strength of which causes suffering to human nature, especially by revealing all the weaknesses and imperfections still inherent in the soul. Infused prayer never *necessarily* implies visions or ecstasies, although these may frequently accompany it. It always leads to peace, to growth in all the Christian virtues, especially humility and charity, and to close union with God.

Father Robert himself did not entertain this concept of mysticism. In consequence, when he comes to consider the possibility that Mother Berchmans was a mystic, he answers that she was, but only on the grounds of two "interior locutions." As to the experience we have just related, after Communion on the 28th of April, 1909, the good priest, with his usual discretion, refuses to commit himself. He recognizes that it was probably not an imaginary vision, and, that being so, he goes no further. The implication is that it was not a mystical grace.

In a consideration of Mother Berchmans' prayer, the documents are most unrewarding. Since she copied out many vocal prayers from the lives of SS. Margaret Mary and Gertrude the Great and others like them, and frequently read them and meditated upon them, Father Robert can quote them in great profusion. But this gives us a distorted idea of her interior life, since he is able to counterbalance it with very little information about her mental prayer, which is the only really important source of evidence in this connection.

Her prayer was not totally unintellectual, for, on the contrary, we know she would often take a sentence from the Gospel, or some words of Jesus to one of His saints, and turn them over and over, peacefully, in her mind, not prying at them with her reason, not studying them analytically, but simply allowing their meaning to sink into her thoughts in a general way, and tasting the simple affections which they inspired. This kind of meditation is often far more fruitful for the intellect, and produces much greater light through the grace of God than any amount of study and concentrated analysis.

For this purpose, she sometimes used a book, but not as a rule. She once kept by her side, at meditation, for a considerable period of time, a book made up of revelations and prayers from St. Gertrude, all of which were simply food for a few acts of love. Most of all, when dryness paralyzed her, she would have recourse to her own anthology of pious thoughts and prayers from the writings of the saints, which she called the "Mirror of My Soul."

And so her prayer is easily and completely described in a few sentences of her own, spoken at random here and there, to those under her direction and to others with whom she came into chance contact in the monastery.

"A few words of love spoken by Jesus to His saints are all I need for my mental prayer," she told one.

To another she confided that her acts were always the same, throughout her whole prayer.

Again, probably speaking to one of her novices (for here we must anticipate a little), she said: "Don't go in for long prayers. Even the Hail Mary is too long (i.e., to say all at once, without pausing). For my own part, I keep repeating: 'Holy Virgin Mary, I love you with all my heart!'"

Another one, having in mind the fact that the manuals of mental prayer recommend that we always have some definite object of petition, asked Mother Berchmans what grace she asked for in her mental prayer. The answer was simple: "I ask for love."

No one who has been trying seriously to lead the contemplative life for any length of time ever needs to stop and wonder what grace he is going to ask for. God usually sends him all the difficulties, trials, and temptations that are required to make his needs perfectly clear to him. As for Mother Berchmans, she had been proved in the furnace of tribulation for many years now, and not only knew all the different graces that she needed, but knew above all that there was one grace that summed them all up and included them in itself. She must have smiled, within her heart, at the fantastic simplicity of such a question.

The same novice persisted: "Of whom do you ask this grace, Mother?"

"I ask the Most Blessed Virgin. I ask her for the grace to die a victim of love before I have the misfortune to offend the good God, and I ask that I may have her assistance in my agony." About dryness in prayer, she told her novices: "When you cannot get anywhere in your mental prayer, unite in one the Heart of the Blessed Virgin and the hearts of all the saints, and offer them all together to God."

Again, she said: "When I cannot do anything at mental prayer, I say the rosary or a few ejaculatory prayers: I love Jesus." But the last statement, as a matter of fact, is a description of all her mental prayer, and of her whole life: "I love Jesus." That was all she did and all she had to do.

Another novice who came to her with difficulties in mental prayer, asking what kind of mental prayer she should make, received the reply: "How did Our Lord pray in the Garden of Olives? Three times over He said the same prayer. So you, too, can very well repeat, with fervor, the same prayer."

Above all, she did not try to constrain her novices to follow any rigid method of prayer, or to keep to the same kind of prayer all the time if they were attracted to something else. She was familiar enough with the workings of the Holy Spirit to know His ways, how He comes and goes as He pleases, giving to each one different gifts as He sees fit.

"If you always eat the same dish, you will get tired of it," she told them, "and if you always take the same subject, or always make the same acts, you will get bored."

We are writing about a Trappistine, a contemplative nun, and one who, even for all her activities and offices, still had far fewer sources of distraction and far less occasion to talk than would be the lot of a Sister in a less enclosed order, even where a partial rule of silence is observed. Mother Berchmans led a life of great recollection; she had learned to guard her eyes and all her senses; she had gained control over her imagination; and her soul was in order and at peace within her. To begin with, her heart had always been perfectly pure and clean of sin, and had never known any of the disturbances of the grosser passions which are at the root of so many difficulties in prayer. She lived constantly in the presence of God, in uninterrupted union with Him. And consequently, it is not only likely, but almost certain, that beneath this simple surface which has been revealed to us in these few, plain, colorless statements about her prayer there remain great depths to be plumbed.

From the time Mother Berchmans came to Our Lady of the Angels, if not a little before, during the last months of her novitiate at Laval, she had probably entered upon what St. John of the Cross calls the "Night of the Senses." This is a period of passive purification which is the introduction, or threshold, to the mystical state, and which, according to the great Carmelite and his contemporary, St. Teresa, is relatively common among religious and persons given to prayer and purity of life. It is a period in which souls are tried in many ways; and if they accept these trials with generosity and without complaint, and if the work of the Holy Ghost is not impeded in them by imprudent advice, they may see a pledge of rapid advancement in divine union. The trials in the period before Mother Berchmans' new stability are all typical of this state. Temptations against patience, dryness at prayer, lack of all sensible consolation, not only for a day or two here and there, but for months at a time and even for years; darkness of the mind, inability to see or understand her way in spiritual things; above all, a constant feeling of pain, a thirst for the vision of God, and anxious uncertainty as to whether or not she was pleasing to God; solicitude concerning the state of her soul, which appeared to her more and more weak and deficient as days went on: all these things had come together in her life to fill her with a deep and obscure suffering. When such trials occur in a soul in conjunction with a great spirit of faith, an intense fidelity to all the duties of her state, and an unshakable, earnest desire to progress in sanctity, to persevere in prayer, and to do anything whatever that God may ask, then the whole combination clearly indicates that infused contemplation has already begun, though in a "dry" and more or less negative state. Such, at least, is the teaching of St. John of the Cross, the greatest and safest authority on Christian mysticism.

Indeed, according to his view, infused contemplation, the night of the senses, might well exist where there were far less clear indications of it than these in Mother Berchmans, always provided there is in the soul that sincere desire to please God which is proved by regularity and humility, obedience and good works. Without this desire dryness in prayer might well spring from laziness and infidelity; and all the other trials, for example against patience, might simply be the result of voluntary tepidity or ill-governed pride.

Father Robert says without hesitation that Mother Berchmans' face seemed, sometimes, to be completely transfigured and illumined by grace in prayer, and evidently he had seen her so himself. Those who have lived in a religious community, especially of contemplatives, where the same individuals are cloistered together for a lifetime, will realize that it may be possible for a novice to delude herself and part of the community, for a while, with manifestations of prayerfulness that are more or less external; but when, after ten or twenty years, the same opinion prevails among most of the Sisters, and is supported by manifest virtue, it is perhaps not far wrong. Nor is it cynicism to say that the average contemplative soon develops a sharp eye for anything false or faked in the piety of his confreres; one only fears that perhaps it may sometimes become too sharp where others are concerned, but remain extraordinarily blunt when he turns it upon himself.

The final result of Father Robert's conservative and prudent examination, based on the evidence and opinion of all the nuns, is that Mother Berchmans could not have arrived at such high virtues without a corresponding ascent in the order of infused contemplation. "The great advances made by Mother Berchmans in the way of perfection would be hard to explain otherwise," he says in his manuscript. "Her real virtue could scarcely be compatible with a merely ordinary degree of prayer." He then goes on to record two or three graces which came to his knowledge and which she considers "mystical." One, an interior locution with which she was to be favored in 1911, another a clearly mystical experience when she received Extreme Unction in September of 1915. Then the experience we have described, in 1909, which Father Robert hesitates to classify. There is every likelihood that Mother Berchmans received a favor she ardently desired, that is the grace of "infused love." In fact, it is not altogether improbable that she received it even before she asked for it, without clearly realizing that to be the case.

It happened that one day, in his catechism class to the nuns, Father Robert described the infused love in the souls of Christ and His Blessed Mother. It was a love, he explained, which was poured into their souls directly by the Holy Trinity, a love that transcended in power and intensity any love that could be acquired by cooperation with ordinary grace. It was a love that stood, as it were, half way between the love with which the Blessed love God in heaven and that with which holy souls love Him on earth. It produced, in the souls that received it, an effect similar to that of infused knowledge of God, which is given to mystics and to the souls in purgatory, and which works a marvelous and powerful transformation in them, preparing them for the Beatific Vision.

He presented the conception of this love to them in terms of dogmatic theology, in such a way that it necessarily appeared to be something remote from the experience of all but a very small number of saints. Nevertheless, as soon as Mother Berchmans, who had been left spellbound by his account, realized that this love was sometimes granted to the souls of mortal men, still in exile, she began to desire it with an ardor and vehemence that were the products of no ordinary movement of grace in her heart.

She consulted Father Robert on the subject. He evidently did not hold out any hope that she would get what she desired. But she thought, surely, if God did not mean these special gifts to give Him special glory, would He grant them to souls at all? Above all—and here she showed by the ardor of her desire what great confidence she had that God meant this gift for her also—if God did not mean to grant her the grace of infused love, would He have inspired her to long for it with such intensity? Had He not said: "Ask and you shall receive"?

Perhaps Father Robert pointed out that God could still refuse her, if He deemed that the gift might do her harm. But this did not concern her. She knew that well enough. But she knew well enough, too, that God saw her intention, and that all she wanted was to love Him more, to give Him more glory, to belong to Him more perfectly. And so he gave his consent and approval.

From that moment Mother Berchmans began to storm heaven with her prayers. From that day on, with loving and humble confidence, as soon as she had imprisoned Jesus within her loving heart at Holy Communion, she began to beg Him insistently but gently, reminding Him of all His promises to those who asked anything in His name, for this grace of infused love. He knew that this was the only way she could love Him as much as she desired—as much as He had made her desire.

"What do I care," she wrote in a letter, "whether I am in exile, or home in heaven, provided I can love Jesus as much as I desire to: provided I can love Him with all the fulness of infused love? I say infused love because it seems to me that this love in which the soul has no part, since it is completely gratuitous, gives more glory to the good God."

In asking for infused love, Mother Berchmans had asked to be nailed to a cross of longing and desire; she had asked to suffer the very thirst that had caused the dying Christ to cry out upon Calvary; and the answer to her prayer would be to hear, with a new and terrible distinctness in the depths of her heart, the echoes of the Saviour's "*sitio*." The sound of that dying voice would be to her as it had been to the Mother of God, standing at the foot of the cross, a sword as sharp as flame, transfixing the roots of her soul and the center of her very life.

There is no reason to wonder at her immediate conviction, upon hearing of this infused love, that this was what she wanted above all other things. Ever since she had become an oblate at Laval she had been trying to express this desire without knowing what infused love was. She had been trying to frame some prayer that would express her longing to love Jesus as He deserved to be loved, and this was the only way.

Were Mother Berchmans' longings for death, for release from this exile, of which we have seen several instances during her early years at Our Lady of the Angels, an expression of infused love?

Taken by themselves, these desires would not be enough to warrant any such statement. The fact of her constant desire to love Jesus perfectly, to give Him everything, to lay down her life for Him, is more convincing. But this, too, would not be enough by itself. But, united with her generosity in sacrifice, her utter forgetfulness of all her own physical sufferings in order to devote herself to others and to the interests of Christ, all the longings she so frequently expressed in her journal and letters give us good reason to suspect that the spirit of God had already begun to pour this intense supernatural gift of love into her soul, several years before she had any idea of what it was, or that such a gift existed.

There is less doubt as to whether she received this grace when we come to consider the period that followed her ardent prayers for it. In the chapters that are to come, we shall find nothing but constant growth in self-sacrifice, in self-forgetfulness, in the desire to die as a holocaust of love for Christ; but above all we shall from time to time see into the depths of the motives behind this generosity. And always we shall find there nothing but the purest and most supernatural love, a love so deep and intense that it outstrips all the limits attainable by the ordinary efforts of a soul cooperating with grace, which clearly testifies to the special intervention of the Holy Spirit.

Let us record at this point only one or two incidents, and a phrase or two from her letters.

"I desire to love Jesus so much! I wish that I were all love: but alas, too often I am nothing but an iceberg....

"I come to ask you to give me a sickness: the incurable sickness of love, which the length of exile can only make more inveterate, and which will never find its remedy until I arrive, in Paradise, at the possession of my Beloved.

"Oh, pray for me that I may come to love Jesus much, but very, very much: that I may become a little Seraph of love in order to console His Divine Heart so grievously wounded by the crimes of our poor nation.

"Oh, I desire to love, and to love much: but what a distance there is between my desires and the actual fact!

"Oh, beg Jesus that I may love Him much. He needs love so badly in poor Japan, where He is so little known, so little loved. In order to make up for all this, I wish I could turn into fire and flames. Ask Jesus that I may love Him much, that I may come to rival the love of His little spouse of Carmel, from whom I am inseparable. I too desire to love Him so much! I would like to love Him completely, if that were possible.

"Oh Jesus! Would that I could make Him some return for His favors by loving Him as much as I desire to, with all the powers of my soul, with all the strength of my heart. I want the perfection of love: its plenitude. Oh, I realize that I cannot arrive at that point without paying the price. My poor heart will bleed for it, no doubt, many a time. But what does suffering amount to, in comparison with so great a gift?

"And yet when I see how little I do in order to obtain it, I cannot make it all out. My cowardice simply astounds me.

"Oh, if only Jesus would pass right over all miseries and satisfy the desire of His divine Heart which wants me to love Him, as well as the desire of His little spouse who so wants to love Him and to be one with Him."

"O love, love," she could cry, "make haste to burn me up! Oh love! Make haste to satisfy my desire…finish what you have begun!"

Again she asked prayers in the following terms: "Remember your unworthy child (she was writing to her former mother abbess) with the intention that she may not only live in the love of God, but that she may be transformed into love, and that she herself may be nothing but love! Oh yes, I thirst for love! That is the precious pearl for which I want to sacrifice all."

When she asked her novices to pray for her, and they wanted to know what grace they should beg for her, she would always say: "That I may become fervent in love: that I may die of love."

She used to explain the way she huddled close to the statue of Our Lady of the Angels in the center of the Sister's choir, during the cold early intervals after night office, by saying that she wanted to catch Mary's sickness, "the sickness of love, and die of it." And she would often exclaim: "*Que la maladie de la Mère devienne celle de la fille!*—Let the daughter catch the same sickness as her Mother."

Once a very simple novice asked her the question: "Mother, what sickness would you like to die of: tuberculosis?"

"I would like," she said, "to die of love."

Later on, when she herself was suffering and gradually sinking toward death in the infirmary, she was never concerned with her own physical torment, never ruffled by any natural contrariety, but she would be found weeping bitterly at the outrages committed against the Blessed Sacrament in the war areas of France and Belgium—for by that time the first World War was devouring her beloved land and beginning that long crucifixion of an impious world that was to drown not one but many generations of our century in blood.

Once, too, a novice entered Mother Berchmans' room after work and found her in tears. Asking what was the matter, the child received the reply: "Have you meditated today on the Passion of Our Lord? Alas! The good God is continually thinking of us, and we have the misfortune to forget Him!"

Often, in her sickness, she would say: "What does it matter to me if I suffer, so long as the good God is not offended! The good God, He receives so much offense!" If she wanted to be a saint, it was purely in order to console the suffering Christ, and to make up especially for the ingratitude of souls dedicated to Him in religion: for the coldness and hardness of heart of His "chosen people," the elect flock of His special pasture, who have so often turned into pharisaical wolves and tried to devour their own Shepherd.

"Oh," she wrote, "let us love Him for all those who do not love Him.... Poor Jesus, He has good reason to be so sorrowful! He

Who is Love, is so little loved!...Oh, let us love Him for all those who do not love Him, and by our love, heal the wounds made in His Divine Heart by the infidelity of so many souls."

Of another, she asked: "Please pray to Soeur Thérèse for all of us, that she may make us saints, and great saints, in order to console the Sacred Heart of our Beloved Jesus Who is so much offended in our days."

If it has been necessary to break the thread of that story, by looking ahead into the years when she was mistress of novices, we may render this excusable by entering almost immediately upon this last, most important period of her life.

But while she is still standing on its threshold, we see her mark this further stage in her spiritual progress by an act of thanksgiving offered to the Sacred Heart of Jesus on His feast day, in the year 1909. This beautiful little document, which Father Robert calls her "Canticle of Gratitude," is a kind of retrospect over the past years, especially before her entrance into religion, and it shows how intensely aware Mother Berchmans was of the constant guidance and loving influence of divine providence in every smallest incident of her life. Her grateful heart could look back on all her thirty-three years, and see in every one of them countless marks of love, unnumbered graces and favors and blessings accompanying her every step forward, her every breath, every movement of her body or her heart.

"Oh Jesus!" she writes, "my dearly beloved Jesus! You Who never cease to pour forth into the soul of Your little spouse the infinite tenderness of Your Sacred Heart, let me, on this day consecrated to You, try to express something of the sentiments of deep thankfulness overflowing in my heart. Oh, yes, my beloved Jesus, I desire to thank You for all the known and unknown graces You have poured into my soul with such profusion until this day, and which I have, alas, so often abused. I am like a child born in the midst of nobility and fortune, unappreciative of the luxury with which she is surrounded, since I have always drunk from the very source of grace. Forgive me, Jesus: I desire to make up for everything by a hymn of love and gratitude.

"Thank You, my dearest Jesus, for having drawn me forth out of nothingness, formed me in Your image and likeness, and made me a child of Holy Church the very day after my birth, by regenerating me in the sacred waters of Baptism. September 22nd, 1876.

"Thank You, my dearest Jesus, for having given me Your sweet Mother for my Mother and Patroness, and for having entrusted me in a very special way to her maternal care.

"Thank You, my dearest Jesus, for the faithful guardian Angel You gave me to be the companion of my exile here below, and to whom You confided the care of my soul.

"Thank You, my dearest Jesus, for having taken me out of the world before my soul was able to tell evil from good, and for having confided me, in my tenderest years, to Your cherished Spouses, that they might form me in virtue. March 24th, 1880.

"Thank You, dearest Jesus, for having called me to live under the same roof with Yourself, in the shadow of Your Sanctuary, just like the little princesses in the old days, who were engaged in their very cradle and grew up under the eyes of their future spouses.

"Thank You, O my dearly beloved Jesus, for that ever unforgettable day when I first received Your kiss of love in the Holy Eucharist, and for all the many hours of solitude and delight before the Holy Tabernacle, in which Your love so amply repaid me for the loss of the joys and affections of family life which were refused me at that time. April 26th, 1888.

"Thank You, my dearest Jesus, for the inexpressible gift of confirmation which made me a perfect Christian and gave me the Spirit of Love with all the plenitude of His graces. 28th of May, 1888.

"Thank You, dearest Jesus, for having chosen me to be the privileged child of Your sweet Mother, and for having clad me in the vesture of her holy service. December 6th, 1891.

"Thank You, sweet Jesus, for all the absolutions I have received in the Holy Tribunal of Penance and for the graces of fortitude which I have drawn from this Sacrament and from the advice of Your priests.

"Thank You, oh my very dearest Jesus, for all the Holy Communions I have had the happiness to receive until this day, and for the treasures of grace which my soul has found in these intimate unions with my Beloved, in this sweet converse, heart-to-heart with my Divine Spouse.

"Thank You, my Jesus, thank You for ever and ever, for that first call which my soul heard in one of Your loving visits, and for the irresistible attraction to the religious life which You implanted in my heart.

"Thank You, dearest Jesus, for having raised my soul above all the things of this earth and for having allowed me to find nothing but deception and boredom among creatures.

"Thank You, dearest Jesus, for having brought me through the desert of this world without letting my heart become attached to anything in it, but having only one desire: Your love, and the possession of You alone.

"Thank You, my beloved Jesus, for all the joys and consolations You have scattered along my way, but thank You too for all the brambles and thorns that have drawn blood from my heart and which have helped me to become detached from everything that was not You, my supreme Good.

"Thank You, Jesus, my love, for having given me the consolation of spending the last hours of my life as a young girl in the world at the feet of Your sweet Mother in her Holy Sanctuary at Lourdes, where I placed my religious life under her motherly protection. May 23rd, 1899.

"Thank You, sweetest Jesus, for having leveled all the obstacles which stood in the way of my vocation, and for having sent me Your angel to show me the way that was to lead me to You and to the blessed cloister where Your happy little spouse was to be immolated for Your love. April 30th, 1899. (The angel was, of course, Father Polycarpe.)

"Thank You, O Jesus, my only love, for that great day when at last all the chains that bound me to my own dear ones were broken and my soul was free to fly to where my Beloved called me. June 7th, 1899.

"Thank You, dearest Jesus, for having chosen, from all eternity, the Feast of Your Sacred Heart as the day when the doors of the cloister were to open to Your little spouse, and for having willed, with the most delicate consideration, to preside, Yourself, in the monstrance over this little private feast. June 9th, 1899.

"Thank You, sweetest Jesus, for that beloved new family You then gave me, in which my heart found all the affection it needed, and thank You for taking all that away again when You saw that my heart was once again becoming attached to creatures.

"Thank You, beloved Jesus, Oh, yes, thank You for having laid Your Cross upon my heart.... (And here Father Robert still refuses to give up the secret, only telling us that she was referring to her "special trial," the cross that had begun to cause her so much suffering all her life, the interior cross, the nature of which we can only surmise.)

"Thank You, beloved Jesus, for having, in a movement of Divine jealousy, made me more like unto You by demanding of me not only the sacrifice of my religious family but also the sacrifice of my dear France, my heart's Jerusalem. January 6th, 1902.

"And finally, thank You, my adored Jesus, for all the known and unknown graces You have poured into my heart until this day.

"O Mary, sweetest Mother! Fill my heart with gratitude like that which overflowed from Your own Heart when You sang the glorious Canticle of Your Magnificat: and so, may I be able to give to Jesus a more worthy expression of gratitude!"

She must have realized, as she put down her pen that June day, in 1909, that her canticle of thanksgiving had barely begun; the greatest graces were yet to come. They would come to her, principally, she knew, in the form of crosses. They would be ever greater and greater crosses—but ever, too, obscure, outwardly unheroic, unspectacular crosses. They would come to her from the loving hand of Mary, together with the grace to bear them, to sanctify her soul by them, to become united on each one of them to Jesus her

Spouse. And soon (how soon she could not tell) would come the last cross, the bitter agony in her soul would fight its way at last free of her flesh to enter heaven by the gate of pain and desolation.

All this, she knew, lay before her, but now the knowledge gave her nothing but peace and joy. "*Scio cui credidi*," she could cry with St. Paul, she knew who it was that she believed in. She knew how much He loved her—one day, she would cry: "*Mon Jésus, vous m'avez trop aimée!*—My Jesus, You have loved me too much!"

Did she have far to look for opportunities to love Him in return? Indeed, no. As the year 1909 came to an end, and the new year ushered in a decade that was to see her own death and one of the greatest tragedies in the history of the world, she received the most important and most difficult task she was ever to accomplish in her life. It was the office she had once so dreaded; the responsibility so far beyond her powers, so inevitably destined, she had once thought, to crush her frail shoulders and to break her utterly, body and soul.

She, the humble and retiring contemplative, who was fit, as she believed, for nothing but obscurity and the humblest tasks, now had to take charge of the moral, spiritual, and intellectual formation of some ten or fifteen confused, but eager, Japanese oblates, none of whom could even make themselves intelligible in the few words of stuttered French they had acquired since coming to the convent, all of whom had been endowed by God with minds and points of view and inherited traits that were bound to be at times completely incomprehensible to her French soul. And, what was most terrifying of all, upon her formation of these inexperienced souls depended the whole future of the Trappistines in Japan.

God had, indeed, given her no small responsibility. But she knew, by now, that He intended and desired to do the work for her and in her; all she had to do was keep her eyes intently fixed upon His will, in all the simplicity and peace of faith, and He would do the rest.

CHAPTER XV

MISTRESS OF THE NOVICES

There was no surprise awaiting Mother Berchmans on the feast of the Purification of the year 1910. She wrote to Laval, at the end of January:

"Next Sunday we will indeed have a big 'purification' at Our Lady of the Angels. Reverend Mother says she is going to make many changes. I am to leave the gate and my charge as cellarer, but I shall probably keep our good Laysisters and the cheese stores, and shall furthermore become—a thing so strange that I scarcely dare to utter it—the shepherdess of our little lambs of the novitiate. Yes, I am to become Mistress of our little Choir-Novices—I who can scarcely stammer a few words of Japanese. Once upon a time the good God willed to make use of the jaw-bone of an ass to destroy the Phillistines. Today He is about to make use of the whole animal, in order to train His spouses. I assure you, Reverend Mother, that I do not fear any temptations to vanity in this charge! If I should ever do any good to these dear little souls, it will not have come from me, but from the Blessed Virgin, whom I am going to make their Shepherdess, asking her to lead her little sheep out to the pasture herself. Poor little sisters! They will have many sacrifices to make, realizing that they do not make themselves understood. But Jesus will be there, and I will rest on His Divine Heart, and abandon myself completely to His Divine Will."

"A few years before," Father Robert comments, "at the

prospect of such a responsibility, she would most certainly have had a tantrum. But now all was different. Love had grown in her soul, and with it abandonment. This extremely difficult and even, in a certain sense, frightening office was accepted with peace and conformity to God's will." From now on, her whole spiritual life was to revolve around this central responsibility and sacrifice. She no longer belonged to herself. In Father Robert's words: "Her greatest and most valuable mortification was, now, to give herself entirely to her work."

Her own comment, extremely simple, speaks volumes. On the 6th of February she wrote in her Journal: "*Mon bon Jésus, je vous aime, et je m'abandonne!*—Good Jesus! I love You. I abandon myself to You."

Before she entered upon her new charge, she had a long talk with Father Robert, a talk which she never forgot. Father Robert was fond of the famous Dominican preacher, Lacordaire, and gave her, that day, some very sound principles he had drawn from the pages of that eminent director of souls. What an immensely important task she had now taken upon herself. If only she realized how much depended upon her!

"The life or death of a religious order depends on the way the novices are formed," he said to her. "And, to begin with, you will exercise your greatest influence by the example you give. If you are obedient, they will be obedient. If you are submissive to your superiors, in your judgment and your will, they will become that way too. If you have a spirit of penance, they will probably acquire the same.

"Another thing: it does not matter if you have twenty novices or only one. Numbers don't make any difference. Supposing there is only one. She is a chosen soul, called to religion. A lot of other souls depend on her perseverance. If she is badly formed, and fails, think how many other people may fall into hell on account of it! If she becomes an irregular religious, the whole order will suffer!

"But above all, never forget this: the care of the novices is your whole life, now. Everything else, your reading, your private devotions, your health, your work—these are merely accessories, accidentals. If it ever happens that your charge of the novitiate becomes an accessory, and something else is the chief thing in your life, from that moment on you will be in a permanent state of prevarication. There would be no punishment too great for such a betrayal of the souls in your care.

"And don't be too soft with them, either," continued the good Father, "don't let them boss you. Don't let them have things their own way. Be gentle but firm. You have to beat a dog and pat him by turns, to make a good dog out of him, and it is the same way with novices. Beat them and then pat them. Not too much beating and not too much patting. But don't let them see that they can boss you around and have their own way..."

Mother Berchmans did, from the very first, give herself entirely to her work, with her whole heart. Whether she managed to combine chastisement and consolation in the exact proportions Father Robert and Lacordaire may have envisaged, we do not know. But she would soon win their hearts and rule and form them by love—a love that was tender but never indulgent, because indulgence is not love. She would never let them ignore the rule which had been given them by God as the sure path to happiness and peace of soul; but she would always make them keep the rule by love, rather than by fear and threats of punishment.

Without a word of complaint or self-pity, she entered peacefully and joyfully upon the immensely difficult task. Thirty-three years old, eleven years in religion, weakened by ill health, she did not fear, with all her inexperience and her ignorance of the language and almost complete lack of "Japanization," to take upon herself the direction of the novices who had fallen to her lot.

"As you know," she wrote to an aged Trappist at Bricquebec with whom she had developed an epistolary friendship while cellarer, when he had been in charge of the shipping of some badly needed supplies from the mother house, "the little bird of the woods has left her solitude and entered upon the command of Jesus' little bird-house. There she is to teach the birdlings of the Rising Sun to fly with their own wings, and to hold their little heads good and high, so as not to see the sorrows of this world of ours."

It appears that the good old Trappist was as enthusiastic a member of the "Little Legion" as Mother Berchmans herself, and was thoroughly enchanted with the style of her letters.

"It is a very difficult task for her in her weakness," continues the little bird of the woods, "and one that is all the more difficult because of the fact that she does not understand the chirpings of these little songsters. And so, although the bars of her cage are gilded by the will of God, still her little heart bleeds. *Mais vive notre bon Jésus et sa croix!* Let us turn everything into firewood to feed the flames of divine love, and like Sister Thérèse, let us make our songs all the more sweet and melodious as the thorns get longer and sharper."

It was not that she had not studied all the grammar. We have every reason to believe that Father Robert gave her a thorough drilling in all the rules, in spite of her evident distaste for such things. What she needed above all was practice, to form her ear to catch all the subtle differences of tone and modulation which so effect the meaning in the languages of the Far East. Only one of a thousand misunderstandings that arose out of her ignorance of the language has come down to us.

The nuns of Laval had sent some pins for the novices. The pins had colored porcelain heads, some red, some green, some pale blue, some yellow, and so on. Great admiration in the novitiate of Our Lady of the Angels! Everybody looked at the pins with awe and delight, especially the red ones and the green.

Then Mother Berchmans began to go into action with her halting knowledge of Japanese, in order to explain that the pins were not to be used on the veils, but only on the napkins in the refectory. (What they could possibly want with pins for the napkins in the refectory, a mere monk has no way of knowing. We can assume that the sisters have some special prettiness about their way of fixing things in the refectory which has escaped the masculine version of the usages.) But when she went to use the word napkin, she slipped on one of the syllables, without realizing that she had done so.

The faces before her remained blank. The vague feeling that all was not well began to come over her, and, uneasily but doggedly, she went over the whole thing again. The pins, she said, were not to be used on the veils but on the napkins in the refectory.

She slipped again, on the same syllable.

This time, however, one of the novices, Sister Francisca, heaved a profound sigh, and said, in a tone of patient resignation: "Oh, I see: you made a mistake. You mean the *napkins* in the refectory."

Light dawned on the other novices, one by one; and one by one they put their hands in front of their faces. One of them giggled audibly.

"Why," said Mother Berchmans, with a dismal sense of void opening up in her heart, "what did I say?"

"You said we should only use the pins for pinning up *our beaks* in the refectory."

Poor novices! They must have had sudden visions of a long, hard Lent, with all the nuns sitting in the refectory before a bare board, with pins stuck through their lips to keep them closed: lovely little pins with red and green and yellow and blue porcelain heads! And nothing to eat at all, just sitting and listening to somebody reading a long, tedious book in a language they could not understand.

But the word *impossible*, says Father Robert, does not exist in the vocabulary of a Cistercian, and Mother Berchmans, with the indulgence and patient sympathy of her novices, soon arrived at the point where she could converse with them fluently and well.

During her eight years in Japan, Mother Berchmans had had little opportunity to acquire any intimate knowledge of the customs and habits of thought of the people of her new country. She may, indeed, have observed some of the special national traits evidenced in the bearing of the postulants, but she had not yet sought to understand them. Indeed, when Father Robert reproached her, in Japanese class, for her failure to develop any feelings for the language and its idioms and for the mental attitudes they implied, she blandly replied: "Well, after all, I'm French."

And she was, indeed, French in her tenacious love for all that belonged to her race and nation. But now she could no longer afford to ignore the peculiarities of another race. It was necessary that she study them and form herself to the same ways of thinking. It was hard for her, but the task was made easier by certain natural virtues of the Japanese which made an immediate appeal to her.

She could not, for example, long resist their innate politeness and delicacy, their sensitiveness and good taste. Then, too, the deep filial piety of her novices and oblates aroused sympathy in her own loving heart, and their sincere and reasonable love of their own country—these harmless girls did not have any of the jingoism of the more militaristic elements of the population—was something she could at least understand.

Soon she discovered in her novices not only rich gifts of intelligence and good sense, but also a deep refinement of sensibility and an innate idealism, which, as their hearts came more and more under the sway of the spirit of Christ, developed into a most beautiful Christian charity, humility, and simplicity. She began to feel intense gratification at their response to her own way of guiding them by love. How docilely they responded to her! How eager they were for instruction! How avid to learn new ways of pleasing God and submitting their souls unconditionally to the beneficent action of His grace! If she had been baffled by one or two of the lay sisters' stolid unfriendliness toward the principles of "spiritual childhood," she was to find her consolation here in the novitiate. These generous, humble, and unspoiled girls were perfect material for formation according to the plain doctrine of the Little Flower, simply because there were none of those stubborn traces of half-conscious Jansenism to be wiped out of their souls, as there are in those of so many European Catholics.

The result of this was that Mother Berchmans rapidly acquired all the sympathy she needed for Japanese customs and attitudes. She was no longer astonished that her novices insisted on taking off their shoes when entering the house, or on greeting one another with demonstrations of politeness that seemed excessive. In consequence of her sympathy, she was quickly able to distinguish what would be necessary in their formation—that is, what was strictly Cistercian and Benedictine—and what was unnecessary, or, more plainly, what was merely in tune with her French training and blood. To have tried to turn her novices into Frenchwomen would have been useless and, perhaps, impossible. Nor does our rule demand the suffocation of national traits. The rule of St. Benedict is for all races, not races for the rule. It is designed with enough latitude to embrace all kinds of life in order that, by following it, men and women of all races and nations may work out their own special potentialities for sanctity implanted in them by God. A Japanese saint will give glory to God differently from an American or a Frenchman; that is why God made us externally different. But nevertheless all can keep the Cistercian usages, all can glorify God with a certain uniformity which He desires of Cistercians.

No doubt, there were some things about Japanese life that were essentially incompatible with our way of life. These had to be sacrificed, and Mother Berchmans did not disguise the fact, nor hesitate to insist upon it. It would not kill the novices if they ceased to bow profoundly to everybody, and kept their deep bows for Mother Scholastica and Father Robert.

So great were her sincerity and simplicity in carrying out her task that Mother Berchmans soon won the hearts of all her novices, and became, according to the testimony of Mother Scholastica, a perfect novice mistress.

One evening, toward the end of her first year in this charge, a novice came to Mother Berchmans' room, and found her gazing with special tenderness upon the pictures of St. Thérèse and Gemma Galgani before her on the table.

"Mother," said the girl, "you are looking at them so lovingly tonight. What is the reason?"

"I was thinking," said Mère Berchmans, "that if I should happen to be changed, and give up this position in February, I would have to be separated from them."

"Don't talk about being changed," said the novice, with tears showing in her eyes, "it would be too hard for me to lose you." "What about me," said Mother Berchmans, "I would have to lose my nine children."

What underlay this love? Was it merely a question of natural sympathy? Had the novices merely succumbed to her natural charm? There was much more than nature on her part. So seriously had she taken Father Robert's advice to make the novices her whole life, that she really loved them more tenderly than a mother. It seemed there was no sacrifice, no attention, that she would deny them.

One of the novices, cleaning the church, had soiled her Japanese-style house shoes, and put them aside to clean them as soon as she could. When evening came around, and the girl went to get her shoes, she found them all cleaned and in perfect shape. So she went to Mother Berchmans holding the shoes.

"Maybe it was your good angel that came and cleaned them," said Mother Berchmans, in answer to the accusation that she had done so herself.

Then one of the postulants, totally unaccustomed to the heavy outdoor work of the nuns, outdid herself at the beginning of the labor, and before the end came was ready to drop with fatigue. She began to think, "If only I could sit down and rest a little and drink a nice cup of milk."

In a little while, she looked around, and Mother Berchmans who had evidently looked out of the window and seen her, came along with a cup of milk.

She never forgot their little troubles and temptations. One of the poor girls was pining away with homesickness. All she could think of was her dear little mother at home; if only she could be with her again! It was not that the life was too hard, or that she minded the fasting and hard work, but she needed to be with her mother. Mother Berchmans convinced her that it would be a good thing to pray to our heavenly Mother, and to get in the habit of liking to be with her by praying, for example, at her statue in the choir; she also did not forget to look in through the curtain of the child's dormitory cell that evening and give her a smile and a little blessing as she lay wide eyed on her hard couch, with the covers up over her chin. Such little acts of tenderness meant very much, sometimes, and the girls never forgot them.

The novices found that the best antidote to their homesickness, and, indeed, to most of their other troubles, was the family spirit which Mother Berchmans was able, through her close union with God, to foster and maintain in her novitiate.

This was one of the most admirable characteristics of her training of the novices, and one which proved how deep and supernatural was her love for them. Led by a kind of spiritual instinct, she knew how to unite all the novices with one another and with herself and with God in the strong, pure power of her own disinterested love. This alone speaks volumes for the purification that her heart had undergone, for nothing so quickly destroys this unity of peaceful charity in a little community of religious or novices, as favoritisms and natural affections when they are allowed to take their course.

Had Mother Berchmans showed preference to certain of the novices, had she seemed to favor them over others, to take more pleasure in conversing with them, to show a singular concern for their needs, this would inevitably have wounded others, and caused petty envies and jealousies and rivalries which spell the end of charity and of peace. Of course there was no question of blind, mathematical equality. The weaker ones certainly needed more attention; she could not conceal a certain special satisfaction that some were more virtuous than others, but because her motives were always clearly supernatural, they were always understood and taken for granted.

The most precious thing she had to give the novices was her time, and she gave all that she had to give, never neglecting the needs of anyone. She was never too busy to listen to one of her novices. There was nothing so important that it could not be interrupted for their sake.

She had once lamented the loss of her "intervals," the difficulty of getting ten or fifteen minutes once or twice a day before the Blessed Sacrament. Now she was fortunate if she could salvage five minutes after supper or collation, or a little time after the night office, when she could throw herself down and pour out her heart at the feet of Our Lady of the Angels. No matter how busy she had been, in past years, she had always managed to say her rosary in peace—perhaps not all at once, but at any rate she said it. Now, there was no chance to do so until she stretched herself upon her couch in the dormitory. Gone were the days of pleasant, solitary meditations and uninterrupted communion with Christ in the tabernacle. That did not mean that she was less united to Him than before; she was more so. He was working in her. Her soul belonged to His spirit. Her mind and will were His instruments for the formation of other souls in His likeness.

She had not given up her lay sisters; she still had to direct them also. And besides, the days were soon to come when, after a sudden turn for the worse in her health, she would move to the infirmary, first to sleep there at night, then to spend most of her days there too. But always she would struggle against every pain, every weakness, every obstacle to get down to the novitiate to give her repetitions and receive novices for direction.

If her kind and tender heart made her quick to perceive all the needs of her spiritual children and to provide for them and comfort them in their trials, she was not a weak and indulgent mistress. On the contrary, she did not allow any of the conscious or semideliberate subterfuges of nature to capitalize on her kindness.

Of one postulant, who was one of those unhappy introverts full of self-pity and always whining for sympathy and attention from others out of pure egoism, Mother Berchmans simply shrugged and said that she might as well be out in the world. She did nothing to encourage candidates who obviously had no vocation, girls who dragged themselves around with no good will and no desire to adapt themselves to the rule and to the life, seeking every possible dispensation and sulking when they did not get it. She had little use for those constant successions of imaginary sicknesses and illusory pains that made it impossible for these newcomers to get up and go to choir, and made them fear death from weakness and anemia before ten o'clock on the morning of Ash Wednesday. After having made every reasonable allowance for them, and finding that they really did not mean to sacrifice themselves in the least, she would suggest that they be sent back home without further delay, which was, of course, the only charitable thing to do with them. They would eventually leave, anyway; it was better that they should not waste any more of their own time and impose an unnecessary burden on the other members of the community by staying longer.

She was equally firm with the stubborn and self-willed among her postulants, and did not do them the disservice of allowing them their own way whenever they wanted it, although she was always gentle and reasonable in her denials. In short, she faced all the situations a novice mistress can face in dealing with souls fresh from the world, with all the prudence and charity and self-possession of one guided by grace, and determined to use all the special lights afforded her because of her very state.

Those who sensed in her that strong vein of humorous vitality were nevertheless never able to break through the reasonable limits separating the Mother from her novices and lapse into dissipation or boisterous familiarity with her. Others who took advantage of her good nature to treat her with coldness or patronage never aroused any sign of ill-will, but they never succeeded in piercing the calm of her dignity or disturbing the peace of her simple humility and love which placed her far above such things. True, she often felt them keenly, but that did not surprise or disturb her, and did nothing to change her supernatural patience and eagerness to serve Christ in the souls of all her novices, no matter who or what they were, or how they behaved toward her. Yet she did not pass off these things too lightly, because she always saw them with the objectivity of pure love, and knew that they were offenses against Christ Himself, which injured Him in the very souls of those who thought they were putting her in her place.

One day, a novice had slighted her in some small way, probably in one of those moments of impatience or ill-humor, and afterward came to apologize for it. The prudence of the world might have dictated a sweet expression and a few words of pious forgiveness calculated to show the child what a patient and magnanimous mother mistress she had. But Mother Berchmans was not working for her own interests. The slight had been directed against her, but it was not she who had been the most injured by it; and she said: "Look: Berchmans doesn't count. It is Jesus Christ that you have slighted." And she explained how this was, calmly and objectively, without denying that she had felt it also herself. In this way, she forgave not only as a Christian but as a guide and mother of souls, whose duty it was to heal as she forgave.

We have perhaps hardly begun to enumerate all the faults and human weaknesses a directress of novices may have to contend with in direction. For instance, there were the flatterers: those who color all their dealings with their superiors with the pink icing of a patently artificial sweetness and savor every sentence with open or implicit servility. Mother Berchmans was armed against such talk by nature, as well as by grace, by good sense and good taste, as well as by humility and simplicity. She did not tolerate it, nor did she countenance any words or expressions that might wound charity. She never allowed her spiritual direction of the novices to degenerate into a session of idle and somewhat critical gossip about all the affairs of everybody else in the community.

She had learned, in directing the lay sisters, to beware of forcing her own enthusiasms upon others, and even now, where the souls who came to her had little or no previous spiritual formation, and she could work almost as she willed with the raw material in her hands, she was careful not to put an emphasis on what appealed particularly to herself in the spiritual life.

The Little Way was put before them, but never forced upon them: it was not even the central theme of her repetitions and direction. On the contrary, she warned them before all else that, whatever their spirituality might be, it must first of all be Benedictine. If they wanted to interpret their rule and the Cistercian traditions in the light of some devotion that had a particular appeal to them, and which was appropriate to their kind of contemplative life, they could do so. But first of all they must live the rule of St. Benedict. "St. Thérèse's way," she said, "is certainly an excellent one. But we have, first of all to keep our own Holy Rule."

According to Father Robert, as the years went on, she allowed more and more latitude to the lay sisters as long as they did not show any tendencies to peculiarity or excessive contention and strain. And while she was always more firm and dogmatic in her guidance of her novices, she respected more and more the special movements of the Holy Spirit in the heart of each one. For the rest, whenever nothing serious was at stake in the interior life of one of her children, Mother Berchmans always became the servant rather than the mistress, studying only how to listen and conform herself to the desires and tastes and attractions and needs of her charge, were she the youngest oblate in the novitiate.

Finally, some of her hardest trials came when, after long and prayerful study of the case of one or another of her candidates for the Trappist life, she was forced to decide that the vocation was illusory and suggest a return to the world. This generally meant much more to Mother Berchmans herself than it could have meant to anyone of her novices. Ever since she had first crossed the threshold of Laval, and indeed, for months before, her Cistercian vocation had been the one great joy of her life. Even now, even to her bed of death, she always had in her heart a cold and secret fear that she might lose this great grace, that she might fail to persevere, that something might happen to separate her from her sisters, from the community, and drag her back into the world. This was something she feared as she feared sin, something unthinkable, yet never impossible as long as she was not safe on the other side of the grave in God's grace or glory. She knew what a thing it was to decide that a soul who had seemed to be called by God to this life of pure peace and joy and love, was not called by Him, but belonged outside in the world.

The signs would be there: There would be some radical deficiency, an incapacity to face the hardships of the life, even with the normal dispensations; or a tendency to overstrain, to excessive introverted concentration at prayer that might lead to nervous or mental trouble; an inability to fit in with others in the common life, together with unwillingness or incapacity to look at anyone else, or smile at anyone else, or make a civil sign at any time or for any reason; or else plain, crass, dissipated laziness; or, again, exaggerated scrupulosity, an incurable love of eccentric devotions: all these things had to be considered. Frequently, she would have to tell some poor girl that she must leave and see her dissolve into tears of the truest and most sincere grief, even perhaps falling on her knees to beg to be allowed to stay, with all the earnestness of a heart filled with desire to live for God alone in the cloister; and yet she would know that it could not be, and would have to say so.

It was a test of charity—a test of the true supernatural character of her love; and it would seem as if God were trying every possible way to test that love. But once again, it was a way of finding out whether she would listen to a more or less natural sympathy, and weaken, and so sacrifice the true interests of God in those of the community and of the postulant herself, both of whom could only be harmed by her staying on where she did not belong. She listened to the voice of true love in the depths of her conscience.

What was the secret of her love? A year before her death she was to write: "I still have our dear little novices, whom I love so much; and here again, in these little souls, I find Jesus. Are they not living ciboria of my Beloved?" Her love was always supernatural because even when she loved creatures, it was only her God and His will and His love that she loved in them. In the souls of her spiritual children she saw reflected the love of Christ for them, by which He had called them to Himself; and in the light of that love she saw also all their weaknesses, their helplessness, their needs. And the contrast won her heart.

How could she best love them? By teaching them to love Christ as she desired to love Him herself, as St. Thérèse had loved Him; to love Him on earth as He was loved in heaven.

"You have everything that you need to become saints," she would often say, to her novices. "You have hearts to love with and bodies to suffer with. Love, love: that is enough. That is all Our Lord asks of you."

This was the ordinary subject of conversation with the novices who came to her for direction. She could never insist too strongly on the importance of habitually doing everything, even the smallest and apparently most trivial act, for the pure love of God. This, of course, was the practical foundation for all the acts and aspirations of the heart that she suggested as a means of continued prayer. It was not enough to tell God that they loved Him, and then deny it by their actions; but even as they raised up their hearts to

Him, there would always be an opportunity of making their prayer completely real and genuine and convincing by ordering their will to His will. Whether they were at work, in the chapel, in the refectory, in the dormitory, or anywhere, they could be sure that there was always something that God desired of them, which they were at liberty either to give Him or refuse Him. They could always please Him by doing His will or displease Him by refusing to do it; that is, displease Him by harming themselves, for to refuse Him His will is not to deprive Him of anything, but only to rob ourselves of a grace that He desires to give us by that means.

At prayer, let them avoid long and complicated meditations, lofty thoughts, brilliant ideas, and intuitions. "It is all right for priests to go in for these beautiful thoughts, in mental prayer," she would tell them, "but as for us women, it is enough to let our hearts do the work."

In all their temptations, there was one sure refuge: confidence in God's love for them, a confidence which was the best motive for loving Him in return. "When you are tempted, say: 'My God, I believe in Your love for me!' and you will be consoled."

What a sure and unerring instinct Mother Berchmans had for the pure essentials of the interior life! The only way we can permanently overcome sin is by love, by preferring the will of God whom we love before everything else in the world, even before life itself. But how can we give our whole hearts to Him without reserve unless we believe that He loves us, that He will never abandon us, that He is with us in all our trials, and has, indeed, already overcome them for us upon the cross, if only we will make use of the graces He offers us? It is our belief in His love that opens the flood gates of His grace into our hearts; and it is our lack of trust in Him, our lack of confidence in His love that almost paralyzes the action of His grace in our souls.

It cannot be too often repeated, however, that for Mother Berchmans love, abandonment, and trust were always positive, always intensely practical. Her faith and confidence were always bringing forth much fruit, in sacrifice and good works.

Once a lay-sister novice went to the choir novitiate on some errand and while she was there, overheard Mother Berchmans say the following words in one of her instructions: "Merely to stoop down and pick up a straw off the ground is enough to help a soul, if we do it for the love of God."

Such a doctrine is unintelligible unless it implies perfect obedience, because, obviously, if a religious goes around neglecting the prescriptions of the rule and the desires of her superiors in order to amuse herself with sacrifices of her own choosing, like picking up straws that do not need to be picked up, when there is something far more important to be done, she will not please God or help her sisters or gain any merit for souls. If Mother Berchmans believed that we could show our love for God by such small and insignificant acts, she always warned her spiritual children that they could never please Him by interfering in things that were none of their business.

One day, a zealous little novice, having observed that the ceiling of some room or shed was full of dust and cobwebs, took it upon herself to clean it up. Mother Berchmans arrived upon the scene just as this self-chosen labor was nearing its completion.

"Who told you to do that?" she asked.

"Nobody, Mother. I just did it of my own accord."

"You are not a soul of prayer," said the mother mistress. "You do not think enough of Jesus!" It was a hard saying, but it was a true one. These private, self-chosen works of virtue, which often imply a subtle criticism of other people in the community, are incompatible with a real spirit of prayer, and a person who develops the habit of them will soon lose all capacity for true union with Christ. But Mother Berchmans hastened to temper her severe criticism with a remark that excused the poor novice by showing how human and universal an instinct she had obeyed.

"I know how it is," Mother Berchmans continued. "I suffer, myself, when I notice such things. But when it is none of my business, I let it strictly alone."

It is easy enough to say that we ought to love God in all that we do, to make reparation for sin. But what did that mean for Mother Berchmans? Her teaching on love was never merely vague and general. She always went into practical details. To a novice who asked her how she might sanctify and supernaturalize her manual work, and turn it into a kind of prayer, Mother Berchmans said:

"When you are working, you cannot always be thinking of Our Lord, I know; but at the beginning, offer Him what you are about to do, and then, as you walk, let Him walk beside you; when you go into a building, let Him go in before you; when you sit down, leave room for Him beside you."

Mother Berchmans always strove to sanctify her day, and taught her novices to sanctify theirs, by doing everything simply at the time and in the way prescribed or commanded by the superiors.

"How should I spend my intervals?" a novice once asked her. "When you work, work with all your heart. When you have an interval, pray with all your heart, because the intervals are not the time for work. Do everything in such a way that when the hour of death comes upon you, you will be able to say to Our Lord: 'I made good use of the work-period by working, and I prayed hard during the intervals.'"

She insisted strongly on private prayer, and we have seen that she had devoted most of her own free time to prayer, in the days when she had free time to spend. But she always insisted that her novices stop work or any other business not strictly contemplative as soon as the bell rang for an interval. "If we do not pray in our intervals," she said, "we will get neither graces nor spiritual strength." To another novice she said: "What did you do today? Were you not too loaded with work? Never be afraid to drop whatever you cannot finish."

She was strict in discouraging her novices from pouring themselves out in useless activities, and from becoming too engrossed in work or the satisfaction of curiosities, to the detriment of their prayer. These Japanese girls all had a natural love of flowers and probably were skilled in the art of arranging them in beautiful bouquets. They would have liked very much to put flowers before the statues of all the saints in the novitiate. Indeed, if she had permitted it, they would probably have festooned the shrines of their patrons with the most elaborate decorations. But Mother Berchmans thought it more important for them to spend their intervals in prayer and spiritual reading, and she considered anything that might interfere with these truly contemplative occupations a waste of time. Consequently, she forbade her novices to decorate the novitiate. She suggested that they supply for the lack of flowers by interior sacrifices and prayer and offer up their obedience and their willing renunciation of this little pleasure.

When novices showed a certain lack of balance in their interests and seemed to be excessively taken up with work or studies or other occupations in preference to prayer, she endeavored to give them a truer sense of proportion. One novice always seemed to be talking to her about the work she had done or would do.

"You are always thinking about work," said Mother Berchmans, "and after that about studies and reading, and only after that comes prayer. It ought to be the other way around. Prayer should be your chief occupation. Never forget the importance of the office. When the bell for office rings, realize that it is Jesus calling you."

And, indeed, it was. Jesus was calling them to do the one thing, the *unum necessarium*, for which He had drawn them apart from the world. Nor should they look at the divine office merely in terms of an obligation. How strange it would have seemed to her to refer to the work of God as "choral duties"! She surely never did so. Such a conception would not be worthy of a contemplative.

She said to a certain novice: "To *love* God: that is why we sing the office. It is not just an obligation. That is why we should take care to recite it attentively." Love is never lazy, love is never careless. For laziness and carelessness can only exist where the desire to please God and the fear of losing Him have been dulled by indifference or routine. Love may make mistakes, and become lost in distractions, but it always comes back with an ever greater solicitude and humbler desire to please God at any price. And such was the love that burned in the heart of Mother Berchmans.

That was why she had no patience with slovenly and careless vocal prayers. She kept telling her novices that it was better to say one Hail Mary attentively and with fervor, than ten of them in a hurry. Nor would she have them rush through the stations of the cross. She told them that if they did not have twenty minutes to spare for the way of the cross, they should not do it at all, but rather say the six *Paters*, *Aves*, and *Glorias* of the Scapular of the Immaculate Conception.

Finally, there was one of her novices who was overcome with stage fright at the prospect of accompanying the choir of the nuns on the harmonium in chapel, but Mother Berchmans pointed out that there was no reason for stage fright since this had nothing in common with anything that took place on a stage. "Don't imagine that you are playing for a human audience," she said. "Play for the pleasure of God alone."

CHAPTER XVI

"VIA CRUCIS"

All that has so far been said of her work as mistress of novices belongs, it must be remembered, to the last five years of Mother Berchmans' life, during which the latent illness in her lungs gradually began to take a more definite and invincible grip upon her, and to drag her inexorably to the grave. All that has been said of her sacrifices, her complete holocaust of all her time, all her desires, and all her aspirations to the interior life, in favor of the needs of her spiritual children, can only be appreciated when we see them in their true setting. They were accompanied by an ever increasing physical weakness and exhaustion, and by an ever more crucifying pain which she refused to heed, but which drove her back, step by step, depriving her of one regular observance after another, until all she was able to do was struggle down from the infirmary to give repetition to her novices and receive them in spiritual direction.

Before we accompany her on her ascent to Calvary, we must consider another offering of her life which she made, in 1910, the year when she became mistress of novices.

In that year, there came to her knowledge the story of a fallen priest. What were the details? Father Robert does not tell us. Was it a missionary in Japan, or someone at home in France? We cannot say. It was another version of an all too familiar story: a story that filters through all too often into the silence of the Cistercian cloister, to move hearts to more fervent prayer and sacrifice. What is behind the story of these men who fall away from the very source of life, to wander for a while on the periphery of respectability, hiding their sin under a kind of hopeless exterior nonentity, like the living dead waiting for hell to engulf them, stupefied as by the torpor of some strange tropical disease, or held fast as by the tyranny of a powerful drug?

Those who have experience in these matters know that it is easier to convert a pagan, or even an atheist, to the faith than to win back a fallen priest. How is one to penetrate the armor of their sluggish and despairing indifference to grace? Only by a miracle of grace. And that is one reason why God calls souls, as He had called Mother Berchmans, to the contemplative life.

Hearing, then, of one of these unfortunate prevaricators, Mother Berchmans was so profoundly stirred that she turned to God with all the earnest faith of her heart burning with love for souls, and offered her life again to Him, urging her claims through the meditation of two most powerful advocates, St. Thérèse and St. Gemma Galgani. Let us read the words of her offering, words of fire:

"My beloved angelic little Sisters, Thérèse and Gemma:

"I come to entrust to you a soul whom Jesus loves: a soul, alas, that has fallen into the gravest sins. It is the soul of a fallen priest, Father X—You must—do you hear me, little Sisters?—you absolutely *must* give me this poor soul. In return, I promise to refuse you nothing, with the help of Christ's grace. I give you the last drop of my blood, the last breath of my life. Take everything, but give me this poor soul. I want that soul at any cost. O angelic Little Thérèse, O seraphic Gemma, you who so loved Jesus here below and flame on high with a far more ardent fire of love, set me ablaze with your heavenly flames, and transform my heart into a furnace of love."

If we begin the account of the final stages of Mother Berchmans' life by mentioning this offering of herself, it is not in order to suggest that it was accepted by God, and that the sufferings which were to follow were its answer. We do not know whether they were or not: we do not know what became of the priest for whom it was made. All we know is Mother Berchmans' own charity. And by it we can see with what dispositions she was now about to take up her last and heaviest cross, and prepare for the ascent to Golgotha.

It did not come at once. Months passed. She was engrossed in her work with the novices. Another year ended. It was now 1911. There was Lent, then came spring. No sign of her health giving way as yet. If she knew what was coming, she did not show it, or think about it.

But her Lord gave her a sign during that year that she might expect something soon. It is a law of the spiritual life that great trials usually prepare us for great favors and consolations, and that, conversely, strong favors are sent to strengthen us and steel us against the onslaught of suffering or temptation.

We do not know when this particular favor occurred. But it followed one of the countless trivial acts of sacrifice, opportunities for which come to us in religion scores of times every day. She had desired to send a little package of picture postcards to her sister and brother-in-law. Then it turned out that someone else wanted the same pictures for other purposes. With her usual alacrity, Mother Berchmans gave up all claim to them, not without feeling the sacrifice a little. God allows even the perfect to pay a little for their offerings to Him, that He might get greater glory from them, and they themselves acquire more merit—which, in the end, comes to the same thing.

This time, however, our Lord rewarded Mother Berchmans' generosity in a more immediate and tangible manner than was His ordinary way with her. The next day—perhaps she was no longer thinking about the affair—she went to Holy Communion. With what dispositions did she approach the holy table? We are not told, but are left to assume that it was without any special sensible fervor, rather with her ordinary dryness, demanding the exercise of constant, peaceful faith. She received the Sacred Host into her heart and was returning to her place, when suddenly Jesus spoke to her.

She knew His voice. How? Ask the mystical theologians. But there was no mistaking it. Between this and the voice that might be produced by her own imagination, there was all the difference that there is between human certainty and divine. It was a voice that did not come to her through her senses, interior or exterior. Yet its evidence was more certain than anything merely sensible, with nothing more to recommend it than that it could be touched or seen. It was not, strictly, a voice that she "heard," for hearing is a sense. It was a voice that uttered itself, not as a sound, but as a vital certainty in the very center and substance of her soul.

Yet did it not utter words, and are not words formed of sounding syllables? Yes, but the syllables were in a certain manner suddenly implanted, spiritually, on the very substance of her mind, and came to it from within, from no known, no understandable source.

What were the words?

Jesus said to her: "I am jealous of thy heart."

That was all. Six words. But so simple and so direct, and having upon them such a guarantee of their divine origin, that they had a profound influence upon her whole life from that day on. Father Robert himself accepts this as a clearly mystical favor. "This locution," he says, "was never forgotten, and it inaugurated a new and more perfect phase in her spiritual life." But, as we have said, it was not our Lord's way, with her, to repay her little sacrifices with sudden, sensible favors.

Summer gave way to fall. The leaves fell from the trees. The cold wind began to blow down from Kamchatka and the Arctic Circle. Leaden clouds raced across the cold sky. November ended. Then came Advent, with its fast.

On the vigil of the Immaculate Conception, December 7, she was sent to help in the laundry. The ground was covered with snow, but the air was cold and dry, and the sun was shining. Mother Berchmans spent the greater part of the afternoon carrying clothes in heavy baskets out of the steaming hot laundry into the cold air, where she set them down and spread the clothes out on the hard, crisp snow to dry. Then she would go back into the hot room, and load up another basket amid the din of the Sisters whacking the clothes in the wash tubs with their heavy wooden paddles. It was almost impossible to work in such an atmosphere, even for a few minutes, without all the pores of her body opening and her clothes becoming damp with perspiration. Then she was out again in the snow. The wind came down from the mountain like a knife, and made her woolen robe suddenly feel as light as gingham.

Mother Berchmans did not mind. She was doing the work she had been told to do. It was God that wanted this. He desired her to be hot and then cold. She thanked Him. It was His love. She made acts of love. As for the way she felt, she paid no attention to that. Work ended. Perhaps she was already shivering with fever when she stood in her place in choir and heard the invitatress intone the first lovely antiphon of the vespers of our Lady's feast.

When she took her blankets and pillow from her cell in the dormitory and went slowly to the infirmary, she probably knew that there would not be a return journey. She was glad, if anything. Indeed, she could easily see in this a great favor from the loving and powerful Mother whose feast was being celebrated. Every favor that had ever come to her in life, had come to her from Mary's hands. And now this sickness, on her feast, was no coincidence. Indeed, the words "coincidence" and "chance" did not exist in Mother Berchmans' vocabulary. Oh, she knew that she could not hope to die and go to heaven at once! That would be too much to expect. Or rather, to put it more accurately, she knew that our Lord loved her too much to let her die without drinking His own chalice to the very dregs.

Now she was very ill. The doctor diagnosed her case as bronchitis, and her whole frame was shaken by a new and tearing cough. There was nothing serious, said the doctor, no real danger. But even after she got well enough to return to the regular exercises of the community, she must still sleep in the infirmary.

A letter she wrote to Laval, sometime before this, will serve to show what were her dispositions on this occasion also.

"I do not belong to myself," she had said. "I am in the hands of the Good Master, Who turns me this way and that, just as He pleases, both physically and morally. It is impossible for me to make any mental prayer.... However, since the good God wants it that way, I can only thank Him." Yes, it was impossible for her to pray. This was to be one of the greatest trials of her years in the infirmary: a trial that was to increase as she came gradually nearer to death.

Souls of prayer! Do not count on consolations and ecstasies in your last sickness. It is then that God will really begin to try your faith. If you think you have suffered dryness and distractions when you were well and strong, count them as nothing in comparison to the frightful darkness and incapacity for the slightest good thought which, if God loves you with a great love, as He does, will probably fall upon you in those days. That was the way it was with Mother Berchmans. But if you fear (and why should you not?), take courage, and learn from her example.

When the Sisters came to sympathize with her in her sufferings, she always laughed, and made the Trappist sign for "good" which consists in rubbing the chest with the flat of the hand; and if it was someone to whom she had permission to speak, she would say: "It's good, it's good; it is God that gives me this." Father Robert adds that she always said this with characteristic liveliness, "*élan*"; she was not the one to moan and force a pale, weary smile, and utter words of painful resignation with all the melodramatic undertones of the dying heroine in a cheap movie.

Having heard that her sickness was, as the doctor said, not serious, and that she was simply to sleep in the infirmary, one of the first things she did was to surprise everyone, one early morning in 1912, by giving the doctor's instructions the most literal possible interpretation. Evidently, he had visited her again and decided that she was better and could return to a more normal way of life. Perhaps he had added the word "soon" and she had forgotten it. However, at four o'clock, after the night office, the infirmarian went to Mother Berchmans' cell to find out if she wanted to receive Communion that morning. To her astonishment, the cell was empty. Yes, Mother Berchmans wanted to receive Communion that morning; in fact, she had already gone down to choir and was making her customary preparation, kneeling in the howling draught before the statue of Our Lady of the Angels.

We do not know if she was reprimanded for this. It seems, as a matter of fact, that she succeeded in persuading Mother Scholastica that she was "much better," for, eventually, either in 1912 or 1913, she was rewarded for her zeal by two new jobs, in addition to her tasks as mistress of novices and mistress of lay sisters. The first was that she was to become sacristan once again, for a short while.

In this capacity she was to have the comparatively heavy work of moving the contents of the sacristy into new quarters when the new building was ready for occupation. But a novice would assist her in all this.

The other office given Mother Berchmans was, by its nature, the most exalted and important that she ever held or was to hold in the convent, but it was not in fact as exacting or as valuable to the community as her work in the novitiate. She became third superioress, or president. If she had been at Laval, where the first superior was an abbess, she would have been dignified with the title of subprioress. Here, Mother Scholastica was prioress, her second in command was subprioress, and the third place in the community, the third chair at the head of the chapter room and the refectory, and the stall next to Mother Scholastica in choir, was for Mother Berchmans, as president.

The duties of the president are less complicated than they sound, and they would not have made any extra demands on Mother Berchmans' time. True, however, they required all her tact and charm and supernatural charity.

It is always a difficult and unpleasant task to correct others, and all the more so when the correction has to be done by a sign. The president ordinarily does not speak to anyone, in her capacity as third superioress. Mother Berchmans' chief duty was to see that everything was carried out in good order, in the choral functions especially, and in everything surrounding the liturgy, but also in all the little practical details of community life. Worst of all, it was her peculiar and characteristic office to persecute the nuns who might allow themselves to be overcome with sleep in choir, or in the chapter room, or anywhere else, for that matter, except the dormitory. She must have been very sensitive about the fact that she herself slept until three in the infirmary. That made it even more of a sacrifice when she had to go and give a charitable nudge to some veteran nun, worn out by long hours of hard work and fasting and vigils in choir from which she herself was dispensed. But Mother Berchmans' conscience had no reason to reproach her! After Mother Scholastica, there was no one busier or more active or more burdened with responsibilities than she was.

Furthermore, even though the doctor said she was all right, she soon discovered that she could not throw herself into all this work with impunity. Soon she began to feel as if there were several long, sharp knives sticking into her back and under her ribs; and every time she drew breath, one or another of these knives would give a sudden, agonizing twist within her. At other times, a breath of cold air would seem to burn her lungs like a red-hot iron. The suffering pervaded her whole chest, and weakened her whole frame, and she was forced to make it known to the doctor.

After having examined her, he decided that it was rheumatism.

Whatever it was, she was glad, and accepted it with her usual enthusiasm. And if it was harmless, then so much the better. She could offer it up to God in reparation for sin, and go about all her duties with a clear conscience, perfectly satisfied that she was in no way disobeying her Lord by an excessive or imprudent zeal.

She wrote, cheerfully: "At the moment, I am paying for my escapes from the infirmary, with rheumatism in the chest. It is painful, but nothing serious, and I am very glad of a chance to suffer a little."

What she wrote at the actual time of this special suffering passes it all off with careless indifference. But we may judge of the severity of these pains by what she was to write, retrospectively, in the following year: "Last year, Jesus certainly put me through the wringer, and I thought He was going to speed me on my way to heaven."

"To one who knew her," Father Robert remarks, "these few words speak volumes. If she found that something was painful, one might have no hesitation in accepting her evaluation! If she considered she had been put through the wringer, we can safely say that she suffered a real martyrdom."

As Lent progressed, although she did not bear the full burden of the fasting, yet the increase of hours in choir, especially concentrated as they are in the morning, made itself felt, and the season was not without its great and increasing hardships for her. It was not surprising, therefore, that when Good Friday came, it brought along another "grace" in the form of a real, unmistakable warning of her condition.

It was sometime during that day. She probably went to choir with all the others at two o'clock. Then the night office was sung, after which the nuns went immediately to their cells to take the discipline. Good Friday is a long, hard day in Trappistine convents. Hours of chanting on an empty stomach are offered in reparation for the sins of the world and in memory of Christ's Passion.

Oh, we know that Mother Berchmans did not look at the physical difficulties of this day. The long office, culminating in the stark, appalling haste in which the last Host remaining from Holy Thursday was suddenly elevated and consumed at the "Mass of the Presanctified," while the nuns looked on with hearts empty and aghast: all this made her want to suffer everything she could possibly suffer for Jesus, because, by it, she not only believed she was near Him on Calvary, but the realization of the fact was darkly but powerfully driven home to her in every moment of that terrifying ceremony.

That day she was to have her desire. She was alone—either at prayer or in her infirmary cell—when suddenly a streak of hot, red blood boiled up into her mouth, out of her choking throat, and spilled over her lips into the handkerchief she quickly raised to stop it. It was over in an instant. She looked at her handkerchief, and read the message in it.

There was joy in her heart, a great and deep and terrible joy. But we should not speak of it as if it were a joy that flooded her with sweetness. It was something dark, appalling, incomprehensible, but it was real joy, nevertheless. The abyss of death had suddenly opened out before her feet; a terror to her flesh, it could not help but strike the very roots of her nature with a thrill of cold excitement, but her heart leaped up at once to God with peaceful gladness in faith, mingled with the mighty exultation of the thought that her deliverance was near.

She interpreted it at once as a "call" from the captain of her legion. It was a message from her leader, Little Thérèse. The captain had seen that her little standard-bearer was ready to advance into the battle, and had sent her warning to be ready for orders to move up to the front line.

Of course she must have told Mother Scholastica about it, and received more than the usual care. The event implied no immediate danger of death. It simply warned her that her condition was really serious. However, she was already sleeping in the infirmary and receiving other minor mitigations, and since it does not seem that any special importance was attached by the doctor to this streak of blood, she was not, it seems, confined to her cell. She continued to attend choir, giving her voice as best she could, apart from the night hours when it was altogether extinct; she continued to sacrifice all her free time and spare energy to directing her novices and lay sisters, in spite of the cough that frequently interrupted her talks and racked her whole frame.

No one, in fact, seems to have realized that she definitely had tuberculosis, except Mother Berchmans herself. And she was so calm and unconcerned about it that she was perfectly willing to accept the doctor's official optimism. Undoubtedly her heart was full of happiness and contentment with the realization that her work would soon be done.

She did her best to keep this a secret, but it had to slip out at least twice. She told one of the lay sisters about it, saying: "Don't tell anybody, but I coughed up a streak of blood on Good Friday, and I think I will soon be going to heaven."

In a letter to a friend, she confided her hopes at greater length without specifically stating the incident on which they rested: "I am going to tell you a little secret," she wrote, "but keep it to yourself. On your visit to Our Lady of the Angels, I asked you, in the event that the good God might call you to Himself before me, to come and build a big fire in my heart and speedily carry me off to the home of love...but since you seem inclined to take root here on earth, I turned to my 'little Captain' and asked her to call her little standard-bearer as soon as the formation of the battalion was well under way. And I believe my 'Little Captain' is calling me, but with a voice so weak and distant that the Good God seems not to hear her at all."

This letter was evidently written some months after the event on Good Friday, for she shows that her hopes of death were not being actualized. The spring weather, the absence of fasting, and all the other factors that make paschal time a season of rest and recuperation for the Cistercian after the hardships of winter and Lent, joined with the special motherly solicitude of her superiors in her regard, had a good effect, and the streak of blood was not followed by any serious consequences. And therefore she adds that, far from listening to Little Thérèse, the good God "sees only the motherly cares showered upon me by Reverend Mother, who is afraid I might leave her. What am I going to do to get out of this fix?"

That did not mean that her summer was to be a vacation from suffering. Not only did her physical torment continue, but interior trials became intensified during this period also.

On the eighth of May she wrote to a priest, lamenting her coldness and dryness of soul. It became more and more difficult for her to pray as days went on. Instead of being able to call forth, with her old facility, so many ardent acts of love from her pure soul, she entered into herself to find nothing but a desert of useless and even frightening thoughts. It seemed as if her heart was cursed with barrenness, abandoned forever, by her Beloved, and left to the specters of the spiritual half-world, to mock her in her helplessness.

"Pray for the poor Little Standard-Bearer," she wrote. "At the moment my course has brought me into the arctic ice-floes. I wish I could tell you how cold, how terribly cold, I am. My heart is a glacier. So please beg Jesus that the warm rays of your blessing may transform this glacier into a furnace of love. How is it, anyway, that in spite of all your prayers for this little soldier, she does not love her Jesus more than she does? One thing comforts me: the desire to love is, in fact, love. And if my heart is all ice, my will is all on fire. How often I repeat to Jesus: 'If you will, you can consume me!' But He who is All-Love has not yet replied: 'I will, be thou consumed!' I think that when He actually does utter that '*fiat*,' my heart, with all the impetuosity of a torrent breaking through a dam, will plunge and lose itself in the depths of Eternal Love. But when will that be? It is up to you, who are so powerful over the Heart of Jesus, to hasten that happy moment. Meanwhile, blow hard on the poor little fire which has almost gone out!"

The year 1912 drew to its close. It had been the most active and most replete with sacrifice in her whole life. Every day had seen a new immolation of herself, both physically and spiritually. The fact of her continued generosity, and her lack of concern for herself and her pains, seems to have given her superiors a false impression of her strength; and when she did make known her special crises, as she was obliged to do, they were at a loss to understand them.

We have so far seen the little community of Our Lady of the Angels through the eyes of Father Robert and of Mother Berchmans herself, and in the light of Mother Berchmans' trials and struggles, her temptations, and her difficulties. And we know how it is with a soul beset by trials: God does not show such a one the good effect of her work, or the bright side of her afflictions. He does not allow her to see the immense good she is doing for His kingdom.

In 1913, however, there was a regular visitation of the little Japanese convent, a record of which has come to us, and which will serve to lift the veil a little on this brighter aspect of things. Dom Edmond Obrecht, the abbot of the proto-abbey of the New World, Our Lady of Gethsemani, in Kentucky, was traveling in the Far East that year, commissioned by the general chapter to visit the various houses there.

Dom Edmond, during his lifetime, was without any doubt one of the most important and influential members of the Cistercian Order of the Strict Observance. To begin with, there were few abbots in the order who had a wider experience and more profound knowledge of its needs and problems. Dom Edmond ranked with such men as Dom Jean-Baptiste Chautard, Dom Hermann-Joseph Smets, and Dom Sebastian Wyart as one of the great Trappist administrators of our century. He had begun his religious life at La Grande Trappe, that is, at one of the most fervent and important communities of the order—the one which, for a long time, even gave our religious family its name and character. From there he had gone to Rome as procurator for the monastery of Tre Fontane, where he successfully battled against the unsanitary conditions of the site, and finally made it possible for the monks to lead the regular Cistercian life. Having then become abbot of one of the chief Cistercian abbeys of America, Dom Edmond continued to serve his order in every part of the world. By the time of his death there was scarcely a house which he had not visited.

This energetic, clear-sighted, practical man, with all his wide experience and deep knowledge, was now on his way to Hakodate, to make the regular visitations of the two communities in the vicinity of that city. It was January. The sea was rough, and Dom Edmond, who was always very famous for his uncompromising frankness, did not disguise the fact that the crossing from Aomori was far from delightful.

"I arrived here, *Deo volente*," he wrote to his prior, Father Frederic Dunne, "absolutely broken up. Six hours in an oil tub with a very high sea, two hours on foot, an hour and a half in a skiff: then two more hours in the snow, on a mare's shank. All very poetical when it's over, but very painful while it lasts. You will ask me, perhaps, whether I was sick. Yes, and never more before. The little boat was pitching and tossing like a cork on the water. I had a high fever, felt cold, and had stomach trouble for three days. We are having a heavy snowstorm just now, and it has been snowing for the last three days...."

The part of the journey in the skiff and on the mare's shank brought Dom Edmond to Our Lady of the Lighthouse, where, although he found the monks very fervent, he was nonetheless depressed by the lack of Japanese postulants. There were only two, at that time, and Dom Edmond felt that the house had little chance of surviving unless matters changed. Consequently, when he climbed back on his horse, and then into the skiff, and came to Hakodate, where he found a sleigh waiting to take him to Our Lady of the Angels, Dom Edmond was in no optimistic mood, and prepared to give in to no illusions.

His first reaction was, indeed, expressed in terms of somewhat guarded satisfaction, qualified by many "ifs" and "buts."

"The Reverend Mother Scholastica," he wrote, "is an excellent nun, very well disposed and very well loved by her daughters...but, alas, overloaded with work. Her health does not seem to be very good, and I think means should be found to lighten her burden. The Subprioress is likewise a good nun, but there is one drawback, she does not speak Japanese. The mistress of lay sisters (that was Mother Léonie, who had succeeded Mother Berchmans) is deaf, but she is a fervent, excellent, and holy nun. The office of chantress is filled by Sister Angelica: there is a lack of voices (Dom Edmond liked to hear a good strong choir), but the singing is very pious and all the pauses are well made. Mother Berchmans, the Mistress of Novices, is an excellent, intelligent, and very holy nun, but she is threatened with tuberculosis."

That was only the beginning. When, as visitor, he entered the enclosure, he found spotless cleanliness, great poverty, perfect silence, peace, recollection, joy, and fervor in every face. This was truly a house of God. But what impressed him most of all were the Japanese oblates. Gone were those first sad days when Mother Berchmans had been somewhat discouraged at the aspect of the poor, unhappy, and bewildered candidates that had first come from outside to join them in their austere Cistercian solitude.

"What dear little children!" Dom Edmond exclaimed, "What a child of God!" And the more he saw of their joy and humility and simplicity and perfect obedience, the clearer it became that all was due, in large part, to the teaching and example of their mother mistress. "And what," added Dom Edmond, with even greater enthusiasm, "shall I say of Mother Berchmans!"

He was not totally at a loss for words. This good abbot, who was one of the most fervent clients of St. Thérèse of Lisieux and later became one of the best friends of her sisters and community, in the Carmel where she offered up her sweet sacrifice to God, did not hesitate to write: "What good souls they are! (At Our Lady of the Angels.) Your saintly Carmelite and your Virgin of Lucca are equalled here, if not surpassed. I never met with souls so utterly abandoned to the Will of God. What self-denial, humility, and obedience! Such souls must bring down upon a wicked world the richest blessings and favors of God. My last stop during this long, painful voyage shall certainly be one of the choicest souvenirs of my life. Oh, the consolations I tasted here!...I had but compliments to pay. This week spent within the Trappistine monastery in Japan was as good as a week's retreat for me."

In another letter he wrote: "It is a great pity indeed that both the Reverend Mother and Sister Berchmans have such poor health. I wrote the Visit card but really there was nothing to correct. But if one of these two Sisters were to disappear, what would become of the community?"

His highest praise was all for Mother Berchmans. Dom Edmond always said precisely what he thought about people and events, and he was no more reticent in her regard than he was about anything else. Having admitted that "Reverend Mother Scholastica is a great woman" he proceeds with: "The Mistress of Novices is a saint. She impresses me more than all your Thérèses and Gemmas!"

And we repeat, Dom Edmond was a practical man, and by no means what one would call a dreamer. He judged by visible results. He believed that a good tree would be known by its fruits, and he had seen the fruits of this tree. He had seen the work of the Holy Ghost in this saintly little community. Above all, he had seen the spirit of God working through the deeply contemplative victim-soul of Mother Berchmans, pouring out graces and forming angels of simplicity and love in her spiritual children. "What sweet little pure and holy children these Japanese oblates are!"

Here, indeed, he had no fears for the future, unless, as he admitted, Mother Berchmans or Mother Scholastica should die. But he had forgotten just one thing: it was Mother Berchmans' final holocaust, her last total gift of herself that was to put the seal of success on the work that had already been begun, and guarantee its fruitfulness for years to come.

CHAPTER XVII

"VIA CRUCIS" (CONTINUED)

Dom Edmond had written that Mother Berchmans was "threatened" with tuberculosis, when nearly a year had passed since her first hemorrhage! However, during the year 1913, her condition began, seemingly, to improve, and soon she had regained a semblance of health which might have made her forget the sufferings she had borne the previous year. In the summer of 1913, she could write the following in a letter:

"You reproach me with having concealed the state of my health from you. What a good inspiration it was, to keep it from you! You would have committed the imprudence of praying for my recovery instead of rejoicing that Jesus did not find me too unworthy to suffer a little for His love; but I was not yet ripe for heaven, and in spite of the reiterated calls of Little Thérèse, our good Reverend Mother won out, with all her practically unlimited solicitude in my regard. Jesus could not resist all this maternal care, and here I am making a new pact with life, a little sad to see that my exile is to be prolonged, but happy to do the will of my Beloved."

We cannot but be amused and touched by the naïve way in which she represents herself as caught in a kind of charitable tug of war between the Little Flower, trying to pull her into heaven, and Mother Scholastica who wanted to keep her on earth. It shows us that, although the mother prioress took the doctor's word and refused to admit that Mother Berchmans definitely had tuberculosis, she did not, for all that, neglect her, but outdid herself in providing for her care in every possible way, though always in the spirit of the Cistercian life of penance.

Mother Berchmans herself, of course, had never had any inclination to pamper her body, and she did not develop one now. When she was offered things that appeared to be superfluous comforts, like a heated brick wrapped up in flannel and placed in her bed in guise of a hot-water bottle, she simply laughed and would not accept them. Nevertheless, she saw to it that her novices had such little luxuries when they were sick.

And when there was question of sacrificing herself for others, when for instance, she had to be in a draught because of the desires or needs of someone else, she did not complain or try to get out of it. Nor did she hesitate, during the last winter of her life, to spend a whole morning shivering in the unheated novitiate, waiting for one of the novices to come to direction, and, afterward, speaking to her there in the same low temperature.

Meanwhile, 1914 brought a much heavier addition to her burden. First her sisters were dismayed at her reappointment as interior cellarer and sacristan, as well as novice mistress; then came a source of interior anguish which, while increasing her sufferings, also powerfully stimulated her desire to sacrifice her very life for a world gone mad with its own lusts and hatreds.

Not much word of the first World War filtered through into the enclosure of the distant convent in Japan, but the outbreak of hostilities was a severe blow to Mother Berchmans. What tension filled the hearts of the nuns that morning in the little chapter room when mother prioress announced the terrible news!

Mother Berchmans responded with characteristic generosity. She was to have so many opportunities for sacrifice, in the last year of her life, which was the first year of the war, that it is quite clear that she died as a victim for the warring nations.

Not only were her own sacrifices offered up for peace, for the souls of soldiers, and for an Allied victory, but she also urged all her novices repeatedly to do the same. But hear her own conception of her role in the war, as she expressed it in a letter of October, 1914, acknowledging the receipt of a new book about St. Thérèse:

"Little Thérèse is always our best-beloved little saint, and the miracle worker of our century. We are praying to her in a special manner, just now, for our dear country. And there is no doubt at all that Thérèse is there, in the midst of the soldiers, sustaining some, encouraging others, helping those in agony to die a holy death, and preserving all those especially entrusted to her from every danger. Do you not regret that you were not sent with the army? (We do not know to whom she wrote; perhaps to her brother-in-law.) As for the Little Standard-Bearer, she offers her frailty as a woman, which keeps her far from the front, and she would like, by her prayers and sacrifices, to do what she is otherwise prevented from accomplishing."

The war also added its increment to the little burdens of community life at Our Lady of the Angels. Several of the nuns and lay sisters from Ubexy were Germans, but the European element in the community seems to have been fairly evenly divided between French and German Sisters. All of them were more or less eager for the victory of their own respective countries, and it is even probable that some of them got a little excited at the fragments of war news that came into the house. Such was the supernatural spirit of the community, however, that this was all kept under control, and the war did not succeed in making any division between the Sisters united in the charity of Christ and in their peaceful Cistercian family.

Mother Berchmans was a model in this respect. Any good news that came from France, but which might imply bad news for the German Sisters, was never received by her with any expression of exultation or excessive satisfaction. On the other hand, when a Sister from Ubexy got good news about a relative in the German army, Mother Berchmans was always the first to share in her joy, even though a French defeat also was involved.

Particular items of news, however, rarely came to Our Lady of the Angels, and the effect of the war remained almost entirely on the spiritual level, where it belonged in a contemplative community: a constant occasion for intensified prayer and sacrifice, not only for single nations but for the whole world.

God had reserved another big sacrifice for Mother Berchmans in 1914. Until the full story of her birth and early childhood is known, we will never be able to estimate the depth of her affection for her mother, nor the importance of her family in her own spiritual life. Suffice it to say that her warm heart was always tied with a deep and supernatural affection to her mother and sister, but especially to her mother, and her prayers were never so fervent as when she was beseeching God's loving protection and every possible grace for this dear soul who had suffered so much in bringing her into the world.

Now, in the early fall of the tragic year of 1914, Mother Berchmans received news that this beloved mother of hers had fallen ill beyond all hope of recovery.

"My heart is very full at this moment," she wrote, concerning this news, to her spiritual mother at Laval, "for Jesus seems to be about to ask of me another great sacrifice: that of my dear maman. Last week I got news that she had received the Last Sacraments: perhaps at this very hour she is in eternity. I am not able to dwell on such a thought. It is too crushing. However, whatever Jesus wills! Maman belongs doubly to Him since I already sacrificed her to Him once when I entered religion. He can therefore take her whenever He pleases."

Word was not long in coming that the sacrifice was consummated. One day in November came another letter telling her that her mother had suffered a long and extremely painful agony, lasting eight days, and had finally died on the third of October. What anguish her poor child must have felt, and yet what consolation too, for did not these days almost coincide with the time when Sister Thérèse had died as love's victim, and gone to heaven?

Nevertheless, this was the hardest blow that death had ever dealt her. It had been quite different, for example, when Father Polycarpe was called from this world some years before. It had been painful, yes, to know that he was gone; and yet the death of such a good and holy and generous soul, after so many years of loving service of God, could not but be an occasion of deep and peaceful joy, at the thought of the magnitude of his reward. But her mother had been a poor, weak woman, and had struggled long in the world, often with all the suffering and confusion of a soul that does not and cannot see things clearly in the spiritual life. She had suffered, perhaps, most from those things that should have been her consolation. Was it possible to forget her brokenhearted tears at the announcement that her daughter wanted to become a Trappistine?

Above all, there were the strong ties of flesh and blood; the natural love for friends and relatives was something so deeply rooted in Mother Berchmans' heart that it could never be extricated without taking with it her very life itself.

As soon as she could, she retired to the little room which was hers as mistress of novices, and let the sorrow in her heart overflow in warm tears as she reread the letter, praying all the while for her poor mother's soul. God, however, would not allow her even this luxury of natural emotion, for presently a knock came on the door, and a little Japanese novice looked shyly in.

It was her time for spiritual direction, and Mother Berchmans, drying her tears, told her to come in. After a few words, considering what must be going on in the heart of her mother mistress, the child offered to get up and go, and leave her to herself. But the kind intention was quite fruitless. Mother Berchmans would hear of no such thing. If her emotion had got the better of her for a moment, that was natural, and did not displease God. Far from it. Had not Jesus wept at the tomb of Lazarus? But what good purpose would be served by indulging these feelings when so much could be accomplished for her mother's soul, and to please the Sacred Heart of her Beloved, merely by attending as best she could to the work that was His will.

She smiled a little and said to the novice: "Oh no, do not go away. I am here just to listen to you, and that is far more important than anything else whatever."

The good child, however, responding to the generosity of her mother mistress with her own charity, talked not of herself but only of the sad news that had just arrived, so that soon, in spite of herself, Mother Berchmans was weeping again, and the little Japanese novice with her.

Then, while the two of them were in tears, another chance came to prove her love of Jesus by the sacrifice of natural feeling.

The bell rang suddenly. It was time to go to chapter for the reading before compline. Mother Berchmans dried her tears again, as best she could, and they were off, with red eyes, to be on time at their respective places in the chapter room simply because the rule prescribed it; it was one of the common exercises.

Had this news come to her two or three years before, it is certain that she would have preserved the letter and reread it many times. Indeed, there would have been no occasion for surprise had she done so at this time. But no. So great was her detachment and her spirit of poverty that she used the blank side of the sheet to write a note, in the course of her day's work, to one of the novices or someone else in the convent, just as they all used any old envelope or scrap of paper for such purposes. Some people might be shocked at this apparent heartlessness; but it shows that Mother Berchmans had achieved that true sense of values which accompanies real interior liberty, without which there is no perfect love of God or of our neighbor. One might say that if she had clung to the letter (which in itself was nothing), with all the tenacity of natural sentiment, we should have to admit that her capacity for loving her mother was less than it was proved to be by this act of renunciation.

What was important was not to weep over material tokens and souvenirs, but to turn to God in the exercise of real charity toward her mother by faithful and confident prayer. And she did not hesitate to ask the prayers of her Father Immediate, the abbot of Bricquebec, and all his community, for her mother's needs. How did she happen to be writing to Dom Vital Lehodey? It seems that in her last years she corresponded regularly with him on spiritual matters, giving him frequent accounts of the state of her soul, in which he had been showing such a lively interest, especially since his last visitation. This, incidentally, is one of the clearest proofs of her advanced spirituality; and we shall see that Dom Vital, beyond question, considered her not only a very saintly soul but also believed her to be well established in mystical prayer, or more precisely, in the passive purifications which are its necessary accompaniment.

Now, however, she wrote to him as follows: "Jesus called to Himself my dear mother on the third of October after a long and painful agony lasting nearly eight days. I am perfectly confident that our good Master has had mercy on her. Dear maman, she was so good and pious. Yet perhaps she is still suffering in Purgatory. And therefore, Reverend and dear Father, I appeal to your charity in favor of this beloved soul."

1914 reserved for her one far more important piece of news. This time, as far as she was concerned, it was an occasion of unmixed joy, although no one else in the community agreed with her in the least. In the last month of the year, what she had long been secretly suspecting and hoping for, became a confirmed fact.

Mother Scholastica had called in a new doctor. He had examined Mother Berchmans with the greatest care. To confirm his diagnosis beyond any possibility of doubt, he took a sputum test. Then, on the octave day of the Immaculate Conception, he told them his verdict. Mother Berchmans had an extremely serious case of tuberculosis. The disease was far advanced, and had taken so firm a hold upon her lungs that it was almost certain that she would succumb to it within a year. Her sputum was full of bacteria, and also gave evidence that she had suffered from the same disease at intervals for some years past, having partially overcome it by her own natural resistance. Now it had definitely got the better of her.

How she received this piece of news! Father Robert declares himself unequal to the task of describing her exuberant satisfaction. And her chief consolation was in the fact that she could so clearly see the kind influence of her sweet Mother Mary in this grace. Now she knew that her prayers were being answered. She would be able to lay down her life for God. She would soon be able to die as a victim of His love. Her holocaust would soon be consummated. Now she would prove that her love was not merely a matter of words or sentiments. Jesus would know that she loved Him more than life itself, and that she would, indeed, put herself entirely into His hands and suffer everything that it pleased Him to send her, for His love, to win grace for souls, to make reparation for sin.

The first thing she did, after hearing the doctor's verdict, was to hasten to the chapel and cast herself down on her knees and recite the most fervent *Magnificat* of her whole life in thanksgiving for what she had just heard. On that December day in 1914, after two years of great suffering and hardship, Mother Berchmans was thanking God for the prospect of even greater suffering and finally death, with greater ardor than that with which the most grateful souls have sometimes thanked Him for delivering them from mortal sickness by a miracle!

Only after her own first transport of joy did she realize that the news had had quite the opposite effect on Mother Scholastica and the rest of the community. Dom Edmond had said that he feared what would happen to the community if they should lose Mother Berchmans, and the good prioress was actually in tears at the prospect. Indeed, all the nuns surrounded the little mistress of novices with tears in their eyes, and the novices themselves were completely crushed at what they heard. Then, seeing the grief and hearing the sobs of her sisters, Mother Berchmans began to repent of showing so much joy, and tried to make up for it by assuring Mother Scholastica that, after all, doctors were not infallible, and that this might prove to be a mistake. Spring would soon come again, and she would very likely regain her strength, and might eventually recover altogether. But her words did not ring true, and few felt able to believe her now. Eventually she gave up trying to console them, but rather reproached them with lamenting her good fortune. "I am so happy that I am going to see God," she would tell them; and when one of the Sisters complained that she spoke so much of leaving them and going to heaven, she replied: "But heaven is our home."

Now, of course, she had not only to sleep in the infirmary, but also take her meals there, and, in fact, make it her permanent abode, except that she continued to follow the regular exercises of the community, and come to chapel, we shall soon see with what difficulty. Above all, she came down to give the novices their repetition in the rule and usages and receive them in spiritual direction.

Thus, says Father Robert, she entered upon that last and most perfect period of her life: a period in which, as he tells us, her love grew beyond all bounds, and she reached such perfection that during these eight months in the infirmary, the last months of her life, only one, half-voluntary imperfection was seen to have escaped her—and Father Robert, as we know, had never been blind to her defects. The imperfection he refers to was that once, when she could hardly even walk, she expressed a little indignation that she should not be allowed to go down to the chapel to receive Communion, considering it too much of an indignity that her Lord should have to be carried all the way to the infirmary on account of her. With the exception of this single fault, which surely had nothing very scandalous about it, and which would, indeed, have been considered by some as a sign of virtue, all her other actions were those of one far advanced in sanctity and union with God.

It soon became evident that her sufferings were going to be multiplied beyond all former bounds. Scarcely a few days had passed, since her definite confinement to the infirmary, than she suffered a painful and humiliating accident. With her usual motherly charity, she was far more concerned with the needs of others than with her own, and one cold morning, about four o'clock, she had just busied herself lighting a fire in the room of a sick novice in the infirmary, when, coming out, she missed her footing, in the darkness, at the head of the stairway that was directly outside the door, and fell down the full length of the flight of steps.

Although no bones were broken, her whole body was to ache for some days to come, and the fall undoubtedly did her ruined lungs no good. Meanwhile, no one being present, she struggled to her feet and made her way at once, though very painfully, to chapel, and fell on her knees at her usual place before the statue of Our Lady of Angels. Then she heard Mass, received Holy Communion, and remained just as long as usual at her thanksgiving, after which she went to the novitiate where a novice needed to speak with her. The child was received with smiles and love, and did not guess that anything had happened to her mother mistress, who did not make the accident known until noon of that day.

Her new status also brought with it a few little humiliations which, although slight, could not help but make themselves felt by so sensitive and loving a nature as hers. She admitted that it cost her a little to have to remind her novices not to come too close to her, and to sit at a distance from her at direction. Then one day, when she unthinkingly approached the door of the convent kitchen, she had to be politely warned, by a gesture, not to enter, lest she infect the food of the community. All this, however, was more material for sacrifice, and that was what she wanted.

The succeeding months, in which the winter weather brought with it no little aggravation to her sickness, probably in the form of high fever and frequent hemorrhages, also saw considerable activity in the little convent where many prayers were offered up for her recovery. In fact, Mother Scholastica realized the seriousness of the situation and determined not to lose her most valuable officer, mobilizing the little community in a series of fervent novenas starting out, naturally, with two appeals to the Little Flower. What is more, Mother Berchmans was ordered, against all her own personal desires, to join in these prayers for her recovery, and make the novena in union with her sisters. She smilingly and peacefully complied.

"What will be the will of God for me," she told a Sister, "I cannot tell. Father Robert wants me to pray for my recovery, and therefore I do so. But I am not so sure that I won't die of this thing anyway. Besides, since suffering is a great gift from God to me, I certainly don't think He is going to work a miracle on my behalf. Miracles are necessary for people in the world, but not for religious. The treasures that religious want to acquire are merits for heaven."

Neither this novena nor the special medicines sent posthaste from France by the Father Immediate seemed to offer any hope of recovery. Quite the contrary. She had said that the best gifts that God could give her now were sufferings to increase her merit in His sight: and that was precisely the answer that Little Thérèse gave to this first novena.

"I have more big news to tell you," Mother Berchmans wrote to a priest. "For in spite of all the excellent remedies that Reverend Father has been sending, in his charity, Jesus has sent me another, and more urgent 'call,' and so, short of a miracle, your little Sister Misery will soon fly away to heaven. But this miracle is something that Reverend Mother is dead set on obtaining, at any cost, from Little Thérèse."

As a result, the good nuns of Our Lady of the Angels soon began a second novena to the Little Flower, this time enlisting the support of the whole Carmel of Lisieux, in a concerted effort to win a miracle from their mighty advocate in heaven. Unfortunately, even Thérèse's sister, Celine, seemed to side with the invalid. She wrote to Mother Berchmans: "To please your sisters, I desire you to get well; but interiorly I leave Jesus perfectly free, and I would not want to delay your joy. I know well enough, for my own part, how much it costs to live on earth."

Once again the novena had the same result. Thérèse knew what was to the best interests of her little standard-bearer. After the nine days of prayer, Mother Berchmans was again appreciably worse.

January was ending. Soon it would be the season sacred to the memory of the first apparitions at Lourdes. The nuns of Our Lady of the Angels decided to change their attack and try to move the citadel of God's merciful favors from another quarter. This time, they began a novena to Bernadette Soubirous, who was not yet called "Saint."

"Her answer," Mother Berchmans tells us, "was even more painful than that of Little Thérèse. For on the day the novena ended, I was so utterly exhausted that I could not even cough, and the doctor declared that I could not last another two months." Meanwhile the indefatigable Sisters refused to give up hope, and, in February or March, still another novena was begun, this time to Our Lady of Lourdes. And this time, it seemed that their prayers were answered.

Yes, this time they had been heard. Perhaps it was even the miracle they had desired, or perhaps God had answered them through the ordinary processes of nature, but on the doctor's first visit after the novena, he was astonished to note a remarkable improvement.

"Our dearest Mother, with her good and tender heart," wrote the secretly disappointed patient, "could not remain deaf to so many prayers and supplications, and to the great surprise of our doctor on his next visit, he noticed that the left lung was entirely cured. As for the right lung, in a few days there will be simply nothing left of it at all, but that does not make any difference, for a person can live very well on one lung, especially if that lung has been renovated by the Blessed Virgin."

Unfortunately for those who exulted at the success of their prayers, and began to claim a miracle, it turned out that her left lung was far from cured. The doctor had simply been unable to make a correct judgment of its condition because of Mother Berchmans' intense fatigue, which made his observation of the lung, at that moment, extremely difficult and deceptive.

Once this was finally made known to the community, the nuns became more or less resigned to the fact that they must soon lose their dear Mother Berchmans, although that did not prevent a few individuals from continuing their ardent prayers for a miracle to save her. As far as the patient herself was concerned, her peaceful and joyous abandonment to God's will emerged from these vicissitudes all the more perfect and more pure. Her comment on the whole thing was: "So now I am back on the high seas. But if the good God wants to give me another forty years, I want only what He wills."

Now, as she realized, and told one of her sisters, she was in the "kingdom of suffering, which is the kingdom of love." Indeed now, more than ever, she studied how to please her Lord by renunciation of herself and her own will in every possible way. And certainly now was the time when her love would be most truly put to the test. Many a fervent and mortified religious may be seen to fail in many ways under the test of sickness. A sister—or a monk, for that matter—may come, after years of regularity and evident fervor, to the infirmary, and suddenly find that the patience and self-denial that came so easy to her when she was healthy and sacrifice was a joy, are now much more difficult when everything is hard, and when her body is broken and her mind has begun to lose its elasticity and clarity, and fever fills the brain with the fogs of imagination and makes faith doubly hard.

It was not so with Mother Berchmans. Her humility and patience and mortification were only the more perfect, in spite, not only of her increased physical suffering, but also of the intensified interior trials that went with it.

One of the most important and revealing documents of this, or any other period of her life, is the letter she wrote on March 8, 1915, to Dom Vital Lehodey, exposing the state of her soul.

"It appears from your good letter, dear Reverend Father," she wrote, "that you think everything is full of joy for your child, and that she is swimming in consolations." She had probably given him that impression by the exuberance of her satisfaction at the thought of soon going to heaven. "But no, this is far from the case. For the last few years, it is my will that does all the work. It is with my will that I believe, and stubbornly persist in believing. But where are my heart and my mind? Prayer, the interior life, have become impossible to me. Everything in me seems to have been reduced to the animal level. Like the Prophet, I can say, 'I am like a beast of burden before Thee,' and I fight hard to add: 'and I am ever with Thee.'" And here we come to one of the most beautiful expressions of her humility. "*I do not even dare to call this a state of trial. No, I simply believe that there are few souls as stupid as mine; and I raise myself above these thoughts, and say: 'Too bad! I will just have to belong to Jesus as His little brute beast!'* And then I start out again, in pursuit of love. That is my sole refuge. There alone do I manage to find rest. It is at such moments that it does me good to read the life of Little Thérèse.

"Reverend Father, what an ugly picture I have just painted! You see how much your little daughter needs your good prayers, and how hard our dearest Mother will have to work, if she is going to make a Seraph out of me. Nothing is impossible to that good Mother, and this would be a miracle worthy of her maternal Heart. And so I place all my hope in her—and my trust is without limits."

It is an indirect tribute to the excellence of the saintly abbot of Bricquebec as a director of souls, that it was he who drew forth from Mother Berchmans' soul this most beautiful and clear and frank and simple manifestation of her interior state. It is evident at once that, far from agreeing with her diagnosis of herself, Dom Vital clearly saw that she was far advanced in that state of passive mystical purification known as the "night of the senses," with perhaps some features of the "night of the soul."

That this was Dom Vital's opinion is not hard to establish, because in his reply to this letter, he misconstrued her statement, that she had been reduced to the "animal level," as meaning that she was besieged with temptations of the flesh. This, as we have seen, was not at all the case. She had never suffered any such temptations in the whole course of her life, and she wrote to tell him so in the following words:

"Reverend Father, in our last letter, speaking about my soul, I evidently expressed myself very clumsily. I was trying to explain the difficulties I encounter in the interior life, and in progressing in union with Jesus, being unable to pray, or get recollected, I place myself before the Good Master like a brute beast, and pray by faith alone, for everything is darkness around me. As for the temptation which you thought afflicted me, the Good God has had pity on my weakness and has always preserved me from such things, although I am not as innocent as my angelic Little Thérèse. He has given me the grace to pass through this life without understanding what evil was, and I am happy to take my ignorance with me to the grave. I attribute this great grace to the Blessed Virgin, whom I have always much loved, and who has watched with jealous care over my poor soul."

Mother Berchmans faced all these physical and moral trials with the same loving and peaceful equanimity, born of faith, and the fruit of true abandonment. Nothing better expresses her attitude than the lines she copied into the "Mirror" of her soul, when she found them in the writings of Elizabeth of the Trinity.

"Always believe in Love. If you have to suffer, the reason is that you are more beloved than ever; so love in return, and ever sing your thanksgiving."

Never did she manifest any regret that she was dying. Never did she take any remedies from purely natural motives, merely in order to get rid of her sufferings. She accepted whatever was given her, and took it out of obedience. When the Sisters suggested massaging her with rubbing alcohol to freshen her feverish limbs a little and give her some comfort, she would not allow them, saying: "What is the use of these comforts, since I am going to die? Leave my legs alone, I won't be taking them to heaven with me."

One of her novices offered to give her limbs a good massage, for the same purpose: to make her more comfortable. Again she refused saying: "Let me be. Why go to all that trouble, just for the worms!"

However, she had not bargained for the spirit of faith and charity in a soul whom she herself had trained. The good novice said gently: "I am not offering this service to you, but to Our Lord." At that Mother Berchmans capitulated.

Her thoughts were always raising up her sufferings in sacrifice for dying soldiers on the battlefields of distant France, and whenever any of her sisters offered her their sympathy, she would say: "It all comes in handy for heaven, and for saving souls. Think of our poor soldiers, how much they suffer! Besides, it is useless to take so much care of me, as I am going to die."

The novices surrounded her, sorrowing at her great sickness, her high fever, her frequent hemorrhages; she only made use of all these things to illustrate a point in one of the repetitions which she still came down to the novitiate to give them.

"This sickness is a great gift from God," she told them. "If I were not sick, I would not be able to go to heaven. Besides, if you wear an article of clothing for a long time, it gets spotted and dirty; and it is just the same with one who lives long years in religion: she picks up the dust and grime of many imperfections."

This last quotation, however, is not characteristic of her except in so far as it reflects her desire to die young, and her belief that it was not necessary to live long years in religion to become a saint. As for the amount of imperfections one might have: we know that it was her firm belief that they could all be washed away by pure love and confident abandonment to God. The closer she got to death, the greater grew her confidence that she would not have to pass through purgatory. Was not everything that came to her from the hand of God an opportunity to prove her love for Him by casting herself more and more completely upon His merciful love?

One of her letters reads: "Jesus knows better than we, what is needful for us. Hence, the logical course to follow is one of complete abandonment: rest upon His Fatherly Heart, and love Him, always love Him. We are very little souls: let us not worry about the morrow. Let us say, with our little Sister (Thérèse) in heaven: 'Yes, my God, I do want trial and suffering, but just for today.'" Mother Berchmans' abandonment in her sufferings was so perfect precisely because she did not worry about the future, and surely, this confidence was the greatest proof of her love. This confidence, if anything, was what would serve as her purgatory, wiping out all the blemishes of her little imperfections.

"I do not know what the good God reserves for me," she said, "but I count on Him, and I am not in the least afraid."

Always, this passive abandonment was backed up by her heroically generous active love, expressed in her insatiable desire for sacrifice. With one lung destroyed and the other far gone, her breathing was always labored, but above all when she walked or moved around. She had a constant high fever, there was pain in her stomach, and her legs and feet were swollen and sore. In spite of all this, she made her way regularly down to the convent chapel for most of the offices. It was with the greatest difficulty that she could be persuaded to go and sit down in the choir of the infirm during Mass. Her day began, now, at four o'clock in the morning, when she dragged herself painfully down the dark stairs of the infirmary, halting at every second or third step to catch her breath, but eventually arriving at her usual place before Our Lady of the Angels' statue, where she made her preparation for Mass and Holy Communion.

Her regular instructions to the novices were remarkable always for their gaiety and animation; more than ever before, she put her whole heart and soul into her words, and not without great strain and great cost for very frequently she had no sooner finished her task and returned to the infirmary than the blood would come boiling up into her mouth from her lungs, seized by another hemorrhage.

Yet she always had time to stay and talk to any novice who needed to see her, to ask her advice and help. "If I do not make sacrifices now," she said, "when will I ever make them?"

One day, Reverend Mother Scholastica was not present at the distribution of work. Mother Berchmans, on the other hand, was always there to get some little task. This day was washday, and everybody went to the laundry, including Mother Berchmans. As she explained later, no one had forbidden her to do so. "You must be very tired, Mother," said a postulant, afterward. "Tired?" she said, "Well, so is everybody else!" And she added: "It gave me much satisfaction to go and work with the community. You too, after your profession, will understand the great joy there is in suffering."

Her ordinary work at this time consisted in keeping the milk accounts, or, when that was finished, she engaged herself in copying out the Japanese translation of the usages for her novices. Later on, when her fingers were so weak that she could not do this for any great length of time, she would employ the rest of the work period detaching and sorting out used stamps from the envelopes that came to the convent. These were then sent to France, where they fetched a tiny sum of money. The convent was poor, and could not afford to ignore even the most trivial source of revenue.

Now that she had more time at her disposal, in the infirmary, she did not mean to neglect the opportunity to practice the private devotions she had so long been forced to sacrifice because of her many duties. Mother Scholastica would not allow her to do the stations of the cross down in the cloister of the new convent, for fear of draughts, and so she remained in the infirmary chapel to follow our Lord along the dolorous way of His passion, uniting her own sufferings to His. And in order to compensate for the inability to go down to the cloister, she did the stations in the infirmary chapel with her arms extended in the form of a cross, until Father Robert forbade her to do so any longer.

There were many other little opportunities for sacrifices, even more valuable because they were not of her own choosing. For example, it happened that for a long time an error of the one charged with the preparation of her food made it so salty that it was not at all pleasant to eat. Mother Berchmans accepted it without complaint, glad of another opportunity for sacrifice that came to her from the hand of God. She never showed any preferences in what was given her to eat. In sickness, as in health, she tried to eat a little of everything. It was impossible to find out what delicacies would give her pleasure. And then, when those who visited her in the infirmary asked her if she did not want something to drink, or some other little comfort, she always replied that the Sister infirmarian would attend to that at the right time.

If, through some oversight, her needs were forgotten, so much the better. She never complained, never played the martyr. In spite of her high fever, and its consequent burning thirst, she never asked for anything to drink—even at the time when her thirst was aggravated by the salt food she was getting by accident. She simply contented herself with admitting that she was very thirsty when the Sister infirmarian chanced to question her about it.

Even when her sickness became so severe that she was allowed to take a little drink before receiving Holy Communion, she still did not avail herself of the dispensation. And when the Sisters offered her a soothing cup of tea, or tried to tempt her with fruit juices, she replied: "You know, I think that the Good God was thinking of me, from all eternity, when He created fresh water. For that is what does me the most good." It was sometime before she was finally ordered to accept other potions more suitable than cold water to a person with a high fever. Even then, the infirmarian could never discover what this peaceful, silent patient preferred. Mother Berchmans accepted everything. If it was good, she thanked God. If it was not so good, she also thanked God. If the infirmarian varied the drink from time to time, so much the better. But always, even in her last days, when her thirst had become a real torture, she often had to be urged to drink a little of the beverage that was there provided for her on the table at the head of her bed.

Undoubtedly her greatest cross, during the last year of her life, was her insomnia, which was to become a terrible torment in the summer months. Her frequent fits of coughing kept her awake for hours, and were often aggravated by hemorrhages and vomiting. The fever kept her body soaked in perspiration so heavy that not only her robe but her scapular and belt and even the straw mattress on which she slept were wet. In her great weakness, it often took her three quarters of an hour to make the complete change of clothing that was needed at least twice a day.

Nevertheless, she was always eager to get up in the morning and get to the chapel as best she could. When the time came for her to make her mental prayer, the Sister infirmarian asked her if she would not prefer to devote that interval to trying to make up the sleep she had lost; Mother Berchmans would hear of no such thing. When the Sister infirmarian advanced certain arguments in favor of such a course Mother Berchmans replied that it was useless for her to try and sleep, for as soon as she lay back on the pillow she began to cough. And so she was allowed to make her mental prayer in peace. We have seen what this meant: she had only exchanged one trial for another. Instead of lying on her bed racked with her terrible cough, she was sitting up, mute, helpless, without a coherent thought in her head, without the slightest movement of fervor in her heart, offering to God by blind act of will in the depths of her being, all her helplessness and confusion and weakness and inability to pray. Yet this, strangely enough, was all her joy: this, and Holy Mass, and Communion, when it was the same helplessness and incapacity all over again.

As the year advanced, instead of getting better, Mother Berchmans grew visibly worse every day. At the beginning of May, she made her last visit, alive, to the little cemetery that was soon to receive her mortal remains. A Sister accompanied her, holding her by the arm. As they returned, no doubt very thoughtfully, the Sister asked Mother Berchmans if she did not want to rest at the Lourdes grotto, about halfway to the house.

"No," she replied, with a sign, "we would be late for work." It was evident, however, that she was almost exhausted. She would not be able to slip away with the community and work in the laundry that day, by any means, nor any other day, as was now unquestionably clear.

May was half over when she was finally forbidden to go down to the convent chapel for office. She was far too ill. Now she was forced to remain in the little infirmary, and there recite her office at the same time as it was recited in choir. This she did with the greatest attention and fervor, especially at the hour of prime, which had always excited her to special devotion by the beautiful prayers of adoration and trust in Providence which it contains. Here, too, as everywhere else, she neglected no little chance to make a sacrifice, even if it were only in so small a thing as disposing herself in such a way that she needed no artificial light unless it was completely impossible to make out anything on the page of her book by the faint vestiges of daylight that still came through the windows.

She had always insisted on going down to church for confession, although this had by no means been necessary. Now this also was forbidden her, but by way of compensation, she had the immense satisfaction of receiving the Sacrament of Penance each day until her death. In the years since their first meeting Father Robert had become lavish indeed! But this was simply a fruit of their great respect and love for one another. Confessor and penitent now realized how much they had both grown in supernatural union, with all their dissimilarities of personality and temperament. Indeed, theirs was a friendship that had a particular supernatural depth and purity, since it had grown up in spite of all these superficial little differences, and had finally overcome them altogether.

If Father Robert thought Mother Berchmans was a saint, it is clear that her respect for him was no less great. And there was nothing she would not do to show her esteem for him, as a man, but above all as a minister of God. So great was her reverence for Christ in her confessor that even when she could hardly walk at all, he had to practically force her to keep her seat, and not try to get up and open the door for him after confession. Once, when trying to do so, she had nearly collapsed.

Meanwhile, paradoxically, her confinement to the infirmary only made her attempts to snatch a little rest for her sleepless and exhausted body even more difficult than before. She could not sleep at night, and she could not sleep during the *meridienne*; there was only one time in the morning when she seemed able to relax and fall asleep at least for an hour or so. However, this was precisely the moment that some of her sisters chose, in their charitable solicitude, to come and visit her. They were always received with joyful smiles; and no matter how long they stayed, in their imprudent zeal, they were never able to guess that they might be unwelcome, or that they were tiring poor Mother Berchmans. On these occasions, she usually conversed by means of signs, if she could.

Another paradox: when she wanted to sleep, it was impossible. When she wanted to keep awake she almost invariably had to struggle hard to keep from being overcome by sleep. This happened most of all when she was trying to recite her office. It would be hard to express what a trial this was to her. One must realize what importance she attached to this central and fundamental work of adoration on which her whole life of prayer was built. It was her whole life, because on it, and on the Holy Sacrifice, her union with God and the salvation of souls most depended. And this was the time when she had to struggle with all her might against the sleep her broken body craved, and which refused to come to her when she was in bed.

However, in the midst of all this suffering, she had one great consolation. At last four Japanese novices, four of her own spiritual children, were ready to make their profession. It was the crowning of her work, the first fruits of success, the promise that the little convent would survive and flourish, that the Trappistines had come to Japan to stay.

And there was rejoicing in heaven, as well as on the earth, that day. There can be little doubt of it. St. Thérèse herself came to give her devoted friends a very sensible token of the fact.

It was the morning of the fifteenth of May—a beautiful morning, we may believe. The convent was quiet and all the nuns were at their work in various parts of the house and on the farm, all except the four little novices who, sitting with a devout and eager expectancy, hungry for divine grace, were listening to Father Robert as he delivered the first conference of their retreat, in the convent parlor.

In choir the sacristan was busy with her broom. Mother Berchmans was in the infirmary.

Suddenly the sacristan stopped sweeping. She smelled a delightful odor of flowers. She raised her head: surely, they were violets! How could she be smelling violets? There were none there, and none anywhere near! But the sweet smell became stronger and more pervasive. It filled the whole church.

The sacristan put aside her broom and hastened to fetch Mother Scholastica who came at once to the chapel and was delighted and amazed with the same miraculous odor. Their hearts filled with joy; the two good Sisters did not doubt for a moment what this meant, or from whom it came. Little Thérèse was in their house, and showed her love for them by this beautiful and consoling gift.

Nor were the superioress and the sacristan the only ones to enjoy this favor. Five other Sisters also were drawn to the church from their work, some even being attracted by the odor of the heavenly flowers spreading out into the cloister.

The exhilarating perfume remained with them, and did not go away at once by any means. Fifteen minutes, half an hour: it was still there. Ten o'clock was striking when Father Robert, who was by no means an emotionalist or given to illusions, entered the sanctuary and was astonished at the strong, pure smell of flowers. What kind of flowers were they? He could not be sure. Possibly violets. What was the explanation of it all? In the end, he agreed with the Sisters that it could only be supernatural.

Meanwhile, Mother Berchmans was lying in her bed in the infirmary, when she heard a Sister bustling down the corridor, to bring the news, by means of somewhat ambiguous signs, to the infirmarian, who hurried away for confirmation—or perhaps for elucidation of the truth thus communicated to her. Soon, Mother Berchmans herself learned of the favor, but she could not leave the infirmary. Of all the Sisters who were actually in the convent at the time, she seems to have been the only one who did not enjoy the privilege of this extraordinary consolation. She leaves us a picture of herself sitting up in bed and sniffing for all she was worth, but the supernatural violets did not send their fragrance as far as the infirmary. By that time, she was used to the ways of the Little Flower with her most privileged devotees.

One consolation however could not be refused her. She could not be denied the joy of assisting her four novices in the ceremonies of their profession, although it taxed every ounce of her strength, and probably prevented her from meditating on the full significance of what was going on. All her attention was concentrated on keeping herself from collapsing and at the same time directing and assisting the four candidates for vows. She was not able to taste the full consolation of this reward for so many sacrifices. That would have to be reserved for heaven, where she would at last know, in all its purity and strength, the great joy of having spent herself to aid in the formation of Christ's image in the souls of His children. All her sacrifices were now just beginning to bear fruit. Already she could begin to grasp with what immense generosity her Lord was going to reward her for what she had done for Him, and it made her all the more eager to get to heaven. She would say, when it was all over: "Now that a few of my daughters are spouses of Christ, I can sing my '*Nunc dimittis*.'"

Before that day was done, however, Mother Berchmans had paid dearly for it all.

In one of her frequent admonitions to the novices who were about to make their vows, Mother Berchmans had begged them that, whatever they did, on the day of their profession, they should not pray much for her recovery: "At the moment," she said, "I am in God's grace. Supposing I got well: I might lose it. So don't pray very hard for me to recover. Every day I beg the good God to take me before I can offend Him...."

The novices had been devoting much time during their retreat to begging the Little Flower for a restoration of their mother mistress' health. The answer was the usual one. The night before their profession day, Mother Berchmans lay sleepless with even greater sufferings, heavier and more incessant coughing, greater pains and exhaustion than usual. Interiorly she kept saying over and over again within herself: "Good. I am glad of it. It will buy a little happiness for my daughters. I am glad to suffer." And she constantly lifted up her heart to God in thanksgiving and praise and perfect love, while her body, incessantly shaken by her dry, tearing cough, ran with perspiration.

How her heart leaped with joy, though, that May morning, when she entered the bright choir of the new convent chapel and saw there, before the grille, the table with the four white cowls and black veils and scapulars, and the gay crowns of flowers that the little Japanese spouses of Christ would wear that day, after their vows! O the significance of that sight! The immense mercy of God, working through these poor weak creatures! A handful of women, exiled far from their native land, had transformed, in a few short years, the wretched abandoned orphanage into a spacious new convent. The novitiate was full of oblates and novices. There were no less than nineteen Japanese candidates for the brown cloak of lay sisters, and many others for the choir, of whom four were now making their vows. These were the first Cistercian choir nuns professed in Japan: four souls, pure, innocent, full of eager and fervent simplicity, casting themselves down before the grille to beg God to receive their offering of their hearts, their souls, their lives. How their faces shone with faith and love and innocent generosity!

Dizzy and weak from having accompanied them to the grille and bowed with them as the usages prescribed, and waiting for her next function in the ceremonies, Mother Berchmans could not but feel her heart flooded with deep peace and satisfaction and joy. Here, before her eyes, was God at work in the souls of His creatures. Here, while she looked on, and indeed assisted the mighty and secret and ineffable work of grace by her mere presence, every moment of which was a prayer and a sacrifice in itself, God was elevating four souls to inexpressible heights in the kingdom of His secret love; and from those souls, powerful waves of grace were being poured out over the whole community and all the world outside. What treasures was Christ, in His ineffable tender mercy, not opening up to these souls and to the whole Church at this moment?

For now, one by one, in their clear little Japanese voices, they were singing the formula of their profession in strange Latin, and again in halting French. How her heart leaped and burned within her when she heard these words come forth from lips so unacquainted with the Church's ancient language, and in the innocent childish voices of these little Japanese women! Here was a conquest and victory for Christ greater than a battle overthrowing an empire.

CHAPTER XVIII

CALVARY

As summer began, the end was clearly drawing near. Both of Mother Berchmans' lungs were now nearly totally destroyed, and worse still, the virulent disease which was consuming her had long since seized upon her intestines. All these things now began to work out their deadly purpose upon the flesh of this heroic nun. She described the progress of her disease with her usual lightheartedness. "My little bugs," said one of her letters, "have nothing left to work on in the lungs, so now they have gone promenading all over the intestines, with their tender ministrations."

Her weakness was now so great that an oblate Sister was appointed to help her in the arduous business of changing her soaking garments twice or three times a day. She would nevertheless have greatly preferred to continue trying to dress herself, not merely because of the repugnance she had in allowing someone else to perform so intimate a service, but above all in order to spare her assistant so much trouble and such a disagreeable burden. However, under obedience, she accepted the first little cross, and made the second a source of many acts of obedience and fraternal charity by her perfect docility and submission to the slightest injunction of the humble Japanese oblate, so that she became, as it were, the servant of the one who was appointed to serve her. It was the same with her infirmarian. It would be hard to say whether the Sister infirmarian worried more about Mother Berchmans, or Mother Berchmans about the Sister infirmarian.

"Dear Sister," the dying nun would say, "you look so tired. You have not slept," or "It is time for dinner; why are you not down in the refectory?" or "Go to bed, do not worry about me; I am all right."

She could no longer struggle down to the little convent church for Holy Communion, which she now had to receive in the infirmary chapel. Indeed, she was often forced to receive her Lord while sitting in a chair, being sometimes too weak to kneel. Every day, however, she still managed somehow to do the stations of the cross, supporting herself against the wall; and when she had more strength she would even kneel at each station.

Meanwhile sad, or if you prefer, glad news came from Laval. In these past months, Mother Mary Angela had been gravely ill. Poor little Mother Mary Angela, whom she loved so dearly! As she sat in her infirmary cell, sorting used postage stamps, the only work she seemed able to do now, Mother Berchmans thought of the sunny days in the garden at Laval, the days in the novitiate, that seemed so distant and yet so near. It did not seem long somehow. Surprising that so many years had really gone by, sixteen of them, since her novitiate, the spring of her religious life! In her memory she heard the chanting of the nuns in the clean, white choir of the French convent, with the flowers banked high around the statue of the Blessed Mother, in the middle of the choir, near the grille. She saw the dappled, moving shade of the foliage on the stones of the Lourdes grotto in the garden. She saw those who had been novices with her, walking singly under the trees, saying their rosaries, or with books in their hands. She saw the smiling face of Mother Mary Angela, so full of purity and candor and simplicity and holiness, looking out from under the shadows of her veil. And now they were both dying.

One might think that Mother Berchmans saw all this through a mist of tears. But no. Her memories of Laval had lost the strange, haunting beauty of the impossible earthly paradise which her homesickness had once made it. Now she remembered it indeed as a beautiful house of God, full of sanctity and charity and peace, but much more did she thank God for having taken her away from there, from all her purely human affections, all the merely natural joys and attachments that kept her from Him.

Was not her heart straitened with a little movement of anguish at the thought of Mother Mary Angela lying on her bed of death? Why should it be? Rather she rejoiced, in deep and quiet peace, in the assurance that her dear sister was about to enter, even before her, into the immense reward which they had scarcely even begun to conceive in their hearts that day when they had received the habit of Cistercians together.

Yet she was deeply touched, even to the profoundest depths of her sensitive and affectionate heart, by the news that came to her from Laval of Mother Mary Angela's last hour. The little nun had offered up what life remained in her, in order that Mother Berchmans might live longer. And then, soon the pure soul had escaped from her body and she had gone to heaven. Her simple, hidden life had at last consumed itself in an act of pure charity, a last movement of that love than which there is none more perfect: the love that lays down its life for a friend.

Of course, what Mother Angela had intended was to procure not only a prolongation of her sister's life, but her recovery. But God in the wise economy of His merciful Providence, saw fit to grant one half of the request and leave the other unfulfilled. Mother Berchmans would indeed live longer, but only to suffer more.

One of the nuns of Our Lady of the Angels, visiting the patient, viewed her ruefully, and remarked, with gentle irony: "I must say, Mother Angela certainly made you a nice present!"

"Oh," cried Mother Berchmans, "if Mother Mary Angela, in heaven, could feel any envy for anything, it would certainly be for my sufferings!"

There was no doubt, now, that she really loved suffering; loved it, not because she suffered with consolation, but precisely because her sufferings were unmixed with sensible inner joy. All her joy was in the will; and when weariness and pain dug deep into her body, she kissed her crucifix, and it was her will that smiled in her white face, no sensible joy. Far from complaining, she had so overcome herself that not even the faintest involuntary complaint escaped her. And yet she took no complacency in this fact.

"It is not due to any strength of mine," she said, "but to the merits of Our Lord." And she added: "Truly, suffering is a great favor," saying these words in a way that indicated how deeply and perfectly she understood the meaning of the words *favor*, *grace*: things of immense value, given to us, and beyond our power to even begin to deserve. For her own part, she was continually asking prayers for the grace to be patient.

Much as she appreciated this favor of suffering, however, it was a constant torture to her soul to be so near the goal of all her desires, and yet to have their fulfillment put off from day to day. She had hoped for the favor of dying on the feast of the Sacred Heart, that day which had played such a dominant part in her life, but the feast came and went, and she was still giving promise of an indefinitely long struggle.

Mother Scholastica and the community, of course, had not completely given up hope of her eventual recovery by some miraculous intervention of God. So intent were they on this, that they conspired with another Sister who was also dying in the infirmary at the same time, and who agreed that as soon as she got to heaven she would busy herself before the throne of God beseeching Him to cure the mother novice mistress whose virtues and talents were so badly needed in the growing convent!

"*Fiat*," said Mother Berchmans, with a wan smile, on hearing of the plot. "Whatever Jesus wills. I am quite willing to live to the age of eighty, but whatever God wills."

The month of the Sacred Heart came to an end. It was evident that Mother Berchmans, whatever else happened, was not going to live to be eighty. She might not outlive the coming week. She was still strong, but considering the ravages of the disease within her, and the fact that she had practically no lungs left to breathe with, a sudden crisis could carry her off at any moment. It was therefore decided to give her the Last Sacraments.

On the first of July she wrote to a priest:

"Tomorrow, on the Feast of Our Dearest Mother, and, what is more, the First Friday of the month, I am to have the happiness of receiving the Sacrament of Extreme Unction. I shall sing my Magnificat of thanksgiving, and pay my tribute of gratitude to Jesus through Mary for all the graces that have been showered upon me all my life. Reverend Mother has been so kind as to have the High Mass offered up for my intentions tomorrow. Truly I am saturated in graces: I am the spoiled child of the good Jesus. For you will easily agree that after so many prayers, death is sweet, and offers no terrors.

"Although I am to receive the Last Sacraments tomorrow, that does not mean that I am *in extremis*. No, it is simply a matter of prudence, because of the fact that my heart sometimes plays tricks on me."

Mother Berchmans was to receive Extreme Unction, not in the infirmary cell, but down in the convent church, after vespers of the feast of our Lady's Visitation.

This was a great grace; but like all the other graces she had been receiving, especially in these last months, it required a special preparation. She had suffered the night before the profession of her first four novices, in May. Her suffering was much worse; this night from the first to the second of July was truly, for her, the *vigil* of the Visitation.

This time it was not merely a question of coughing and vomiting and sleeplessness and burning thirst and perspiration and the purgatorial fires of an intense fever. She could not even pray. In past years, she had amply redeemed her sleepless nights by raising up her heart to God, but now—as all that year—raising her heart to God was like beating against a stone wall. Until now she had at least been able to repeat the words of vocal prayers. This night she could hardly begin a prayer when a violent attack of coughing would seize her and immediately make all prayer impossible. This was not once, or twice, or a dozen times. Mother Berchmans estimated that at least one hundred times in the course of that terrible night, she had begun the *Magnificat* without being able to finish it.

Yet what a powerful, unquenchable fire of love was burning in her heart, if, all through such a night, helpless, lost in abysmal darkness of the spirit, racked with bodily pain, she nevertheless leaped up over and over again in strong flames of desire and thanksgiving, trying repeatedly to penetrate the wall of darkness that separated her from her Beloved, with the words of Mary's canticle of gratitude and love!

The liturgy of the Visitation was God's answer to her desires. The God whom her heart longed for would not keep her waiting long. "Behold He cometh, leaping over the hills." Yes, He was close by, His time was near at hand. "Behold He standeth behind our wall, looking through the windows, looking through the lattices." He would soon be knocking even at the doors of her senses with the Sacrament of last anointing, calling her to come out and leave the house of her tired body, and follow Him to the green hills of heaven. *En dilectus meus loquitur mihi....*

Without the assistance of anyone, Mother Berchmans came slowly down the infirmary stairs in the late afternoon, as vespers were beginning in the choir. The peaceful, level measures of the little office reached her as she and her companion entered the convent church, and made their way to an armchair prepared in the middle of the choir. Having first fallen on her knees for a few moments of adoration of her Saviour in the tabernacle, where He awaited her coming, she took her place and followed the canonical office which now began. The high, clear voice of a nun intoned the *Deus in adjutorium*, that long, sweet cry rising in peaceful supplication as from the very heart of the Mystical Body. It flew along the sunny walls and vaulted ceiling and was gone, and the opposite choirs of nuns, like two white waves, bowed profoundly toward the desks at the *Gloria Patri*. Another solitary voice rose up in the sunny choir, to proclaim, in a few notes of clear joy, the triumph of Mary's charity, intoning the antiphon: *Exsurgens Maria....* Then the psalm: "The Lord said to my Lord, sit thou at my right hand...."

But there was no more solemn or more moving moment in that beautiful office than the intonation of the *Magnificat*, by the strong, pure voice of the chantress; and at last, no doubt, Mother

Berchmans was able to offer to her Lord the canticle of thanksgiving she had tried a hundred times, in vain, to offer Him the night before. Now, too, came the sudden unfamiliar sound of the great bell of the convent ringing above them. Perhaps when she first noticed that it was ringing, and asked herself the reason why, she suddenly felt a strange, deep movement of excitement and exultation, at the realization that it was ringing for her, for her own anointing. *En dilectus meus loquitur....*

Yes, it was the bell for the Last Sacraments, for now came the short pause, and the sudden repetition of the ringing. The ear of every Cistercian is all too well attuned to the tremendous note of urgency that is communicated by that short spasm of silence between the two bursts of ringing. Her Beloved was speaking not only to her, but to the convent, and to the fields and barns, where perhaps some of the lay sisters were still occupied at some necessary task, telling all to come in haste, because the Last Sacraments were to be given, at once, to the dying Mother Berchmans. All this was ten times more solemn because it was mingled with the measured chanting of the nuns in choir.

Father Robert appeared at once, approaching the door of the grille, with the sacristan bringing the holy oils. *Behold, He standeth behind our wall, looking through the windows, looking through the lattices.* Now the nuns were chanting psalms for her again. The sacristan placed the oils on the table at her side. Father Robert stood before her with a violet stole over his white alb, and presently, as the psalm ended, began the moving little sermon he had prepared.

It was the last sermon she was to hear among her sisters. It was the last time she would be with them in the church, in community. Her heart was open to the words of her spiritual Father. Every beat of her pulse said "*Fiat*" to the secret voice of Christ that kept calling to her louder and louder, through all these ceremonies, but most of all in her own heart.

Before she recited her own *Confiteor*, in firm, deliberate tones, though in a voice softened by weakness and sickness, Father Robert did as she had so earnestly commissioned him, and begged the pardon of the community for all her faults, all the disedification she thought she had given them in the last thirteen years.

In short, Mother Berchmans received the Last Sacraments, as everyone had expected, with all the dispositions of a saint. Peaceful confidence and joy shone from her every movement, from every line of her pale, thin face, but above all from the depths of her eyes that burned with holy love. And when it was all over, she rose from her chair, turned to the statue of Our Lady of the Angels, and fell on her knees there for the last time to make her thanksgiving.

What was in Mother Berchmans' heart now? She did not remain long kneeling there, but left the choir and returned, unassisted as she had come, to the infirmary; there had never been an evening meditation like this one in her life!

For now, indeed, it was no longer she who did the talking. *En dilectus meus loquitur mihi....* It was her Beloved who spoke to her. Nor did she listen to Him, as she had for so many years, in the hauntingly vague and general certitude of His presence: that confused and dark and general presence which belongs to the early stages of mystical prayer, in which the Beloved is present, and the soul is on fire with love at His presence, but every time she moves to come closer to Him, to apprehend Him with more intimate clarity, He cries: "*Noli me tangere,*" and draws away, and even vanishes altogether into the shadows from which He so suddenly and inexplicably came.

Now it was no more so! The fact that Mother Berchmans was able to walk back to the infirmary was wonderful, not because of her sickness, but because of the depth and intensity of the joy and vivid light that entirely possessed her and all but robbed her of the use of her senses and her limbs. No, she was not in ecstasy. She was not bereft by rapture of her exterior and interior powers. But she must have been as close to it as one can get, without losing control of one's faculties.

She was able to come down again to the church, that evening, to enter the confessional and thank Father Robert for all that he had done for her. But he, remarking the wonderful change in her soul, and questioning her about it, and then observing her more in days to come, was forced to the conclusion that she had been granted the grace of full mystical union.

In the first place, God had alleviated one of her bodily sufferings (but not any of the others) in such a way as to make it possible for her to be continually occupied with Him. He delivered her from the terrible headaches that had so constantly been besieging her. Now, for days at a time, she was able to be absorbed in the profoundest and most peaceful and simple state of recollection, occupied with God who was almost continuously present to her more vividly than she had ever imagined possible, in the course of all her most ordinary actions. Earth seemed to have fallen far beneath her feet. She dwelt in another atmosphere. The din and activity of the world, of human desires and passions and sufferings, meant far less to her than smoke in the air or shadows on a wall. Even her own physical sufferings could do absolutely nothing to distract her from the presence of her Beloved, or to make her attention to Him any less constant, less peaceful, or less sweet.

This was the thing that made her present state an anticipated heaven. All distractions were gone. Nothing seemed able to take her mind away from God. Not that she was lost in a sort of pathological state of apathy to everything that went on around her, she was more cheerful, more lovingly attentive to her sisters than ever before, but she had been given the inestimable grace of that liberty which is the sign of the true mystic: the freedom to come and go, passing from God to the creature and back again, doing His will, and never losing His presence, and at the same time never offending others by any abnormal shyness or reticence. She had become, indeed, a little less than the angels, and, like them, she was always before the face of her Father in heaven, yet always able to go forth to His creatures when His will demanded it.

This holy freedom, this peaceful and constant absorption in God, this beautiful union with Him, so full of inexpressible joys, and often lapsing into so deep an absorption in His delights that she again was lost completely to the world and to herself, all this did not make her rest content with what she had, as if there were nothing more to desire. Far from satisfying her, this increased intimacy only stirred up the blaze of her desires to the most insatiable longing for heaven. If she had longed to be with Him in His kingdom before, when she had known Him only darkly, now that she had seen Him more intimately, though still in darkness, it was almost a miracle that her craving to be with Him most perfectly, and without fear of ever losing Him, did not kill her altogether, then and there.

The only thing that could equal the intensity of this craving in her soul, was the ardor and desire she now felt to serve Him perfectly, to sacrifice herself altogether. If she did not show any peculiar or offensive tendencies to avoid the company of those who sought her out in her infirmary cell, she nevertheless sought more and more silence and solitude. But here again, there was no need for remarkable effort, for any apparent concentration or struggle. She just seemed naturally to remain in perfect silence and recollection; if it was necessary to emerge from it and enter into contact with others, she was able effortlessly to do so in the most economical way, by the clearest and most obvious sign, or by a word or two if speaking could not be avoided. Otherwise, she was simply, unnoticeably immersed in God.

A sentence from a note to one of the nuns is one of the few documents from her own hand that have come to us from this most important period in her life. "Pray for me," she wrote. "I am no longer of this earth, and not yet in heaven, except by my desires. My soul is, as it were, suspended between them."

Hanging between earth and heaven! That is the true picture of her soul! And while she tasted the joys of her Beloved's presence, and was already looking, so to speak, in through the lighted doors of paradise at the angels and saints enjoying their eternal festivities, and beckoning her to come and join them, nevertheless this very joy was a source of immense sorrow and suffering to her. Now, indeed, she began to taste the full effect of that infused love which she had so earnestly prayed to obtain. And it was by means of this love that the last three months of her life became the most intense period of purification she had ever suffered. In these last three months she was destined, as she had obscurely foreseen, and as she had always taught was possible, according to the Little Way, to be so purified by desire of heaven that it was to serve as her purgatory on earth.

Each new feast that came, in the ordered course of the liturgical cycle, added fuel to the flames of desire that were tormenting her. As July turned into August, she began to look forward to the great day of our Lady's Assumption. Perhaps her dear Mother would come on that day and take her into heaven—we must observe that now the feast of the Sacred Heart was passed, Mother Berchmans was quite convinced that she could only die on a feast of the Mother of God. But on the vigil of the Assumption, Mother Scholastica, who by now well knew the mind of the dying nun, came to her with the categorical injunction not to die on that day.

After warning Mother Berchmans that the whole community was praying frantically that she might not die, the prioress added: "After all, tomorrow is the patronal feast of the order and of the house. And three oblates are receiving the habit of novice. So please resign yourself to the fact that you are not going to die on this feast!"

So Mother Berchmans cheerfully obeyed her superioress and united her prayers to those of the community, and the rest of August went by without event, except that she was growing slowly worse. The days were long, the nights were longer still. One morning she greeted the new day with the cry: "My God, here is a day that is going to seem like a century: so let it be a century of love!"

Yet, even now, Mother Berchmans never spent entire days in bed. On the contrary, she still struggled out of bed at four or five or six in the morning, and began her day as she had always done by kissing the floor. She was generally able to hear Mass. She even managed, somehow, during the course of the day, to make the stations of the cross. She always did a little work, sorting stamps or untangling thread. There were many things she was forbidden to do. As soon as she raised her arms to try and open a window, she would get a hemorrhage, so she could no longer perform such services for herself. She spent most of her day sitting in a chair, instead of lying in bed, although it was much less comfortable for her. But she did not mention this to anybody, until it finally slipped out, somehow, before the end of her life. All this time, she had been taking each little opportunity to crucify herself still more for the love of God and to win grace for souls.

Probably her strength and capacity for suffering were greatly increased by the consolation of her close union with God. When one of her novices asked her: "Mother, do you suffer as much as Sister Thérèse did?" she replied: "Oh no! True, I suffer physically, but interiorly not at all!" But the intensity of her physical sufferings, daily increasing beyond her wildest dreams, was now beginning to surprise even her. "But I am glad of it," she added, "for the good God keeps account of everything." She never tried to deny that she suffered much, but she would always show that she realized that it was a grace from God. "Yes, I am very tired," she once said, "but God is good. It is because of His mercy that He gives me these sufferings! Oh, how merciful He is!"

The violent fits of coughing that seized her over a hundred times a night were all offered up, each one for the conversion of a sinner. One day, before her Last Anointing absolutely exhausted, she had asked St. Thérèse the favor to obtain for her a good sleep, just once, during the *meridienne*, if it happened to be God's will that she recover. The answer to her prayer was indeed quite definite: the *meridienne* that day was even more of a torture than it had been before, with her raging fever and perspiration and attacks of coughing and vomiting all the time. Now that heaven was in sight, she made no more such requests.

As days went on, she could not even drink a little water to cool her burning throat, without her whole stomach searing her as if it had just absorbed a sheet of living flame. But she said: "Since the good God gives me the grace of patience at the same time as this suffering, it is really a great benefit to me!"

"Now," she said, "I am suffering much. Will I suffer more tomorrow? I do not know. But since, along with every suffering, the good God gives me the strength I need, I never worry about what may come." And she added: "I do not ask for any more sufferings than I have already. I simply pray that I may courageously bear those that come to me."

As day succeeded day, although her heart was ever more and more raised to heaven in eager desire, still she lived, as far as her waning earthly life was concerned, more and more in the present moment, without worrying about the future, without looking back into the past. The suffering that was actually there to be borne, at that very moment, was enough to keep her busy, loving and adoring God in her mute and helpless patience with her eyes always raised to Him in wordless supplication. Wordless, indeed: she could no longer even say the rosary. Instead of that, she would mutely offer her body and soul to Mary, that the Queen of heaven might give them to God her Son in union with her own prayers and merits, for the praise of His holy name.

Meanwhile, all the Sisters, by means of notes, if they could not visit her in person, were giving her their last-minute instructions on the errands she was to perform for them in heaven. We have one of her last letters, written in a trembling hand, as a reply to one of these "*commissions pour le Paradis.*"

"My Dear Little Mother:

"In spite of the difficulty I have in writing, I have not the heart to make you wait for a reply to your good letters, until I am dead. I am truly grateful for all the nice things you say about me. But I know it is Jesus you see in His poor little spouse, and I refer all to our Beloved for His glory. Yes, dear little Mother, I assure you that when I arrive in heaven, you will have one more real friend up there, and do not worry: when the hour of suffering strikes for you also, you will certainly not be alone. Your little Sister up in heaven will overshadow you to alleviate your pains: but above all Jesus, our Divine Spouse, He will be there with you, and in His company, how insignificant creatures become!

"Goodbye, dear Little Mother, and may Jesus ever be more and more the 'all' of your dear soul."

August ended, and the Sunday on which is celebrated the feast of the Most Pure Heart of Mary went by, and still Mother Berchmans was singing her "*Heu mihi quia incolatus meus prolongatus est!*" The Nativity of Mary was the next feast on the calendar, at the end of the first week in September. Would that be the day?

Someone said to her: "Supposing the good God were to cure you after all?"

"Oh!" she cried, "will the good God ask even that sacrifice of me?"

About September 15, the doctor came to see her, and she asked him to tell her honestly how much longer she had to live.

The good man hesitated a moment, looking into the earnest, dark eyes that burned in the pallor of her emaciated face.

"Do not be afraid to tell me the truth, I am not scared," said Mother Berchmans.

The doctor shrugged, and said quietly: "Oh, about another week!"

So great were her joy and satisfaction to hear, officially, that her death was only a few days off, that a visible improvement was soon manifested in her condition, and stayed with her several days. However, it was only transient. Her body, literally devoured by tuberculosis, simply could not support life any longer.

"Do not weep," she said to the Sisters who were much affected by the news, "do not cry over my happiness. I am going to heaven." And with her face bright with joy, she added: "Just a little while, and then I will go and see my Beloved Jesus. But I certainly die hard! I am impatient to get to heaven."

Once she looked up, her face filled with the same radiant joy, just after she had kissed a picture of St. Thérèse, and cried: "Oh, I shall see her soon, now!"

In all this, there was no shadow of fear or doubt in her trustful certitude that she would go straight to heaven. She never asked for prayers that she might escape purgatory; she did not solicit them in case she should fall into those flames after she died. She rested in simple, blissful confidence that her Lord would have pity on her nothingness, and, for His own glory, lean down and lift her up in His loving arms, and take her to Himself without further delay. Her confidence was perfect, not because it rested on any merits of her own, any past achievement, anything that might be considered especially virtuous in herself; on the contrary, it rested more on her weaknesses and imperfections, and the unshakable assurance that Jesus, now that He was asked to wash them all out of her soul by His merciful love, would do so at once, according to His promises. She had asked, now she rested peacefully in the hope that she would receive. She had knocked, and now she would hold Him to His word; she knew the doors of heaven would be opened to her because she depended entirely on Christ's promise and that was all.

When they asked her if she was making any special prayers for her own needs, or following any special practice, her reply showed that she was far beyond relying on any given "infallible" prayer, or any of those "guaranteed" devotions. She did not even give any particular thought to the death that was so fast approaching, or to her past life, with its many little imperfections, although it is well known that, at the hour of death, souls are apt to be haunted by the past. She did what she had always been doing in the past seven or eight years: she simply loved God, desired to be with Him, longed for the accomplishment of His will in her, and for the completion of His work, trusting in Him blindly, abandoning herself completely into His hands.

"I do what I have always done," she said, "I follow my little way as usual, and I think neither of life nor of death."

Did she not fear that the devil, or some latent weakness within herself, would be let loose against her soul in her last, bitter struggle? No. "I do not know what the good God holds in store for me," she said, "but I rely on Him, and I have no fear."

Nevertheless, there was a slight change in her attitude, in that she was willing to have someone always in the room with her, and that she accepted all the cares that were offered her without remark. More and more grateful did she show herself for the daily visits of her Father confessor, to administer the Sacrament of Peace, and now also she showed herself anxious to avail herself of his offer that he drop in to her infirmary cell two or three times in the day, as opportunities offered themselves, to suggest a few good thoughts and give her his paternal blessing. Her confidence, in other words, far from ignoring the ordinary means of grace that were offered her, eagerly and gratefully accepted them, but with perfect peace and detachment. Always, her reliance was not on the means in themselves, but on Jesus, whose grace came to her through them. Indeed, all these things helped to increase her trust. How could it be otherwise? Daily in confession and hourly through her aspirations and spiritual Communions and the prayers of the Sisters and the blessings and repeated absolutions of her Father confessor, Jesus was pouring out His love into her soul, constantly purifying it more and more, in preparation for that last hour when she should take her flight to Him in the glory of His kingdom.

"How good and merciful God is," she said to the infirmarian, thinking of the fact that Father Robert so often renewed the absolution he had given her already in confession. "If Our Heavenly Father is so good to me in this life, what will He be in the next? His goodness will be simply unutterable."

It was Saturday, the eighteenth of September. Although the dying nun was not beyond joking, that night was almost her last. Toward evening, her weakness was so extreme that the infirmarian warned Mother Scholastica that the agony might begin at any minute. But Mother Berchmans apparently knew better; she assured them all that she would not die that night.

Her words were fulfilled. She spent a better night than she had for some time past, but the following morning, Sunday, the nineteenth, she said, at seven o'clock: "I had a pretty good night, but I think this little improvement is just a sign that death is very close now. Oh, yes, it is all over. I can't hold out much longer."

Nevertheless, she began that day by struggling from her bed and kissing the floor, and invoking Mary's blessing, according to her usual custom. Indeed, it was only four or five days since she had finally had to give up her stations of the cross. Now, however, there could have been no question of such an exertion as that. She was so weak, when mealtime came, that the Sister infirmarian thought she ought to stay and help her eat the few spoonfuls of food that she was able to take, but Mother Berchmans would not hear of it.

"Look," she said, "I do not like to keep you during the regular exercises of the community." That night, and many other times besides, when the infirmarian wanted to stay up with her, Mother Berchmans said: "Go and sleep. As for me, I will have plenty of time to rest when I get to the cemetery."

On Monday, the twentieth, she was still able to get out of bed, and even kiss the floor, but now at last she did not even try to get up and do a little work sorting stamps. She simply spent most of the time in mute, helpless prayer; powerless to use words or even to elicit any formal affections, she prayed with her suffering and trustful heart, holding in her hands a crucifix or a little statuette of the Mother of God.

Even now, she would not accept the offer of those who took care of her, to shake up her straw mattress a little: and indeed, in her condition, she might long since have availed herself of the dispensation allowing the sick a softer mattress and even a regular bed with springs. But Mother Berchmans still lay on straw and boards.

It was not until Tuesday, the twenty-first of September, that she was finally forced to keep her bed the whole day. It was no longer possible to get up at all. She would have liked to kiss the floor. But now she was too far gone.

That did not prevent her from spending her waning strength in one last act of charity. In order to give Mother Berchmans a drink, before midnight, to help her last more comfortably until two in the morning, the Sister infirmarian had recently been waiting up until ten o'clock. Unfortunately, after her hard day's work, she often fell asleep, and so another of the sick nuns was charged to watch and wake her up if necessary. All this caused great pain to Mother Berchmans, and so, on this day, in handwriting made completely unrecognizable by her utter exhaustion, she wrote a note to Mother Scholastica to try and remedy this state of affairs.

"I believe it would not be imprudent for me to wait from eight at night until two in the morning, for this drink," she said. "However, I will do just as you decide. Thank you, Reverend Mother, with the Heart of our Beloved Jesus, for the care you take of me. Rest assured that when I get to heaven I will express my deep gratitude to you. Your traveler on the way to eternity."

On that day, too, all the novices came to pay Mother Berchmans a visit that filled her with great joy and consolation. No doubt there were not a few tears, and all of them were eager both to ask her prayers for them in heaven, as well as to obtain some little relic of her earthly presence. On the previous day, one of the four newly professed had asked for a holy card to remember her by, and had been told to help herself in the breviary that was on the table. She opened it, and found exactly three—enough to mark the place of the office, and no more.

Even now, as she lay dying, Mother Berchmans showed that she would never, under any circumstances, neglect her duty as novice mistress. One of the young professed had been unable to be there with all the other novices, and had received permission to go up after the evening meditation, at suppertime.

Exercising her natural acumen, however, the young Japanese nun wisely calculated that at that time the infirmarian would probably be there; and she might not be able to get in. So she left choir a few minutes before the end of meditation. She was destined to meet with a great disappointment. As she opened the door, she was greeted by the voice of her mother mistress, saying: "What are you doing up here at this time? You are supposed to be making your meditation, so you just turn around and go back to choir."

The approach of death had not weakened Mother Berchmans enough to allow her to accept even the slightest merely natural consolation that might possibly be in conflict with obedience or with the spiritual welfare of her daughters or herself.

On Thursday, the twenty-third, all the novices came once more. This time it was to say good-bye. They all realized it. Mother Berchmans was as cheerful as ever as long as they were in the room, but after they all had left, and the door had closed upon their tear-filled eyes, Mother Berchmans herself turned her face to the wall, and the tears overflowed onto her pale cheeks. But it was soon over. Even in death she was master of all her feelings.

And now she seemed to know definitely that the end had

come. Someone had suggested that she might live another ten days, to the feast of the Holy Rosary. She made a sign that God would not ask of her that sacrifice. This Thursday, however, was the eve of a minor feast of the Blessed Virgin: Our Lady of Ransom. This was the day sacred to the patroness of an order devoted to the ransom of Christian captives and slaves in pagan lands. This was a day sacred to *Nuestra Señora de la Merced*, "Our Lady of Mercy," the Mother whose loving tenderness ever went out to seek the Christians languishing in the dark prisons or in the galleys of the Moors, slowly losing their life and even their faith in the chains and vermin of Mohammedan captivity. Surely it was most appropriate that, on this day, the Holy Mother of God should come and pay, at long last, the ransom of the loving little captive who had so long languished in exile in a strange country, for the glory of her Son. Yes, this was to be the day on which her exile would end in glory.

But it was not only Our Lady of Ransom who was to come and unlock the cell of her captivity, and bring her home; this day was also an important anniversary in the life of St. Thérèse. Besides, it was Friday and Friday is always consecrated to the Sacred Heart.

"Tomorrow," said Mother Berchmans, that evening. "Tomorrow is Friday. And it is the feast of Our Lady of Ransom. It is also the anniversary of Sister Thérèse's reception of the veil. *She will come to get me tomorrow!*"

That evening, too, one of the young professed asked for, and obtained, Mother Berchmans' blessing. Mother Scholastica also knelt and asked for the same favor, but was refused, until she at last blessed the patient, and, upon insisting, finally received a blessing from the dying nun. Mother Berchmans took her beloved statuette of our Lady and gently made the sign of the cross with it on her mother prioress' forehead. Then she sank back in bed, sighing: "It will be tonight."

At four-fifteen in the morning, after a night of bitter suffering, Mother Berchmans was lying quiet in her cell. The infirmarians came in to change her clothes. They had barely begun to do so, when a spasm seized Mother Berchmans' frail body, and she cried:

"My God, I love You, I am all Yours," and entered into her last agony.

Father Robert was summoned and came at once, giving her absolution, and afterward began reciting the prayers for the agonizing.

It then became evident that the agony might drag on for some time. Mother Berchmans was in full possession of her faculties and able to speak a little. One of the Sisters, therefore, suggested that she be given Holy Communion. Father Robert demurred at first. Giving Holy Communion to a person in the middle of the last agony was a risky thing to do, but after having received the advice of a Sister who had considerable experience in such matters, he decided to go and bring the Holy Eucharist.

"Oh, I am glad!" Mother Berchmans sighed.

Immeasurably strengthened by Communion, she was able to enter with her whole heart into the glorious struggle of this last hour for which she had so long prayed. She had reached out for it a hundred times and more in symbolic death, sacrifices that could never actually be more than partial; but now they were all to be consummated: now she could keep all her promises. She had offered her life so many times; now, at last she was being accepted.

She was dying of love, in so far as she was accepting every new suffering with conscious and free and ardent and perfect love. Her Spouse had reserved for her the grace of perfect lucidity of mind through it all, in order that her merits and His glory might be multiplied a hundredfold. It was a grace of which she availed herself with the utmost generosity.

Although this was, in a very true sense, a special favor, it did not mean, as far as we know, that she received any extraordinary grace in the sense of *gratia gratis data*. At one point her sisters almost thought she had, for she exclaimed: "Oh, how beautiful she is, the Most Blessed Virgin!"

"So you see her, then?" someone said, quickly.

"Oh no," said the dying nun, simply, and with a little note of surprise in her weak voice, "I do not see her!"

She had not seen her with the eyes of flesh, but the eyes of her faith were never wider open than they were now, and their strong dilated gaze had no difficulty in seeing the Holy Mother of God, her Mother and constant Protectress, there at her side. Yes, she had most truly seen our Lady's beauty, when she had cried out thus. And she saw, too, Jesus waiting for her behind those veils that were fast becoming transparent, and would soon altogether give way.

Yet the agony dragged on. Father Robert was always there. She heard his earnest voice from time to time, solemnly and distinctly repeating ejaculatory prayers, close by, for her to hear and understand and make her own.

"Father, into Thy hands I commend my spirit." "Behold the handmaid of the Lord, be it done unto me according to Thy word." "Not my will, but Thine be done."

From time to time, she would raise her eyes to him. It was something she had scarcely ever done before in her life; but now this was the signal that had been agreed upon between them, and each time she did so he gave her absolution once again. How many times, during those hours, was her soul washed of every smallest stain by Christ's most Precious Blood!

And Father Robert's voice would go on, quietly, seriously, between brief pauses: "Jesus, Mary, Joseph." "Jesus, Mary, Joseph." "Father, into Thy hands...."

When a sudden stab of pain almost wrenched her soul from her body, she would still be able to raise the crucifix to her own lips unaided, or to kiss the little figure of Mary that was also in her arms. Then Father Robert would say: "He hath done all things well." "He hath done all things well." "*Fiat mihi secundum verbum tuum.*"

There was one ejaculation he took from Scripture which seemed to be the one she preferred in her last hour: the words of David, in the Second Book of Kings: "I shall not offer to the Lord my God a holocaust that does not cost me something."

Around ten o'clock in the morning, Mother Berchmans was seen to strike her breast lightly with her closed hand, and reverend mother, thinking perhaps she desired to make another confession, was about to clear the little cell and leave the dying Sister alone with her confessor. But Mother Berchmans simply shook her head and smiled. She feared nothing now. Her spirit was in perfect peace. And if anyone doubted it for a moment, the smile on her silent, drawn face was enough to prove it to them. As a matter of fact, all she had done was renew the consecration to the Sacred Heart that she carried in a locket on her breast.

She had now lost the power of speech, and it was evident that the long agony could not go on much longer. Father Robert had not left her side all morning, except to say his Mass. The novices had been with her much of the time, and were with her now, as the morning drew on. The bell had rung for the end of morning work, and it would soon be time to sing none. At eleven o'clock, the novices had to leave to go to choir. As they arose and filed out one by one, Mother Berchmans turned her face toward them, and her eyes followed each one to the door in a last, loving farewell.

Presently, Father Robert, overcome by the insistence of the nuns, consented to leave and get something to break his fast since he himself was also unwell. A few moments after his departure, Mother Berchmans manifested a desire to speak to reverend mother, but could not quite make herself understood. Mother Scholastica, thinking that she wanted something to drink, took a spoon, and gently lifted it to her lips, but the only reply was a little smile.

The last, tired words that had fallen, in an almost indistinguishable murmur, from the lips of Mother Berchmans were: "*Je me meurs*—I am dying."

Father Robert was called and came in haste, arriving in time to give absolution one last time to his dying penitent. And then, a few moments afterward, without struggle, without sound, without word or movement, Mother Berchmans peacefully closed her eyes and her body sank into the deep, deep sleep of death.

No need to describe the last, beautiful Cistercian rites with which her body was laid to rest. The community came at once and sang the *Subvenite*. Mother Berchmans' body, in her white cowl and black veil and crowned with flowers, was borne to the convent church. Night and day, by her side, her sisters recited the psalter, until her burial the following day, at two in the afternoon. Once again, the beautiful psalm *In exitu* was intoned, as the four nuns who were pallbearers lifted their not too heavy burden, and the procession to the cemetery began. Did anyone recall that first day, thirteen years ago, when the little group of volunteers from France had first stood outside the grille in the old wooden chapel, and someone had intoned these same words inside the tiny choir?

"When Israel went out of Egypt, the house of Jacob from a barbarous people....

"Judaea was made His sanctuary, Israel His dominion.

"The sea saw and fled: Jordan was turned back...."

Thus the exile of Mother Berchmans ended in glory, great glory in heaven, and rich and visible fruits on earth; for was not this strong psalm swelled by the voices of many Japanese novices, four of them already nuns, formed by her to the life of penance and contemplation?

When the poor frail body was lowered into the grave, and the spades in the hands of the appointed Sisters began to gently let fall the first consignment of earth about her feet, and the voices of the choir rose in the beautiful, earnest supplication of the antiphon *Clementissime*, her novices raised their dark almond eyes full of tears over the tops of their processionals and gazed down at the body of their dear Mother.

But when the whole community bowed low, on their knees, with their knuckles in the grass, and chanted the last, threefold *Domine, miserere super peccatrice*—Lord, have mercy on this sinner—Mother Gertrude said to herself with a deep and interior joy: "Good Jesus, if You had only such sinners as this one to forgive, You would be pretty well off!"

EPILOGUE

Days passed. Mother Berchmans was far from forgotten in the little convent on the hill outside Hakodate, whose new brick buildings now rose among the pines and faced the flashing sea.

No one who had seen her in those last months in the infirmary doubted her sanctity. Mother Scholastica wrote of her to Laval: "You have seen those pictures of Jesus dying with an expression that hurts when you look at it: well, that was what the agony of our little saint was like."

Father Robert, however, was eminently practical about it all. He was already busy gathering material for his book, the biography of this little penitent of his. Busily, in every part of the convent, the nuns, the lay sisters, the novices were all writing down their impressions and memories of Mother Berchmans, and letters were already on their way to France, to Laval, to Lyons, to the Convent of the Redemption, asking for information about her earlier years in religion and in the world.

It was not surprising that they began to look to her for favors, and that prayers were sometimes addressed to her in moments of need. They were not without answer.

With all her ardent love, Mother Berchmans leaves one with the impression of a strong and idealistic personality, which indeed was hers. But we know that in the annals of Catholic sanctity—in all the history of the liturgy, for that matter—God has not disdained to take care of even the most material needs of His children through the intercession of His saints. It is the mind of the Church that we should seek such help from them as a matter of course. And since Mother Berchmans spent most of her years at Our Lady of the Angels managing the finances of the dairy farm which was the community's chief support, it is not altogether surprising that the first notable favor gained through her intercession was granted—in the cow barn!

Sickness had got into the herd, and one of the cows had been stricken with paralysis in the midst of having a calf. The veterinarian had been called, and said there was not much hope for the cow's recovery. This was something that Mother Scholastica could not take lightly. She could not afford to be losing cows. She turned instinctively to the Little Flower. But St. Thérèse did not hear the prayers. Then Mother Scholastica got an idea. She took one of the hairs of Mother Berchmans that she had kept aside for just such an emergency, and went out to the barn. With the hair concealed in the palm of her hand, she went over to the ailing beast and began to stroke her back, saying at the same time, within herself: "Little Mother Berchmans, you shared all my worries: so now in memory of your love and sufferings, show your power."

Two minutes passed. Then the cow began to move and struggled to her feet. The veterinarian was standing by. Mother Scholastica turned to him with an expression of satisfaction, but he merely shrugged, and said: "She'll fall down again in a minute."

But the cow did not fall down. In fact, she was cured.

Mother Scholastica walked back to the convent, smiling to herself, and turned her gaze to the pines at the top of the ridge, to the little cemetery, with the white cross just inside the gate, on the left as you go in....

That was in 1916, and in Japan.

In 1922, in the convent of the Trappistines called Our Lady of Good Hope which then went under the name of *La Cour Pétral*—it has changed its location since that time—there was a certain Mother Margaret seriously ill with nephritis. She was subject to frequent and violent attacks, and the bile, having passed into her blood, had caused a cerebral congestion which passed off without further complications, but the attacks were becoming more and more frequent. At the beginning of the New Year, 1922, the convent had called in a new doctor. Their earlier physician had been ineffectual, but his successor was a positive menace. He put the poor nun immediately on a starvation diet, in which she received no other nourishment than Vichy water and a glass of Madeira and milk every few hours. On this regime she was soon reduced to the condition of a living skeleton. Her mother abbess, who had some stomach ailment or other, was subjected to the same ruthless treatment. In a few weeks they were walking around like a pair of ghosts. At this juncture, Dom Vital Lehodey happened to visit the convent, and taking pity on the two poor nuns, advised them to give up this starvation diet. By way of a substitute he told them his opinion of the sanctity of Mother Berchmans and left them some sort of a third class relic of the holy Sister.

After the departure of Dom Vital, without saying anything more about the affair, the mother abbess of *La Cour Pétral* began a novena to Mother Berchmans to ask for the recovery of "any one of the sick in the convent"—leaving the choice to Mother Berchmans. A few days later, Mother Margaret—who had not joined in the novena, since she knew nothing whatever about it—suddenly felt herself to be much better, so much so that she thought herself bound to go and inform her mother abbess of the fact.

"Reverend Mother," she announced, "I am so much better that I really think I am cured...."

The mother abbess showed her surprise.

"Why!" she exclaimed, "Do you know, it is the seventh day of the novena?"

"What novena?" cried Sister Margaret, and then the whole thing came out.

It did indeed appear that she was cured. The attacks ceased altogether, she rapidly regained her strength and her normal weight, and after the end of that year she could write to Our Lady of the Angels with the declaration that there had not been the slightest recurrence of her nephritis.

In 1926, Mother Berchmans made her appearance as an intercessor in the new world. On the eighth of February, in that year, the nuns of the tentative Cistercian foundation at Novo Friburgo,

Brazil, fearing the death of a prize cow, flung themselves on their knees and recited a Hail Mary in honor of Mother Berchmans, begging her to avert the tragedy. And to their great satisfaction, they awoke the next day to find the animal completely cured. By this second intervention in the affairs of Cistercian dairies, Mother Berchmans seems definitely to have signified her intention of trespassing upon the territory of another Cistercian, St. Guerin, the twelfth-century abbot of Aulps, to whose shrine, each year, the French Alpine peasants bring their cattle to be blessed.

Mother Berchmans was not long in showing her power on the North American continent, where she had a fervent client in Dom Edmond Obrecht, the abbot of the Cistercian monks at Gethsemani, Kentucky. One of the most able monks in the community had been rushed to the hospital with a ruptured appendix. The operation had been performed, but his condition was so bad that the doctors doubted that he would survive.

In fact one of them, in calling up the abbey one evening, offered very little hope for the Father's life. "If his fever does not abate during the course of the night," he declared, "I am afraid he cannot live."

Dom Edmond instantly turned to Mother Berchmans and begged her, with the most fervent prayers, to preserve the life of his spiritual son. The next day, much better news came from the hospital, and soon the patient was well on the way to a recovery which Dom Edmond attributed entirely to the intercession of the little Cistercian nun in heaven.

There are many others who claim that they have received favors by her prayers. A Sister of St. Paul, at Chemulpo, Japan, who badly needed money to provide her convent with a reliable water supply, managed to get the money she needed out of an American Protestant businessman who was very unfriendly to the Church. She was convinced that the only reason why she was not shown immediately to the door, instead of being so well treated, was that she had a photo of Mother Berchmans with her, and prayed to the "little saint" at the crisis of her begging expedition.

A young Trappist monk at Our Lady of Gethsemani had an

attack of stomach trouble which led to vomiting in the night and early hours of the morning. He went to choir, but had to leave during the little office and again during the meditation. Returning again to the church he prayed to Mother Berchmans to help him, and make him well enough to receive Holy Communion that morning. Within ten or fifteen minutes he felt much better and an hour or so later when the canonical office ended and he went to serve Mass he felt perfectly normal, and received Communion.

Spiritual favors are also attributed to her intercession at Gethsemani. A monk made the best monthly day of recollection he had made in over a year when he put the day under her protection, and having asked her to help him overcome a certain interior spirit of restlessness, made marked progress and acquired such a degree of peace that his spiritual director remarked on it a few months later.

But these are only details. Surely, the most powerful and efficacious work that Mother Berchmans has done in heaven had been in the protection and guidance of her convent on earth. By the 1930's, Our Lady of the Angels had grown to such proportions that a foundation became possible, and so a colony was sent to the neighborhood of Nagasaki, where Our Lady of Lourdes was established, and the foundation, which was made by some who had known Mother Berchmans and one who had been trained by her, Mother Bernardette, began entirely in her own joyful and enthusiastic spirit. The Sisters embraced their poverty with all the "*élan*" that had been so characteristic of the exile from Laval, and the first time they rang their new bells, one Holy Saturday morning, the local fire department arrived posthaste and nearly battered down the front door in their anxiety to get to the "fire."

Mother Berchmans' work as novice mistress was put to its sternest test nearly twenty years after her death. In the second World War, the Japanese government deported all the European nuns from Our Lady of the Angels, except old Mother Léonie, who had been there even before Mother Berchmans arrived. Her health was too poor, and they allowed her to remain in the house she helped to build. The time had now come to see whether the novice mistress of 1913, 1914, and 1915, who had trained the first professed Japanese nuns, had really laid a firm foundation. Would the community be able to survive and stand on its own feet? The answer is unquestionably: Yes. Two of those nuns who had gone on retreat that day in May, 1915, when the convent chapel was filled with a mysterious scent of flowers, and who received the black veil eight days later, were Mother Cecilia and Mother Agnes. Today they are respectively abbess and prioress of the flourishing convent of Our Lady of the Angels—the flourishing *Japanese* convent, which not only can support itself and its daughter house, but is the edification of Japan. But what is far more important even than that is that the Japanese community of Our Lady of the Angels now numbers over a hundred and is the largest Trappistine convent in the world.

More than that, American soldiers and chaplains stationed at Hakodate discovered, in this community, something that opened their eyes to new depths in the religious life. Most of them had never seen such a thing as a community of contemplatives before, and one testified that he has spent "the happiest days of his life" listening to the chanting of the Trappistines in the choir of Our Lady of the Angels. The reasons for this fervor are to be found in the sanctity and unquestioned ability of the superioresses, Mother Cecilia and Mother Agnes, in whose hearts burn the great fire of love that was fanned to bright flames, thirty-five years ago, by the nun who had so greatly feared the responsibility of becoming mistress of novices.

Surely, now that we are beginning to hear projects of the first convent of Trappistines in the United States, it is not hard to see that Mother Berchmans is one whose assistance will be of the greatest value in this hour. And, indeed, it is partly due to her that such projects exist at all. A year or two ago, the very thought of a Trappistine convent in the United States was considered to be "out of the question." But prayers to Mother Berchmans have changed things somewhat since that day, and the site is already chosen. Perhaps by the time this book reaches the American Catholic reader, a colony from Ireland will already be established on our shores.

When they do come, let them be sure that they will not be alone. There will be many others working at their side, lightening their burdens, removing obstacles, winning graces for them to bear their obscure and hidden crosses; hundreds of unknown saints will be there, contemplative monks and nuns, men and women, boys and young girls who left the world before they had even known it, who preferred to die to the world before they lived to its futility and wickedness. Hidden souls, "little" souls, souls who were not afraid of their own nothingness, but who treasured it, and gloried in it, with the great St. Paul, that the power of Christ might dwell in them, and that He might be glorified in them.

And of all these spirits there will be few that will assist them with a more joyous and more fervent and a sweeter charity than that of Mother Berchmans, whose exile has long since ended, and given place to endless glory.